THE DARK SIDE OF THE BRAIN

Harry Oldfield is the Founder and Principal of the International School of Electrocrystal Therapy. He was an early pioneer of Kirlian diagnosis in Britain, the inventor of ESM scanning, and is now researching and developing electrocrystal sound, and crystal laser therapies. An international lecturer, Harry Oldfield is the holder of diplomas in homoeopathy, biology and physics. He also holds a place on the editorial advisory board of the Journal of Alternative Medicine.

Roger Coghill holds an Honours Degree in Psychology from the University of Cambridge.

THE DARK SIDE OF THE BRAIN

Major Discoveries in the Use of Kirlian Photography and Electrocrystal Therapy

HARRY OLDFIELD
and
ROGER COGHILL

ELEMENT BOOKS

© Harry Oldfield and Roger Coghill 1988

First published in 1988 by
Element Books limited
Longmead, Shaftesbury, Dorset

All rights reserved. No part of this book may be
reproduced or utilized in any form or by
any means, electronic or mechanical, without
permission in writing from the Publisher

Typeset in Linotronic Palatino
by Character Graphics, Taunton, Somerset
Printed and bound in Great Britain by
Billings, Hylton Road, Worcester

Designed by David Porteous Associates
Chudleigh, Devon

Cover design by Ray Smith
Cover photo: Michel Tcherevkoff
Image Bank

British Library Cataloguing in Publication Data

Oldfield, Harry
The dark side of the brain : major discoveries
in the use of Kirlian photography
and electrocrystal therapy.
1. Psychical research
I. Title   II. Coghill, Roger
133   BF1031

ISBN 1-85230-025-6

Contents

Acknowledgements		7
Preface		9
1	The Dark Side of the Brain	11
2	Experiments with an Earthworm	20
3	Life Energies: The Pioneers	42
4	The Work of Harry Oldfield	76
5	Life's Secret Mechanisms	92
6	Electrocrystal Therapy: Diagnosis and Treatment	128
7	Nutrition: Pictures of Health	160
8	The Birth of Electronic Medicine	178
9	Conclusions: 'A Thinge Worthe Ye Tryalle'	221
Appendix: How to Make Kirlian Pictures		226
Bibliography		246
Index		258

The improver of natural knowledge absolutely refuses to acknowledge authority as such, for every great advance in natural knowledge has involved the absolute rejection of authority.

T. H. Huxley, physician and agnostic philosopher, 1826-1895

Very little of the day to day work of science is discovery, so the fact that scientific routine can be carried out by teams, can even be published by teams, says nothing for sure about discovery.

In defence of scientific individualism, it must be said that in the process of discovery there comes an unique moment: where great confusion reigned, the shape of the answer springs out, – or at least some form of the question. The insight occurs in the mind of some person ... Yet it must be said that the insight, however exalting, is not the discovery.

What the insight touches off, even before anything gets published, is the familiar and most characteristic work of the scientific community: criticism, modification, and the development of consequences.

Horace Freeman Judson, 1979

Acknowledgements and Permissions

It is impossible to identify in a few paragraphs all the people who have had a formative influence on us in producing this book.

Were we to do so they would fall naturally into three categories: the first would include great scientific thinkers of the past like Goethe, the father of morphology, Pythagoras, Heraclitus, and Plato from a more contemplative age, Sir Isaac Newton and Johannes Kepler the pragmatic enquirers, and Hippocrates and Paracelsus the fathers of orthodox and alternative medicines. The second category would embrace the pioneers of life fields such as Lakhovsky and Kirlian himself and their counterparts the practical and theoretical developers of electricity and magnetism like Clerk Maxwell and Tesla. And finally we would acknowledge the many modern influences from all walks of physics, chemistry and biology; names as diverse as Gary Zukav, John Gribbin, Francis Crick, Julian Kenyon, Rupert Sheldrake, Peter Tompkins and Christopher Bird, Max Perutz, Albert Einstein, Jacques Monod, Bernard Watson, Steven Weinberg, Robert Gallo, Leslie and Susannah Kenton, and Guy Murchie.

In addition to these, however, are the small but vital band of people to whom we have turned for guidance and practical help: Ra Bonewitz, Rosemary Steel, Ian McGibbon, Colonel McCausland, Jamie Pridmore, and Fred Bentham, Paul Devereux, Glen Rein, John Steel, John Merron and Caroline Wise, and to Harry's patient wife Eileen.

None of this would have reached the printed page were it not for Sheila Lawler's perseverance in typing our drafts and adding her own touch of northern common sense; the illustrative skills of Carol Ross; finally and above all without the encouragement and patient enthusiasm of Michael Mann, our publisher, not only would the quality of the work have been lacking, but its clarity would also have suffered. Our debt to him and the many hours he spent in discussing the concepts and detail of the book cannot easily be conveyed in a few words.

We are also grateful to the many other publishers and authors who gave us permission to quote from their work, in particular to Julian Kenyon, John Gribbin, Charles Berlitz, Horace Freeland Judson, Lyall Watson, and Rupert Sheldrake. They often expressed concepts far more elegantly than we ourselves could have ever done.

Though we accept the intellectual donation they have bestowed with enormous gratitude, we must emphasise that the views and opinions contained in this book, and any factual errors which may have crept in or points which have been wrongly left out, must always remain our sole responsibility.

Roger Coghill and Harry Oldfield

Château de Laveau,
St Georges du Bois

Preface

Natural science is the study of 'that which is or can be known'.

A good definition of the aims of natural science is based on the overview by Gary Zukav in his book on the new physics, *The Dancing Wu Li Masters*: '... to discover principles in Nature which unify large tracts of experience by reference only to sound experimental evidence, and to formalise these mathematically'.

This is what we are attempting with this book.

If one thing stands out in the history of scientific progress it is that careful observation of small discrepancies has often uncovered fundamentally better scientific principles than those existing beforehand. The solving of the Mars equations by Kepler, who had refused to accept a discrepancy of only minutes of arc, led in turn to the replacement of a circular planetary orbit theory by the elliptical laws of planetary motion.[20]

So the first aim of this preface is to ask the reader to cultivate an attitude which does not reject or condemn evidence, however small, simply because it does not accord with received opinion. Very few of us, in any case, have actually carried out those experiments which have changed man's view of his environment: we take them on trust and on the perceived results which they produce: atom bombs, penicillin, space shuttles, or whatever.

Newton, who formulated 'the laws by which the great machine of Nature runs' is often quoted as saying *'hypotheses non fingo'* (I don't make hypotheses), and he demanded reproducible experiments to support any hypothesis offered. Yet both Newton and Kepler studied astrology assiduously,[154] a science difficult to replicate. Replication indeed is the cry of the normal scientist in defence of any breach through which fringe or frontier science threatens to invade. But the mechanics of scientific acceptance may be more difficult than such a simple and innocuous demand as replication implies.

First, to gain credence, the original experimental results must appear in a reputable journal, and such articles are usually only accepted if emanating from a recognised academic body or university research department. Once submitted, the findings are quickly evaluated by other research establishments, and sometimes the tests are published at the same time as the initial work, since there is a delay between submission and publication. This is patently a problem for a frontier scientist not attached to any particular establishment. Nevertheless some of our greatest advances have come precisely from those who were not involved in full-time academic research. Einstein was working in a patent office when he proposed the theory of relativity.

Another problem for researchers in frontier areas is not only that projects of less than central interest are unlikely to get funded, but that it is almost impossible to get the establishment to take them seriously. The absence of any 'rival' institution who can check such work by itself may lead to oblivion, simply through lack of interest, or inability to respond. Should the frontier scientist seek to get his message across via a specialist publisher, then the commercial demand for profitable sales becomes the bridegroom of the innocent exposition of truth; and the child of the marriage is often sensationalism.

We have chosen the medium of a popularist book rather than a more academic means of publication not because we are in the slightest biased against the Establishment: we are simply not a part of it; and our contribution can be tested as sandcastle or rock, untrammelled by any need on our part to safeguard career or reputation.

In recognising, on the one hand, the Scylla of an over-zealous and underfunded scientific corpus, without the resources to examine small discrepancies or flaws in the received body of scientific knowledge, and aware, on the other hand, of the Charybdis of sensationalising the evidence which we wish to present, we aim to sail through the straits to safer waters with our experimental and theoretical contributions still afloat. We only hope that we have succeeded.

1
The Dark Side of the Brain

Today you will listen to a radio set, more probably watch TV.

You may use a phone, switch on an electric light, boil an electric kettle, or microwave a hamburger. All these things could be affecting your brain and your body.

This is because the brain and body of every living creature relies on a wireless telecommunications system which controls, repairs, organises and renews its body's cells and tissues. And any nearby electromagnetic field can affect it.

We will demonstrate how this brain-to-cell mechanism works, and that if it goes wrong or is disturbed by outside influences the animal, whether worm or human being, wasp, or whale, will die, or at least become very ill. Other life forms which do not have brains, such as plants, are dependent on a similar mechanism, except that local cell-to-cell communication replaces the brain.

More than that: we propose that the body's diseases can not only be brought about by external electromagnetic waves, but can also be cured by them. We will try to show you that your brain, like the moon, has an unseen dark side, whose workings are not revealed easily, but without which your life as an organism would cease immediately.

*   *   *

We start by proposing the hypothesis that the brain's transmission to, and reception from, its individual cells can be intelligibly received externally by electronic instruments, or even by other people. We use the word 'intelligibly' because of course EEG records through the skull are already being monitored as part of routine medical investigation. But their intelligibility is very limited, and the records are as if the transmission of a radio programme had been converted into a graphic printout of the digitally encoded broadcast information, and the listener expected to understand the squiggles on the page.

There are some grounds for believing that the brain's transmissions can be detected externally, and the possibility has been explored seriously both in the West and more importantly in Russia. It has, however, been often overlooked in attempting to explain certain well-replicated but puzzling phenomena of everyday life.

Take the common cold, or rather its big brother influenza, as an example.

The very word 'influenza' (which comes from the Italian word for influence) should have given us all a clue: originally it was thought that the disease, common since the time of Hippocrates and clearly described by him, was transmitted through the air. Even today the *Concise Oxford Dictionary* refers to influenza as, among other things, 'a mental epidemic'.

In their speculative book *'Space Travellers, The Bringers of Life'*, Fred Hoyle and Chandra Wickramasinghe[135] give an account of influenza epidemics known in this century, and explain the puzzling fact that the epidemics spread much faster than can be explained by case-to-case (that is person-to-person) transmission, or even by the wind, by suggesting that the influenza virus falls onto a cluster of people from outer space. It is a suggestion which certainly merits consideration. But they are wrong to ignore the possibility that influenza – and possibly even the common cold – *is transmitted by the brains of affected persons*. The chilling prospect of this possibility would revolutionise medical procedure overnight if it were found to be correct. It would also lead to the cure of the common cold: and the transmission pattern necessary for such a cure might be remarkably similar to that of ascorbic acid,[71] or Vitamin C as it is more usually called!

The actual epidemics of influenza described by the two authors support this incredible possibility:

'As well as having variations in their fine genetic detail', they say, 'influenza viruses have larger differences which are classified into types A, B, and C, and into sub-types of these main classes. Sub-types of A are particularly common, and it was a new sub-type of A that first appeared in Sardinia in 1948. Commenting on this first appearance, Professor F. Margrassi wrote:[188] 'We were able to verify ... the appearance of influenza in shepherds who were living for a long time alone, in solitary open country far from any inhabited centre; this occurred absolutely contemporaneously with the appearance of influenza in the nearest inhabited centres.'

'This observation shows', continue the two authors, 'that influenza can be contracted without connection being necessary to another human.'

'In 1918 there were only some 45,000 people living in Alaska, which is two and a quarter times larger than the state of Texas' they say elsewhere. 'In November and December of 1918 a lethal epidemic of influenza passed over the whole of that vast thinly populated territory, when human travel from the coast to the interior was essentially impossible because of snow and ice. Here again then we have an example of the spread of influenza by some means other than person-to-person contact, and as before there are the same three possibilities [wind, animals or birds, and that the virus came from space] for explaining how the spread occurred.'

It is also possible that the disease was spread electromagnetically, as we shall see, and this possibility the authors have unfortunately ignored.

Louis Wienstein, writing about the same epidemic,[299] says:

The lethal second wave, which started at Fort Devens in Ayer, Massachusetts, on September 12 1918, involved almost the entire world over a very short time ... Its epidemiological behaviour was most unusual. Although person-to-person spread occurred in local areas, the disease appeared on the same day in widely separated parts of the world on one hand, but, on the other, took days to weeks to spread relatively short distances. It was detected in Boston and Bombay on the same day, but took three weeks before it reached New York City, despite the fact that there was considerable travel between the two cities.

Commenting on this, Hoyle and Wickramasinghe say:

Here we have a third case where influenza was not spread by person-to-person contact, for nobody in 1918 could travel from Massachusetts to Bombay in the day or two which elapsed between the appearance of the new wave at Fort Devens and its appearance in Bombay. Nor could the fastest flying birds, the shearwater swift, or even the albatross, make the journey in that time, even if Boston and Bombay were on the customary flight paths of these birds which they are not. Nor are there winds that blow over such a route, with such a speed, and over such a distance.

If this disease is transmitted electromagnetically, like radio, the implications are frightening. But remorselessly the facts pile up: in their book *Influenza* Stuart-Harris and Schild in 1975 pointed to the same feature,[269] saying: 'Studies in schools have shown that epidemic occurs explosively in such a manner that it is difficult to explain the rapid build-up on a case-to-case transmission basis.'

'Doctors are familiar with sudden outbreaks of influenza in families, institutions, and other circumstances in which people are closely associated together, and from such observations they convince themselves that influenza is being transmitted from one person to another,' say Hoyle and Wickramasinghe. 'But since the incubation time of influenza is three days, person to person transmission would be drawn out by the need for this to occur at each link of the chain.' The authors' [Hoyle *et al.*] own survey of an influenza epidemic in British boarding schools in 1977/1978 with 100,000 victims show that despite conditions for case-to-case transmission being ideal, the real incidence was random and there was no case-to-case transmission.

The idea of viral infection from space cannot be ruled out, however, nor can the possibility that influenza is an electromagnetically transmitted disease. And if this applies to influenza, what of herpes, the common cold, and other cerebrally induced dysfunctions, some of which have not in our opinion even been properly identified by medical science?

We are not the first to notice the special characteristics of influenza. In his book *The Modern Practice of Physic*, published in 1813, Robert Thomas commented: 'By some physicians influenza was supposed to be contagious; by others not so; indeed its wide and rapid spread made many suspect some more generally prevailing cause in the atmosphere.'

In their detailed analysis of Headington School's flu epidemic Hoyle and Wickramasinghe unwittingly provide evidence for a radiative explanation. Following up their work, we asked the school to tell us the physical distances apart of each of its house dormitories, and correlated these with the onset and incidence of influenza. The results show the same attenuation as that of an electromagnetic field, suggesting that influenza is radiating out from specific epicentres. Only further research with other locations will test our prediction that all local epidemics of influenza can be measured in this way. Perhaps other 'cluster' diseases spread in a similar way: there is a large tract of experience of such diseases from which our hypothesis can be tested.

Another quite different effect of this 'influence' could be its ability to create so-called 'telepathic communication' as a result of transmissions intended for internal consumption by one organism being picked up sympathetically by another. We approach this subject with considerable caution, since most of the data concerning telepathy are anecdotal, and in any case, the quality of information transfer is extremely high, involving highly defined images, complex human emotions and identified concepts. To say, 'I was just thinking of you when the phone rang and it was you' invokes cerebral mechanisms of a very high order of complexity. The receiver of such telepathic information will have to have held a mental picture of the telephoner, and this picture will have to have been translated into an electromagnetic wave-form spreading probably over time. The wave-form will have to have been recognised, in the brain of the recipient – but by what? Our model has no construct for the conscious mind. So we are in the invidious position of investigating a non-phenomenon without any hypothesis to help us, save the possibility that a 'radio' transmission system is somehow involved.

The idea that a three-dimensional form can be translated into a specific complex wave-form has already been demonstrated by Hans Jenny.[144] Once this is accepted as a building block then the concept of image transmission is possible. The central problem is, however, one of transmission power: if the transmitter is emanating any kind of electromagnetic wave then these waves will attenuate (weaken) with distance (and there are specific formulae which calculate the fall-off rate[182, 191]), unless the signals are re-amplified somewhere along the line. Normally this is done by means of a repeater station. Perhaps in the case of telepathic energies[143, 187, 218, 296] the mechanism could account for poltergeistic phenomena,[247] or the role of the spiritualist or sensitive invoked and adapted to fill such a function. Or transmission and reception might occur spontaneously as a result of a phenomenon known in atomic physics as Brownian Motion where all atoms are constantly jiggling in any organic or inorganic form.

The number of incidents of telepathy are legion. But the ability to replicate them at will is almost zero. Much Russian research into telepathy[215] has centred round investigation of specific individuals claiming telepathic power, such as Yuri Kamensky, and Mikhail Lomonosov. Empirical evidence is also available: a change in the brainwaves in one identical twin has been shown to cause a similar shift in another in experiments documented in Philadelphia in 1965 by doctors Duane and Behrendt.

Another explicable feature of reports of telepathy is the incredibly long distances over which information can apparently be transmitted: Bernard Kajinski, an early Russian pioneer in telepathy, noted the transference of bodily symptoms from a daughter to a mother when the daughter was undergoing abdominal surgery 1,400 miles away.[215] Another feature, long observed by Western researchers, is that spontaneous telepathy flashes most often between members of a family, people in love, and childhood friends. The power of prayer can have beneficial effects on the distant recipients of its benison, and at football matches the encouragement of spectators seems to have an influence on players' performance. Paralleling these observations are the more sinister implications of magic spells, incantations, and the whole paraphernalia of psychic attack. All these are forms of telepathic communication, and all imply that the cerebral mechanism designed to control form and emotional reaction to harm has extracranial transmissive by-products. To quote William Blake,

> Each outcry of the hunted hare
> A fibre from the brain does tear

Within the context of an apparatus designed to preserve the morphology of an organism none of these seem unduly out of place as alarm signals which have been too powerfully transmitted. The same mechanism could be responsible for people 'falling in love', where it is said that such afflicted couples gaze directly into each other's eyes, surely the most direct way of intercommunicating cerebral wave-forms, given that the eye is directly connected to the cortex!

More specifically, we have the result of an experiment in 1959 in which doctors Serov and Troskin demonstrated that the number of a patient's white blood cells can be altered by autosuggestion. If taken to its logical conclusion this must be a cause of grave concern for any physician. This fundamental discovery of a cerebrally controlled and non-neural immunosensitive system at work deserves more attention than to be buried in a work on psychic discovery.[215]

In 1963 Dr Konneci of NASA told delegates at the 14th International Astronautic Federation meeting in Paris: 'The nature and essence of certain phenomena of electromagnetic communication between living organisms is reportedly being pursued with top priority under the Soviet manned space program.'

The Americans themselves were not slow to investigate the effects of electromagnetic impulses at a distance from human and animal subjects. Indeed as we shall relate, they had been aware of the possibilities for decades, but had chosen to squash any research in that area. Some of the more recent researchers, like Robert Becker[26] and the similarly named Robert Beck, have reported horrific results from the use of electromagnetic weapons in crowd control. The pernicious effects of high-tension cables, which by their nature emanate electromagnetic fields at right angles to their current flow, on creatures human or otherwise living near to them, are only just being recognised. The truth is we live in a world which during the last fifty years, through the arrival of radio, television, electric power generation and transmission, computers, cathode ray tubes, microwave cooking, communication and telecommunications, and an amazing variety of domestic electrical appliances, industrial electrical machines, and other hardwired and wireless systems, has created a sea of electromagnetic traffic around our heads never before experienced in the known history of the world. If our bodies are subject to the sort of mechanisms propounded in this book, sooner or later such traffic will start to disrupt the work of these delicate biological systems, if it is not already doing so. The first sufferers may well be those with the least protective epidermal tissues.

The evidence is already there: the famous case of Sam Yannon illustrates the dangers. In 1954 he started running a television programme for local stations from the 87th floor of the Empire State building. In 1961 he began complaining to doctors that his sight and hearing were deteriorating, and that he believed the radio waves to be responsible. He died thirteen years later, in 1974, some twenty years after the start of his electromagnetic irradiation, at the age of 62, weighing just five stone, having suffered cataracts of the eyes, loss of balance, premature senility and remembering no one, all signs of cerebral destruction. A

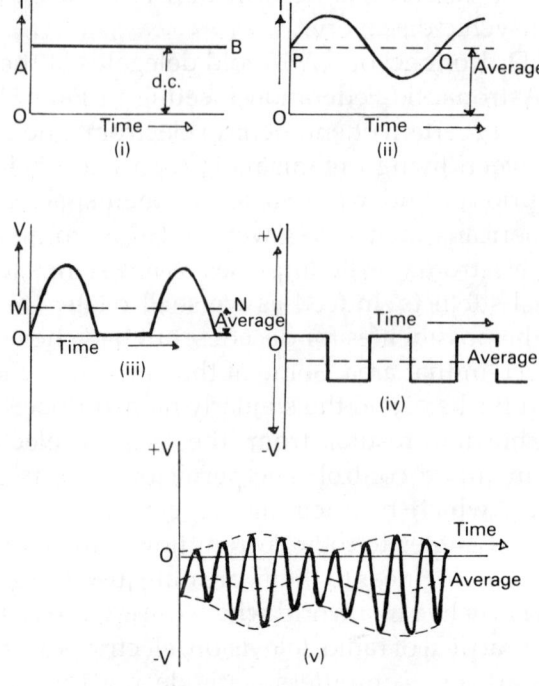
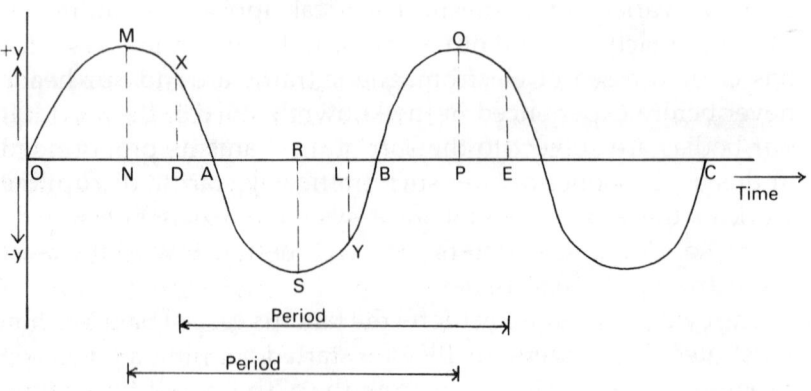

Fig 1.1 Various waveforms.
i. Direct currents
ii. A varying direct current (flowing in one direction)
iii. Positive half-cycles of a pure alternating voltage
iv. A negative rectangular pulse
v. A wave with voltage variation (not of constant amplitude)
vi. A sinusoidal waveform from pure alternating current

doctor testified that Yannon's symptoms were identical to those found in many patients exposed to long-term microwave doses.

Today an increasing percentage of British households use microwave cooking devices to heat food, blissfully unaware of the potential dangers caused by leaks.

Dr Jean Munro works at the Lister Hospital in London, treating allergies with specific electromagnetic frequencies. Together with her colleague Dr Cyril Smith of Salford Hospital, she believes that many allergies are caused by electromagnetic pollution, in other words that they are electronic diseases. She quotes twenty-six cases where the evidence is clear-cut.[203] Just as intriguing was her report on another five patients who were themselves able to affect electrical equipment: causing light bulbs to blow when in an extremely hypersensitive state, producing background noise on tape recorders and television sets up to ten yards away, and so on. Actually this is not particularly amazing to any physicist. Anyone with a cordless telephone knows that it will pick up the click of a refrigerator as the thermostat comes into action, or if you turn the light on. Electromagnetic waves are flowing everywhere around us, affecting everything. (Fig 1.1.) 'Everything flows' is still the most modern statement of observation in this electromagnetic age, just as it was thousands of years ago when pronounced by an ancient Greek philosopher.[127]

The deliberate use of non-ionising low level electromagnetic irradiation, stated the *Observer* in March 1987, is known as zapping in the United States, and a book, *The Zapping of America* by Paul Brodeur, was published as long ago as 1977. Its effect on organic life – including human life – can be devastating.

To conclude this introduction we quote from the British journal *Public Health* whose editorial in 1982 proclaimed: 'Comparable alternating magnetic fields do not occur in nature. They only appear as a by-product of man's industrial activity, and comprise an influence to which there has been no opportunity for evolutionary adaptation.'

This book explores the effects of a hidden mechanism of the brain which works on none other than electromagnetic principles, and the understanding of which is becoming vital to our continued existence on this planet.

2
Experiments with an Earthworm

My advice to a young writer – who is merely thinking of fame – is to concentrate on one subject. Let him, when he is twenty, write about the earthworm. Let him continue for forty years to write of nothing but the earthworm. When he is sixty, pilgrims will make a hollow path with their feet to the door of the world's greatest authority on the earthworm. They will knock at his door and humbly beg to be allowed to see the master of the Earthworm.

Hilaire Belloc

There are moments in one's life which suddenly seem ludicrous.

Why, at the age of 46, am I, Roger Coghill, passionately interested in what is happening to an earthworm, which I have dug up from the back garden and cut in two pieces, christening the rear half 'Ollie'?

My wife has long since established in her mind that I am in need of urgent psychiatric attention. My youngest child is only slightly more interested in my mad experiment: after all, cutting worms in half is part of the everyday apparatus of many young lads with even a modicum of curiosity, paralleled only by pulling the wings off hapless flies.

But my purpose has a more serious objective than sheer curiosity. I am trying to solve an important problem of natural science. By the time that you have read this book, you may accept that without such research we are unlikely to solve problems as huge as the pandemic of AIDS which currently threatens mankind. (See refs. 48, 108, 119, 256, and 257.)

Let me explain why. It is a story which will take us back into pre-Christian history, make us struggle through the intricacies of our own bodies' cells, cause us to speculate about the dematerialisation of human beings, and whether gout is caused by a failure of communication between foot and brain.

Arguably the most important scientific challenge facing physicists and biologists today is the largely untackled question of morphogenetic biological fields. These fields are the fields by which our bodies' shape stays the same, even when, as they inevitably do, some of its cells are dying every day of our lives.

When we cut our finger, what makes the fingerprint cells

grow and heal exactly where they were before? How is it that, even though every cell in the human body has changed in six months, we can instantly recognise the face of a friend whom we bump into after a year's absence? What causes cells to run amok and refuse to toe the morphogenetic line, dragging malignant cancers in their train? How can we eliminate the AIDS virus which is insidiously damaging the immune system of mankind?

The problem is not simply a biological one: it brings subatomic physical knowledge into the fray. It cannot be solved by a closer look down an electron microscope. Restated, the central question asks just how an unknown non-physical influence organises and controls at a distance the growth and maintenance of organic tissues, perhaps even inorganic ones too. The answer is bound to embrace the theoretical frontiers of the physical sciences, because we are dealing with sub-cellular components; with hydrogen bonds within DNA macromolecules; with the electronic transmission of information; with wave mechanics; and with the origins and properties of light and other electromagnetic and electrostatic energies.

Even psychology, demography and social economics have parts to play in this giant quest for the key to morphogenetics. Tackling such an undertaking requires the kind of scientist more common in the eighteenth than the twentieth century. A breed which has largely disappeared in the two centuries of specialisation which followed that enlightened age. Today we stand in need of generalists with open minds: Newton, tough empiricist though he was, still studied astrology passionately. So did Johann Kepler, if only to eke out a frugal living when times were hard.[154] In Christopher Wren's day a dinner party might be equally at home in discussing Robert Boyle's new Law as they would the philosophy of Aristotle. Aristotle himself was a great biologist, carrying out pioneer work on the egg embryo.[12] And Wren too attained eminence as an astronomer before embarking on a career as an architect at the ripe old age of 30. Did you know that Wren also acted as an illustrator to a book about the brain?[28] Figure 2.1 shows his illustration of the cerebrum and its features, revealing its di-pole nature. Joseph Priestley discovered oxygen, but he was primarily a teacher. In those days, science meant knowledge of all kinds, not just maths, physics, and chemistry.

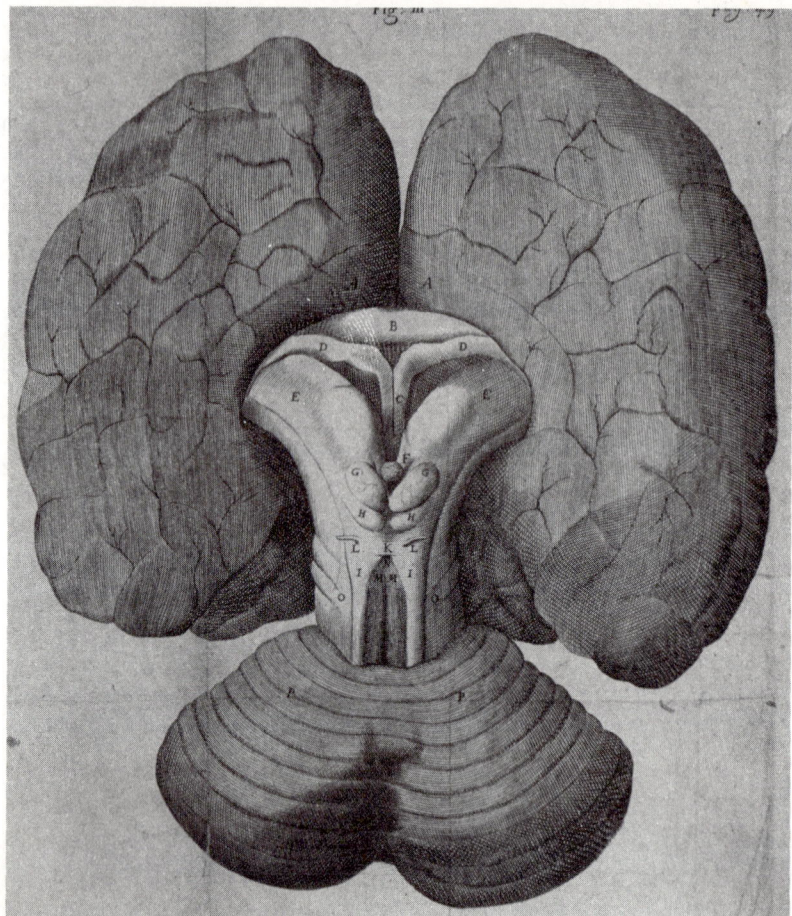

Fig 2.1 Wren's drawing of the brain taken from Cerebri Anatome. *(British Library)*

Not that we disparage the tremendous progress made as a result of specialisation: the coordination of large teams of specialists have put men on the moon, measured the smallest particles of the atom, built giant oil rigs, launched supersonic transport planes, developed virtually instant global telecommunications and constructed powerful computers the size of a matchbox.

But only in the last thirty years has scientific attention turned seriously towards the science of genetics. Crick and Watson, (and some would add Rosalind Franklin and Maurice Wilkins[111]) pieced together the double helix structure of DNA only in the early fifties.[291] The study of nucleic acids is still in its infancy with new discoveries appearing monthly in *Nature* magazine. The science of nutrition is only just gaining momentum, and getting more and more complex. Genetics too seems to need a combination of biology, chemistry, electronics, medicine, sociology, and even geographic economics for its advancement. Archaeology and anthropology have been relegated to the third division.

Perhaps the age of the generalist is returning.

Like all these problems of natural enquiry, to study biological morphogenetic fields we must construct the tools for the job and bring the data into one place. Only after this may hypotheses emerge to explain the collected phenomena. In such a field of study there might also be 'non-phenomena' to contend with; gravity for example is something which you know is there but cannot actually see, and, to avoid being led down the blind alleys of dogma, it is well to anticipate this.

But first back to my earthworm. The common earthworm, *Oligochaeta lumbricus terrestris* to its biologist friends, and 'Ollie' to me, happens to be one of the most populous animals on our planet. Charles Darwin, who sensibly devoted the last years of his life to the study of earthworms, estimated that there were between 6 and 13 million of them in every square kilometre;[64] and more recent estimates suggest that there are actually between 120 and 600 million in every square kilometre of grassland and fertile farmland.[284]

Before you say 'Ugh', you should know that these quiet battalions do us such a signal service that we would probably all starve to death if it were not for their quiet devotion to duty. They oxygenate and aerate the topsoil of the world, balance its acidity or alkalinity, help decompose rotting leaves and other detritus, supply natural guanin and urea thereby improving the soil's fertility, and cost absolutely nothing.

Ollie the earthworm has other endearing features: most important to me right now is his incredible power of regeneration. Biology textbooks are not certain on the subject, but whilst most agree that the front (anterior) part of a severed earthworm can regenerate itself, there is some doubt as to whether the back (posterior) part can grow a new brain, mouth and pharynx, not to mention the five hearts with which every decent *lumbricus* is blessed.[302]

Why should we care?

If it can be shown that an animal has the capability of regenerating all those organs, then it is saying something about the mechanics of life and the way in which cut fingers get repaired. It could help to prove in fact that the cells of an animal not only carry a blueprint of the whole animal – this much we know from studies of DNA – but that those cells can broadcast, as it were, that blueprint to new cells so that they develop in precisely the right places to reform the animal in its entirety. This is why the process is called morphogenesis, and the broadcast network can therefore be labelled a morphogenetic field.

And here's the point: if we can succeed in understanding the mechanics of morphogenetic fields, we have a window onto the mechanisms occurring when morphogenesis goes wrong, as it might be with diseases like AIDS, multiple sclerosis, arthritis, and cancer.

More of that anon. Let me now tell you a little more about Ollie.

The other thing that interests me about him/her is that Ollie is incredibly sensitive to vibrations; not just to the tread of the farmer's Wellington boots, but also to the electromagnetic vibrations of visible light, which are enough to paralyse the poor creature, and as for ultraviolet light, well it is just lethal to *lumbrici*. When you see a dead worm in a puddle of rainwater, its death has not been by drowning but from ultraviolet radiation. That is why worms stay well underground, coming up only at night. They can live for months under water, and for up to fifteen years in a harmonious atmosphere.

So as a test-bed for experiments with ultraviolet and visible light, and any other electromagnetic non-phenomena, Ollie is perfect. And as we shall see, electromagnetics and ultraviolet light seem to play an important part in morphogenetic field studies.

I do not want to go into Ollie's private sex life. Except to say that he can be a she whenever he wants, simply by lying head to tail with a friend, and if nothing else, is therefore more procreative than most animals would dare to hope for in their wildest dreams.

For now, let us concentrate on finding out whether Ollie can grow a new brain, using only his lower half.

If we are right that it is by means of a broadcast signal, then we further suspect that human ingenuity and technology will be capable of developing electronic equipment which can mimic this process by artificial means using equipment which can generate the complex wave-forms of morphogenetic fields. And this would be the start of electronic medicine.

What has led us to this suspicion? It is because of what we call the 'phantom leaf effect', a strange phenomenon we have observed by means of an even stranger process known as Kirlian photography,[201] which we shall soon describe in detail.

The phantom leaf effect has by accident allowed us to chance upon a mechanism in Nature which could provide an important clue to morphogenetic fields. More than that, it offers an opportunity to explain in a few principles large tracts of experience which are currently an almost complete mystery. As an example let us apply the resulting hypothesis to a new way of looking at the AIDS retrovirus, and a few other diseases currently defying the attempts of researchers to find a cure – cancer, multiple sclerosis, arthritis, and psoriasis, to name but a few.

Let us suppose for one moment that our brain acts like a di-pole radio aerial. After all, it looks a bit like one: there are two fat, but highly separate, hemispheres with a plate wrapped round each one (called the cerebrum and cortex respectively). Connecting the two halves, which are neatly insulated from each other by a membrane and ventricles, is a thick connecting band called the corpus callosum. Underneath this appear to be some signal detectors and also some signal generators, called the limbic system, thalamus, and other specialist components. The cerebrum is set in its entirety like a jelly in an upturned bowl (the skull) so as to be sensitive to the slightest mechanical vibration, let alone electromagnetic ones.

Let us next suppose that this relatively vast and complicated transmitting and receiving station services an immense number of small radio sets, each one being one individual cell of our body: and that the receiving aerial of each radio set is the nucleus, packed with DNA in helical windings. A helical winding is ideal for picking up a radio signal, and all modern radios have a similar device inside. The difference in this case is that instead of having a separate tuning device the station has been programmed to a fixed frequency and cannot therefore easily change its station. The way it has been programmed is that along the helix are a number of different bumps: they are tied to the helix by hydrogen bonds and bases (chemical molecules), each three of which represents a specific bit of information. Thus only a specific wave-form can be received by the helix, and more than this the distance between one complete winding of the helix is also fixed by hydrogen bonds which ensure that it doesn't stretch or contract,[217] which might also have the effect of making the aerial go out of tune.

Apart from acting as a radio receiver, however, let us further suppose that the other part of a double-stranded helix acts as a local transmitter of exactly the same signal as that which it receives. This kind of structure, we speculate, is like a two-way radio: other types of single-stranded structures of DNA (and all RNA) may only be receivers.

The strength with which the cell can broadcast its signal will depend on how much energy is pumped into the cell by a sort of biological battery called the mitochondria.

And the strength with which the brain can send and receive signals to all its cells will also depend on the amount of energy available to it. This energy is protected by an insulator called myelin which insulates the whole central nervous system from the rest of the body. If this sheath is destroyed then energy can seep away, the brain's radio signal strength falls off, and the body starts to malfunction, as in the case of multiple sclerosis.

If the brain's specific signals are weakened by its having to use up a lot of energy, through stress for example, then the cells start mishearing, or worse, not hearing the signals at all. So they either start doing their own thing and go wild, or start doing the wrong thing and re-broadcast incorrect instructions, allowing for example a build-up of uric acid in the feet which we call gout; or letting in foreign bacterial infections; or wrapping themselves in a mucous coat so that they go completely deaf to the signals coming to them from the brain. When one considers that the real problem in understanding morphogenesis is that there are millions of cells dying and being born in one human being every day and that it is necessary to replace each one correctly, then it must be immediately obvious that this sort of traffic could never be handled by a chemical-electrical system whose speed of transmission down neural axons is 40 metres a second if you are lucky. Nervous transmission is simply too slow by a high factor: the number of transmissions to and fro down the spinal cord necessary to keep the brain and its cells in touch with each other would exceed the capacity of the spinal cord to carry the information. Even the spinal cord needs a rest to recover from electro-chemical transmissions! The cord would have to cope with some 15,000 million brain cells alone.

Sometimes an aberrant effect is pellicular, that is to say it affects the skin, as in a sarcoma (a tumorous skin disease) or psoriasis. Here's where we can actually test to see how the mechanism works, because we can overtly see the effect of any treatment. With multiple sclerosis it isn't so easy: everything is inside and hidden from view.

In our postulated radio network a number of things can go wrong: a virus for example could get into the nucleus and alter the signal by inserting its own signal into the DNA chain. In consequence the structure starts sending out the wrong fixed signal to other cells, which start to ignore the brain's normal signal – unless the cells are brought back to normality by an even more powerful transmission from the brain in retaliation. The effort of engaging in this electronic warfare causes the headache which might for example accompany a stomach upset or the onset of influenza. Usually the brain can overcome these local invasions, except when it is already weakened by stress loops or lack of energy resources.

Another way the system can go wrong is if the cells are miscoded in the first place by reason of hereditary translation of the sequence of bumps along the DNA. Phenylketonuria is an example of this 'point mutation'. And a miscoding can also be caused to an already grown animal by ionising radiation, leading to cancers: even excessive sunlight can cause mutations of the skin pigment and accompanying skin cancers, [271] as a recent study by the Royal College of Physicians entitled 'Links between Ultraviolet Radiation and Skin Cancer' pointed out in April 1987. Chemicals can also cause mutations by altering the structure of the DNA and its hydrogen bonds. Finally there can be direct mechanical damage to cells by burning or cutting. In such cases the brain has to send out specific instructions to the repair squad, and this hurts when the pain mechanism is brought into play. Pain is simply the after-effect of the radio distress calls from the cells to the brain.

The more one starts thinking of the brain and the cells in this way the more it explains a lot of different things.

But in one case there is a really serious problem. Some particular viruses which are very small, including the AIDS virus, can penetrate the blood-brain barrier or the myelin sheath and establish themselves in the brain from where they can start altering the brain's signal ever so slightly and slowly. This virus then operates specifically to alter the signal to the special class of cells designed to seek and destroy foreign bodies. In more dramatic terms it has infiltrated behind the lines, captured the enemy's machine guns and is turning them on their owners. Down in the trenches the cells then start doing precisely the reverse of what they were programmed to do: they attack when they should defend .

The other cells cannot stop it: as the signal strength builds up they are progressively weakened, even though it takes a long time. Antibiotics cannot stop it: they act by having a fixed radio signal of their own which cancels the cells' signals, but with this signal it is uniquely different for each body, and unless the signal is exactly right it will not be obeyed. DNA is different for everyone in the world, just like a fingerprint.

So what on earth is the solution?

It very much depends on the way these signals work. And that is why I am so interested in Ollie the earthworm .

Right. We've put an idea forward. Now we are going to stop just there and ask you to read the following account of a dreadful plague:

> The season was universally admitted to have been remarkably free from other sicknesses; and if anybody was already ill of any other disease, it finally turned into this. The other victims who were in perfect health, all in a moment and without any exciting cause, were seized first with violent heats in the head and with redness and burning of the eyes. Internally, the throat and tongue at once became blood red, and the breath abnormal and fetid. Sneezing and hoarseness followed; in a short time the disorder, accompanied by a violent cough, reached the chest. And wherever it settled in the heart, it upset it; and there were all the vomits of bile to which physicians have ever given names, and they were accompanied by great distress. An ineffectual retching, producing violent convulsions, attacked most of the sufferers; some as soon as the previous symptoms had abated, others not until long afterwards. The body externally was not so very hot to the touch, not yellowish but flushed and livid and breaking out in blisters and ulcers. But the internal fever was intense; the sufferers could not bear to have on

them even the lightest linen garment; they insisted on being naked, and there was nothing which they longed for more than to throw themselves into cold water; many of those who had no one to look after them actually plunged into the cisterns. They were tormented by unceasing thirst, which was not in the least assuaged whether they drank much or little. They could find no way of resting, and sleeplessness attacked them throughout. While the disease was at its height, the body, instead of wasting away, held out amid these sufferings unexpectedly. Thus most died on the seventh or ninth day of internal fever, though their strength was not exhausted; or if they survived, then the disease descended into the bowels and there produced violent lesions, at the same time diarrhoea set in which was uniformly fluid, and at a later stage carried them off with a few exceptions. For the disorder which had originally settled in the head passed gradually through the whole body and if a person got over the worst, would often seize the extremities and leave its mark, attacking the privy parts, fingers and toes; and many escaped with the loss of these, some with the loss of their eyes. Some again had no sooner recovered than they were seized with a total loss of memory and knew neither themselves nor their friends.

No, not Bhopal. Not AIDS. It was a description by Thucydides of the great plague of Athens in 430 BC.[278] But it illustrates what we mean by what can happen when the brain starts to mis-transmit its signals as a result of a cerebro-viral infection: progressively the signal works its way down the body from the eyes to the feet. Thank goodness we haven't had many plagues like that.

It seems that the wavelength the brain is using is not a low one as one might have supposed by listening to EEG recordings; we are used to being told that our alpha waves are about eight to twelve Hertz, which is only eight to twelve cycles per second. But a glance at the wavetrains and their irregularities will convince any electronic engineer that the frequencies are much higher, more probably in the low ultraviolet wavelength range. At this wavelength certainly we can see many effects on DNA and on skin sarcomata too: psoriasis for example yields to certain ultraviolet light wavelengths. Yet the psoriasis returns in a few weeks when the UV light stops. Ollie's regenerative powers are completely smashed by ultraviolet light. With other organisms, however, mutation or growth can result. We just do not know enough yet about which frequencies and wavelengths work most effectively. All we can say is that there is considerable evidence that when ultraviolet radiation comes into contact with organic tissues it starts to affect DNA. And that this is a clearly radio (or radiative) effect.

The essential task in all healing is to normalise the brain so that its signal gives the proper instructions once more to the particular cells which are not doing their job. With AIDS it is the T4 helper cells, which are part of the platoon of fighters programmed to destroy enemy viruses and other foreigners. Unless we can reprogramme these T4 helper cells, the patient is increasingly prone to opportunistic diseases any one of which can take over the cells and swamp their signals until death is the only possible result.

Under this hypothesis AIDS is not an ordinary viral disease, it is a cerebroviral cellular dysfunction. It eventually kills by destroying brain tissue, and its immunosuppressive qualities are merely a secondary symptom. Pharmaceuticals cannot penetrate the blood-brain barrier and get to the virus without damaging the brain itself. And even if they did they would not be able to reproduce the individual signal necessary to bring the T4 helper cells back to normal, since each patient is different.

The only answer is to send an artificial signal into the patient's body which mimics its unique healthy brain signal. Or to send a signal which precisely cancels out the incorrect version put there by the retrovirus. Fortunately the retrovirus cannot itself broadcast. It is made of RNA not DNA and does not have a transceiving capacity. Even DNA cannot broadcast all the signals it would like to: it lacks a codon called Uracil, so cannot ever manufacture the so-called 'essential' amino-acids, which have to be ingested from outside the body.

Remarkably an instrument which can mimic the brain's signals has already been developed. In fact prototypes and early versions have been around for over fifty years. But that is the subject of the next chapter.

Before that let us now take a fresh look at cancer, or rather cancers: even the common wart is a cancer of sorts. If you look at a wart under a microscope the most amazing thing you will surely notice is that it has little square crystals in it.[41] Actually these are probably viral infections too, called papovaviruses from their longer name papilloma polyoma – vacuolating virus (Fig 2.2). Let's not be frightened of long medical words: papil-

EXPERIMENTS WITH AN EARTHWORM

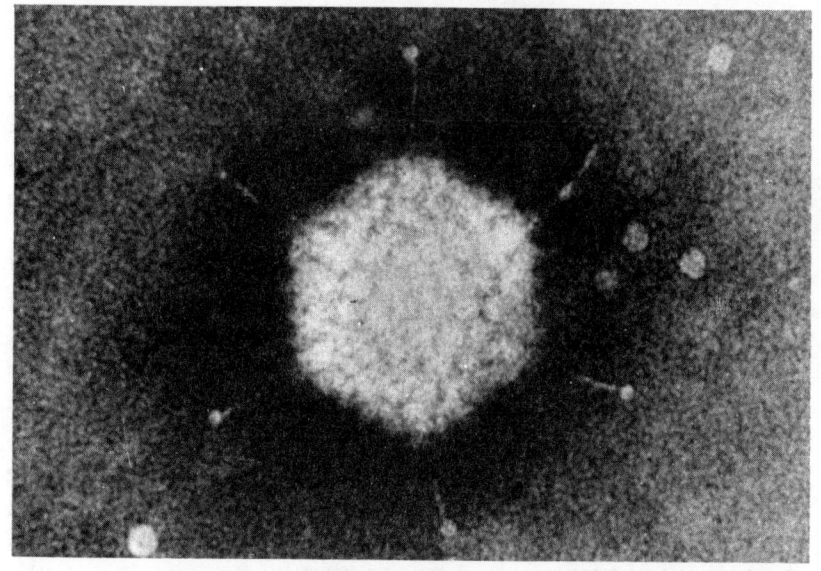

Fig 2.2   Adenovirus (Valentine and Pereira, J. Mol. Biol. 13, 13-20, 1965)

loma simply means a wart or similar skin growth, polyoma is a type of animal tumour, and vacuolating refers to the ability of many of these viruses to produce spaces or vacuoles (vacuums) within the infected cells. Indeed, most medical terms are simply Latinised descriptions of the symptoms or appearance of the structure or disease. (Surely the most inadequate medical description of all time must be the word 'chromosome', which simply means 'a coloured body', because that is what it looked like to the first observers.) The interesting thing about crystals is that they can act as very good receivers: ever heard of a crystal radio set? And the interesting thing about warts is that they can appear and disappear very quickly, sometimes overnight.

If the cells of a wart are retrained by the brain to become normal again then the virus is evicted or destroyed – phased away – according to our hypothesis. The question is, how does the brain do it? We suspect it is by first finding out what is the viral wavelength and then broadcasting a resonant wave-form which cancels it out; and that this is sometimes a difficult calculation for the brain to make, so that warts will persist then suddenly disappear. Since time began people the world over have been amazed and puzzled that warts can mysteriously disappear overnight. Now we are beginning to understand why. Indeed many other viruses also have a crystal-like array similar to a wart virus (Fig. 2.2): the adenovirus, for example, which gives us a sore throat. If, as we suggest, warts are eliminated by the brain's correcting signal, then could it be possible that a sore throat too might be cured by broadcasting its normalising frequency?

Other cancers are not so easily dealt with.

In such cases the cells continue to run amok, and are not contained. The signal is growing steadily, or is being misunderstood; or not being heard at all. There is a clear connection with the brain in that cancer very often strikes within two years after a mental trauma has occurred.[252] There appears to be a fatty coating round some cancerous cells. Using Kirlian photographs it is possible to identify a chaotic effusion of uncontrolled energy at the tumour source. Clearly the cell's radio tuner has gone out of tune. Eating fresh fruit seems to give the cells normalising energy, and surgery seems literally to cut out the aberrant signals. Other suggested causes and helpful treatments for cancer can all be traced back to an explanation in terms of our proposed radio network as a later chapter will show. One of the most powerful of these is will-power: the power of the brain to override the wayward signals and reimpose normality.

An example of this is the work of Carl and Stephanie Simonton who have used techniques of visualisation to help cancer patients combat their problem. In one case Simonton suggested to a naval officer that he should imagine the white cells as frogmen putting limpet mines on the side of cancerous cells and blowing them up. It worked: the officer was cured of cancer.

Getting Well Again[261] describes the Simontons' approach to cancer, and their self-awareness techniques, with many examples from their cancer counselling and Research Centre in Fort Worth, Texas. In discussing the search for the causes of cancer the Simontons and their co-author, James Creighton, accidentally relate an interesting example (among many) of our mechanism in action.

Such a case was reported by Dr Ronald Glasser in his book *The Body is the Hero.*[102] In a rare incident, even though everything had been done to ensure that the kidney donor was healthy, a kidney with unobserved cancer nodules was placed in a person who had received drugs to suppress his immune system for the transplant. After the operation the patient was given further medication to continue suppressing the immune system, and thereby prevent the body from rejecting the kidney. Within days the transplanted kidney began to enlarge. The reaction looked like some form of active rejection. A few days later, a routine X-ray revealed a tumour in the patient's chest. Since chest X-rays taken four days earlier had showed no such mass it was clear something had developed since the operation. A day later a similar tumour could be seen in the other lung. The physicians concluded that the masses in the lung were metastic cancer (that is, malignant cells had broken away from the original cancerous mass and had begun to reproduce in other parts of the body). The startling thing was the speed with which the masses had grown. Within days cancerous masses had appeared that would normally have taken months or even years to develop. There was no choice but to stop administering the drug that suppressed the body's defences.

Glasser reports: 'Within days, as the patient's immune system came back to normal the masses in his lung began to disappear, and the transplanted kidney began to shrink in size.'

Simonton and Creighton point out that this research led to the general medical acceptance of what is called 'surveillance theory'. What we argue in this book is that the surveillance system is a brain-cell telecommunications system based on electromagnetic wave-forms. In the example above the 'metastasis' was simply the unchecked re-broadcasting of an aberrant wave-form which was received by cells in other parts of the body. There was no physical transfer of cancerous cellular tissue.

Simonton, not realising this, was admittedly baffled: 'External agents, radiation, genetics, diet', he said, '– all four factors may play a role in the causation of the disease, but none of them is a full explanation without considering why particular individuals, at particular points in their lives, contract cancer.' He identifies stress as a major underlying contributive factor – thus linking immediately the brain of an organism with cellular dysfunction, and we shall explore the nature of that link throughout this book. Simonton, we would add, goes so far as to link pathological conditions with the limbic system, the hypothalamus, and pituitary activity.

Of course, it is easy to be dogmatic about the cause of any phenomenon, and we talked just now about the 'blind alleys of dogma'. As an example take that potentially blind alley in physics whose entrance was first unwittingly opened by Thomas Young in 1803 – the particle/wave duality of light. Young discovered that light passing through two slits in a board produces an interference pattern when it falls subsequently on a screen. This pattern, of alternate bands of light and dark, is a wave mechanics phenomenon, suggesting that light travels in waves. About a century later it was found that 'photons' of violet light act like particles to knock electrons loose from a metal plate (the photo-electric effect). So is light composed of waves or is it composed of particles? The ensuing debate has occupied theoretical physicists ever since as they struggle to rationalise these seemingly inconsistent sets of phenomena. (See notes 110 and 204.)

Suppose for a moment we deny the existence of a photon as a particle, but regard it simply as a harmonic of the same wave. (The Schrödinger equation in fact revealed quanta essentially as waves of resonance.) This harmonic could also dislodge an electron from a metal surface. If the light were of a violet colour it would do so more easily, in fact, than a red one, being of a shorter and more powerful wavelength.

No one has ever seen a hydrogen atom: millions would sit on a pin's head. But we think that the spaces between hydrogen atoms in a covalent resonant hydrogen bond can be changed by temperature and by other attachments to the hydrogen atom, which serve to pull the atoms apart slightly. Exciting a hydrogen atom's electron with a specific electromagnetic frequency causes it to move from one harmonic to the next. This is what produces the photon of light perceived by us to emanate from the hydrogen atom. So it isn't a particle after all: we just perceive it to be one, because we perceive only certain electromagnetic frequencies. If the source of the electromagnetic waves is subject to interference – that is if the crest of one wave is cancelled out by the simultaneous trough of another, then we will perceive no light at all. Some say the photo-electric effect may be explained without recourse to the invention of a new concept, the photon; being entirely a wave-mechanical phenomenon, the 'shells' round an atom are simply the harmonics of any particular electromagnetic frequency. They even follow a molecular equivalent of Bode's Law of planetary distances.

While such sorts of hypothesis would allow the wave-particle duality to be synthesised, they are unlikely to be a correct guess. We use the duality problem as an example of the need not to ignore those realities which may not be perceivable. And also as an example of how one wave can cancel out another by means of interference.

Magnetic fields, gravity, radio waves and the vacuum are other examples of non-phenomena, perceivable only by their effects on other phenomena, and yet we are quite used to accepting such fields now that they have been identified and defined mathematically.

By and large science is suspicious of non-phenomena, and it is not adept at understanding them even when they are known to exist.

'Modern scientists', say Tompkins and Bird,[281] 'still have no idea of the composition of electro-magnetic waves. They simply use them for radio, radar, television – and toasters.' Remember the concept, long rejected, of the ether? It was rejected because nobody could measure its effects. Such suspicions, moreover, are usually redoubled at the frontiers of science.

Not always, fortunately.

Great scientists occasionally acknowledge the unknown. This quotation from James Clerk Maxwell is suitably tinged with humility:

> Mr Airey has found that a large proportion of the disturbances at Greenwich correspond with the electric currents collected by electrodes placed in the earth in the neighbourhood, and are such as would be directly produced in the magnet if the earth current were conducted through a wire placed underneath the magnet. It has been found that there is an epoch of maximum disturbance every eleven years, and that this appears to coincide with the epoch of maximum number of spots on the sun. The field of investigation into which we are introduced by the study of terrestrial magnetism is as profound as it is extensive ... When we consider that the intensity of the magnetisation of the great globe of the earth is quite comparable with that which we produce with much difficulty in our steel magnets, these immense changes in so large a body force us to conclude that we are dealing with one of the most powerful agents in nature, the scene of whose activity lies in those inner depths of the earth, to the knowledge of which we have so few means of access.[191]

(It subsequently transpired that such magnetic disturbances had their origin outside of rather than inside the earth.)

But back to Ollie the earthworm. After four days Ollie's severed rear half is still alive. We have kept him moist, and remembering his sensitivity to light we have put a china cup over him. He moved in both directions during the first few days, as if uncertain which way was forwards or backwards. But now all the residual earth in his little gut has moved right down to the end of his body without passing out of it, and his front end has as a result got cleaner and redder. Could this be a hopeful sign? The front end of complete earthworms is where their light sensitive pigments are concentrated and the same could be happening to Ollie. But he hasn't eaten a thing. He no longer moves backwards when provoked but tends to move more normally forwards. Concerned that he has not for obvious reasons been able to eat anything, we are surprised that he has not expelled any earth either. Perhaps he is making the most of the food already in his gut. Or ingesting the air like a plant; or taking in nutrients through his skin? Meanwhile Ollie's front half is as lively as if the divorce had never occurred. Are the two halves still in radio communication? According to our hypothesis they should be, since their DNA is identical. This is not incidentally such a daft question: if an earthworm is severed and then retied together with cotton, movement will continue normally.

A brief glimmer of support for our hypothesis.

Moreover, if only the nervecord is left unsevered the wave of contractions will continue down the segments posterior to the cut. What we are really trying to see, however, is whether Ollie can generate a new brain. Now an earthworm's brain is hardly a mighty affair: it would look to us no more complicated than the eye of a needle, the interesting thing for our hypothesis being that it has two flanks with a hole in the middle – a prototype di-pole transmitter (Fig. 2.3)?!

So we are not asking a lot of Ollie if we ask him/her to generate a new brain. What is more complex is for Ollie to generate a new mouth, pharynx, oesophagus, and five hearts. If he can get these all back together then we have a clone with identical DNA to his better half. And with these two identical clones we

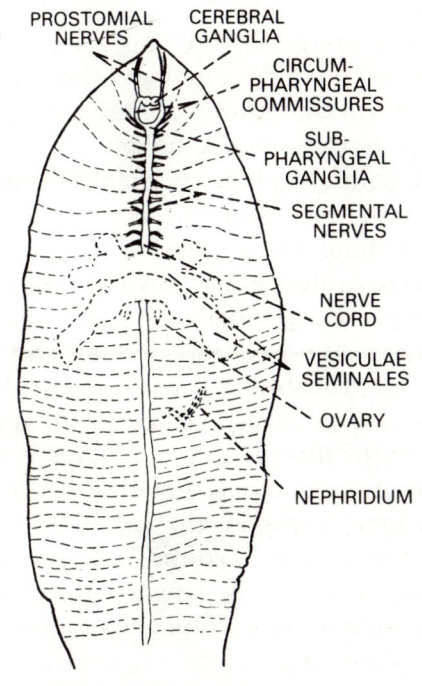

Fig 2.3 Ollie's nervous system.

might be able to carry out some interesting experiments on the effect of electromagnetic radiations on organic cellular tissues.

Overall our book gives an account of developments within the leading edge of research into morphogenetic fields, one of science's few remaining great unknowns. It attempts to survey, between one set of covers, most of the previous research and hypotheses in this field, much of which has been vehemently ridiculed or denied by orthodoxy and commercial interests. It describes the specific work carried out by Harry Oldfield with Kirlian apparatus and related equipment. It proposes our general hypothesis of morphogenetic fields based on and within the framework of accepted subatomic and atomic physics.

And finally it applies our central hypothesis to certain tracts of experience such as nutrition, disease and the alternative medicines,[140] and reaches towards some areas of the so-called paranormal sciences.

This is going to be an exciting journey. But the prize is the better understanding of how nature works, the explanation of important unsolved questions, and just possibly a curative solution for some of the most mysterious and uncheckable of human diseases.

Whilst Ollie is wriggling down his yellow brick road in search of a brain, let us take a brief look at other examples of regeneration in animals in the hope that they may give us clues to the mechanism of morphogenetic fields.

The most commonly known example must be the tails of lizards. 'Gotcha', we cry, only to see the creature dart off, while we are left clutching a small piece of its tail. Reptiles are in fact the highest vertebrates which possess any substantial powers of regeneration. At the other end of the scale, amoebae seem to do nothing except feed and divide. And in between these the sponges are probably the most spectacular of creatures, in that they were never really one organism at the outset.

The common feature of all regenerates is that their replacement limbs are never quite as good as the original, like a video re-recorded from a video. Furthermore, studies both in animals and man reveal that if the wound is closed by a suture, regeneration will fail to occur. Regeneration can only begin after a scab has been formed from clotted blood and dead tissue, which can take a week or two. When a new skin (or epidermis to be precise) has been formed underneath it, this scab falls off. Occasionally regeneration goes wrong, and double or even triple new tails are produced. The regenerated scales are often abnormal in colour or arrangement, and tend to be smaller than normal scales, again as if the template from which they were made was at one stage removed. Digits of lizards do not regenerate, but a limited amount of cellular tissue or cartilege overgrows the wound. A turtle can replace about one-third of an injured shell within a year, and shells which have been completely restored have also been reported.

No one knows how the regenerative mechanism works, except that in the higher life forms it is somehow dependent on the nearby presence of nervous tissue, an essential for regeneration. Planaria, for example, a common species of a tiny flat worm found in nearly every pond, stream or canal, and just as careful to avoid light as the earthworm, have the amazing capacity to regenerate the whole of their body after it has been starved to almost nothing, leaving only the epidermis and the nervous system. A small piece of planarian cut from its centre will regenerate a head at the correct anterior end. (Hear that, Ollie?) But as in other higher organisms, even the humble algae can only regenerate if medullary cells are present; and, though the hydra is able to regenerate a complete animal even after being cut into fifty pieces, the pieces must have the two components of nerve and cell.

The champion regenerators, however, are the sponges.

If a sponge is sieved through a cloth into a dish of water the cells will soon regenerate into small clumps, and each clump will slowly develop into the mature form. Apart from this, sponges have no other form of co-ordinating mechanism: they have no nervous system or special receptor cells. In consequence, every single cell of a sponge must carry with it any communicative mechanism with which it is equipped, and the intercommunication between cells must rely on a mechanism other than via neural pathways. In our investigations this feature of primitive organisms may prove to be an important clue.

If we now trace the development of how animals control their shape starting with the sponges, our account might appear like this: The cells of sponges have a non-neural intercommunicative system, something like citizen band radio. When the cells have been divided they subsequently reform as before, even when mixed up with another different variety of sponge. Lyall Watson recounts[296] the experiment where a red and a white sponge are sieved together into a pink mixture. After a day the two sponges have reunited into separate red and white shapes. This tells us something about the mechanism at work. The two sponges must have their own unique and separate call-sign, so do not confuse each other's signals. Higher up the ladder of life a nervous system starts to develop which exercises overriding control: without its presence the individualised and therefore now much more specialised cells cannot seem to operate completely independently as before, but get lost without the central controlling mechanism. They can still intercommunicate with each other or amplify and relay signals emanating from the nervous system. Since the nervous system is not in physical contact with all of its cells, some non-neural mechanism must be in operation. It is not so effective as direct transmission, however, and regenerated tails or claws are not likely to be as large as or differentiated as the originals which they replace. If the epidermis is interfered with or sutured, this has an inhibitive effect on regeneration. Indeed one purpose of the epidermis seems to be to shield internal tissues from external radiative influences, and this function may actually be working against the organism's own radiations when a suture has been made.

The epidermis is special in animals: its cells are highly impervious to ultraviolet radiation by comparison with internal tissues. They cover the entire outer structure of plants, protecting them everywhere except in the growing root-tip area. (Later we describe an experiment where the root tips seem to emanate radiations.) The epidermic cells sometimes produce oil, resin, crystalline salts, or silica for protective purposes, exactly like a car wax: they are impregnated with a waxy substance called cutin.

Normally in invertebrates the epidermis is only one cell thick, but frogs by contrast have an epidermis several cells thick, constantly renewed by division. Normally blood vessels do not penetrate into the epidermis, which tends to become scaly and hardened with age. Multiple sclerosis is so-called because of the scaly cells which are a feature of the disease. In plants the epidermal cells do not generally contain chlorophyll. In short the epidermal cells of plants and animals serve as their armour, and are an unfeeling protection against the hostile outside world. They may also serve as a barrier against the incursions of electromagnetic waves which would otherwise interrupt interior intracellular communication.

Ollie the posterior earthworm has now been alive for a month. He/she has crawled out from the small saucer and is decidedly more lively if touched. He looks a little fatter and redder at the front. And what is quite pleasing is that he has voided the earth from his rear end. He/she rests with his new nose touching the earth, as if somehow ingesting the moister liquids of the soil, or about to start burrowing. He/she avoids magnetic fields, and definitely crawls in the original direction of his/her previous self. Do we detect signs of something forming under the front end of Ollie's skin? Let us leave Ollie there while we look back over the history of research into the fields of life, and see how those early versions of wave-form broadcasting machines came to be developed, and the remarkable results which were obtained from their use.

3
Life Energies: The Pioneers

Doktor Franz Anton Mesmer, *struck off.*
Ruth Drown, *suicide.*
Wilhelm Reich, *died in prison.*
Upton, Knuth and Armstrong, *forced into bankruptcy.*
Dr Albert Abrams, *slated by the Establishment, died of shame.*
C. M. Allen, *driven insane.*
Dr M. K. Jessup, *suicide/murdered.*
Bill Moore, researcher and author; *fled into retreat.*
George de la Warr; *nearly bankrupted by legal proceedings.*

Such has been the fate of early researchers into bio-electric life fields. Why?

The answer may lie buried for ever in one sentence of a letter[54] from Albert Einstein to a fellow scientist, Otto Stern, in the dark days of World War Two: 'I can report no more on this matter than we are not the first who have faced similar things, ... and that it would in no way help, at the present moment, to bring it to public notice.' Cryptic words indeed from one of the most lucid of scientists. Subsequent commentators believed that Einstein was referring to the secret atomic development known as the Manhattan Project. But as we shall show, he may have had quite a different experiment very much on his mind.

*   *   *

The fundamentals of physics are unchanging. It is only the way we use them which has changed.

Like an echo from some previous technological age, Joshua fought the well-celebrated battle of Jericho, using the principles of resonance to bring the walls tumbling down. Tesla, the inventor of wireless telegraphy, would have been proud of him. Archimedes, the inventor of so many things, would have been grateful that Joshua hadn't passed the idea on to the Romans besieging him at Syracuse. (Not that Archimedes noticed even when they did break in.)

LIFE ENERGIES: THE PIONEERS

But Joshua was the first we know of to bring resonance into the human battlefield. Here's how he did it:

> And Joshua had commanded the people saying 'Ye shall not shout, nor make any noise with your voice, neither shall any word proceed out of your mouth, until the day I bid thee shout; then shall ye shout. ...
>
> And Joshua rose up early in the morning and the priests took up the Ark of the Lord. And seven priests, bearing seven trumpets of rams' horns before the Ark of the Lord went on continuously and blew with the trumpets; and the armed men went before them, but the rearguard after the Ark of the Lord, the priests going on and blowing with the trumpets. And the second day they compassed the city once, and returned into the camp.
>
> So they did six days.
>
> And it came to pass on the seventh day when the priests blew with the trumpets, Joshua said unto the people, 'Shout; for the Lord has given you the city. ... So the people shouted when the priests blew with the trumpets: and it came to pass, when the people heard the sound of the trumpet, and the people shouted with a great shout, that the wall fell down flat.

These verses from Joshua describe perfectly the critical features of his Divinely inspired experiment with resonance. By first establishing a specific frequency with the trumpets, and then overlaying it with the frequency of his men's shout, he could have set up a powerful resonance effect no less devastating than that by which Tesla once nearly brought down a New York building with his oscillator.[214] (We describe this in more detail later.)

Offshore sailors will understand the principle immediately: every few waves or so 'the big green one' comes rolling up from behind, threatening to poop them, and fill the boat with water.

The idea that every organic particle has its own particular resonant frequency or 'call-sign' which can be transmitted and received at a distance, is one of the few which never occurred to the ancient Greeks, except, perhaps, to Pythagoras of Samos.[241] However, the 'evil' uses to which wizards and witches of the Middle Ages put a lock of hair to damage a distant victim are well documented; and it is said that the ancient Egyptians were afraid to portray a person's full face in case enemies could weaken him from afar.

Historical evidence for the existence of a human energy field dates right back to ancient Chinese and Indian cultures. But probably the first well documented account comes from Paracelsus[118, 216] in the Middle Ages, around 1530. Though Athanasius Kircher, one hundred years later, was interested in magnetism, and wrote several papers on it,[158] he never seemed to connect magnetism with health as later writers did, nor with any vital force.[103]

Paracelsus was a rebel from medical orthodoxy. In 1527 he burned the famous textbook of medieval medicine, *The Canon of Avicenna*, which became a symbol of rebellion against pedantry and unthinking acceptance of ancient doctrines. According to his new 'doctrine of sympathetic resemblances', all growing things reveal their usefulness through their shape and physical characteristics: everything that lives radiates light, and plants with high vibrations are able to raise the low vibrations of man. He advised all physicians to sense the natural energies of plants, advice which was developed later by Edward Bach, a London doctor, into the well-known Bach Flower Remedies.[15] Paracelsus probably inspired Bach with his habit of gathering the dew under various configurations of the celestial bodies, believing the water to contain the energies of planetary aspects. Bach too believed that the dew contained a power of some sort.[21]

Perhaps one of the earliest scientific approaches to bio-electrical radiation was that by Maimbray in 1746. He put two myrtle shrubs next to an electrical conductor in Edinburgh and was amazed to see the shrubs grow three-inch branches and buds at a time when most other buds were dormant. (In a later chapter we discuss the impact of electricity on nutritional processes.) A few years later Jean Antoine Nollet,[209] physics tutor to the Dauphin of France, discovered that plants in metallic pots increased their rate of transpiration and that seeds grown in electrified containers grew more rapidly. By 1783 Abbé Bertholon had published a complete work, *De l'éléctricité des végétaux*,[32] and had collected atmospheric electricity with what he termed an electrovegetometer, which was then passed through plants growing in a field. His suggestion that 'one day the best fertiliser for plants will come in electrical form, free from the sky', should strike terror into the hearts of fertiliser manufacturers, and comfort the minds of conservationists. Happily for Bertholon there had been no massive demand for nitrites, the stuff of First

World War explosives, and the consequent nitrate fertiliser industry had not become the lobby it is today, otherwise his name might have been added to the list of ill-fated pioneers which heads this chapter.

Round about 1780, the time that Luigi Galvani discovered that not only plants but also frogs' nerves could be excited by 'the electrical fluid',[96] a Hungarian Jesuit, with the colourful but unfortunate name of Maximilian Hell, and his Viennese physician friend, Franz Anton Mesmer, came to the conclusion that 'living matter has a property susceptible to being acted on by earthly and celestial magnetic forces'. They called it 'animal magnetism'. They were subsequently expelled from the medical profession, and Mesmer retired to the cold of Switzerland to write an infamous treatise[193] in 1814, which protested the truth of his assertion.

Unlike Galileo Galilei, his muttered rebellion in the cause of his belief hasn't yet been given much of an accolade.

The bio-electrical baton was then taken up by a more prestigious personage, the mighty Baron Karl von Reichenbach of Tübingen, who in 1845 invented the wood-tar product since known as creosote. Reichenbach perceived that 'sensitives' could actually see a strange energy emanating from human beings; he called this the Odyle or Od – but even the Baron's attempts to prove the existence of the 'Odyle energy' were discredited. He did at least succeed in having his message translated into English through the good offices of one William Gregory, Professor of Chemistry at Edinburgh, under the somewhat Teutonic title of *Researches into the Forces of Magnetism, Electricity, Heat, and Light in Relation to the Force of Life*.[245] Meanwhile the list of fellow researchers into the beneficial effects of electricity on plants was growing.

In 1844 William Ross reported on *Galvanic Experiments on Vegetation*, and Edward Solly, an agronomist, recorded *The Influence of Electricity on Vegetation* a year later.[263]

But more attractive subjects were beckoning the scientific minds of the second half of the nineteenth century: scientists were quite rightly concerning themselves with atomics, rather than holistics, which were to be left for the next century, and a wide gap developed between physicists and students of the life sciences, a gap which was necessary at the time if the massive quantity of new knowledge was to be assimilated, but which is now fortunately closing again.

In the first three decades of this century interest in bio-electrical studies became intense, counterbalanced only by the efforts of the establishment to prevent the spread of innovation from this source. A similar ludditism had delayed the introduction of alternating electrical current in America during the late eighteen hundreds, thanks to the machinations of Thomas Edison who favoured the unworkable direct current method of transmitting electrical power.[148] The fear which gripped the establishment was, and perhaps still is, that established markets for fertiliser and pesticide products would be lost to them should electrical/electronic methods be allowed to gain a foothold. There were also more insidious factors to consider which threatened the very fabric of life itself, as we shall see.

As early as 1904 the battle commenced with the publication by Lemström of his *Electricity in Agriculture and Horticulture*,[178] and even this early work had been anticipated two years previously by Sylvanus Thompson's *Magnetism in Growth*.[277] Just one year after Lemström's book, Raoul H. Francé came out with *Das Sinnesleben der Pflanzen*, published in English as *The Love Life of Plants* and also *Germs of Mind in Plants*.[90] Thus the battle lines were arrayed for one of the most unfortunate confrontations in the history of scientific endeavour.

Lemström, a Finn, had made several expeditions to Spitzbergen and Lapland, and was an expert on earth magnetism and polar light. He firmly believed, as a result, that the luxuriant vegetation of that region owed more to the radiations of the Aurora Borealis than to the long summer days.

'The sharp points of plants', he proposed, 'act like lightning conductors, to collect atmospheric electricity, and facilitate the exchange of charges of the air and the ground' – an ion effect, to be precise.[264]

It was Lemström who first correlated high sunspot activity with tree growth by reference to fir tree rings, adding to the observations of Clerk Maxwell a quarter of a century before. He also carried out confirmatory experiments in which 'electrified' plants grew 50 per cent taller than normal. He reported these results in *ElectroKultur*, published in Berlin.

Back in England this book inspired that great scientific frontiersman, Sir Oliver Lodge,[181] and John Newman among others, to replicate the results successfully.

Why, the reader may then ask, does no one use these techniques today?

Actually, they do: the Electroculture Corporation was formed only in 1970 by Dr Len Cox of Denver, Colorado – a region so beloved of Nikola Tesla for its huge thunderstorms and atmosphere heavy with electricity, that he built a laboratory there – to market a magnetised fertiliser powder with exceptional properties to encourage plant growth.

However, probably the most tragic story (amongst many) concerning the early pioneers is that of Dr Albert Abrams,[2] and the subsequent invention of the homoeotron.

Abrams was a very rich San Franciscan who studied advanced medicine at Heidelberg in the last decades of the nineteenth century, gaining top honours and the Gold Medal from that eminent university. Abrams had already witnessed, while in Naples, the great Caruso perform the trick of shattering a glass with his voice by singing the same tone as that given out when the glass was tapped with a finger.

One day a Professor mentioned to Abrams that onions uprooted and left adjacent to others still planted, seemed to have adversely affected the onions still in the ground, whereas onions further away were unchanged; and Abrams wondered whether this too might be a resonant radiation effect: were the dying onions damaging their growing neighbours? He came across the same effect again much later when, having returned to America, he began teaching pathology at Stanford University. As a matter of course he would tap a patient's abdomen to test for reflex reaction, and noticed that he obtained a resonant sound from a healthy patient. When the patient was diseased in some way, however, the sound became dull. Experiments with this technique brought Abrams to the conclusion that unknown waves from diseased specimens of tissue could be received by another person and reflected in the muscular tonality of his tissues, particularly the muscular and nerve fibres in the stomach region. When, for example, X-rays were pulsing from nearby equipment, the tone produced was that of an unhealthy body: when the apparatus was switched off the tonality improved immediately!

It is significant to recall that the ancient Greeks considered the stomach to be the seat of the emotions.

Abrams, after some further months' research, produced the

hypothesis that the cellular origin of disease should be abandoned: it was only because the molecular constituents of cells are altered by radiated changes in the composition of their electrons that disease occurs. He found that radiation from a pathological specimen could be transmitted, like electricity, over a six-foot wire; and he then set about developing a diagnostic instrument to replace his finger-tapping technique, which he called a 'reflexophone'. This instrument, claimed Abrams, could differentiate between the wavelength of different diseased tissues.

If this account is beginning to sound far-fetched, the reader should note that the most modern method of pest detection uses radar to identify the specific wave-form radiated from different types of insect flying up to a thousand feet above the apparatus, thus exposing its feeding and flying habits. Insecticides can then be sprayed at only those times when the offending aphids are known to be on the wing. The same detection apparatus is used to provide a map of migrations by insects, each of which has a quite distinguishable wave-form.

Abrams went further than this in 1924, however, with a claim that was to bring him into direct conflict with medical opinion, and eventual disrepute. He said he could diagnose disease and to what extent it had taken hold of a patient simply from a drop of that patient's blood. Shades of witchcraft again!

Today we are beginning to use DNA 'fingerprints' from a single blood sample to identify individual human beings. DNA stands for deoxyribonucleic acid, the genetic encoder of life. To a conservative America in the twenties, however, Abrams' claim must have smacked of black magic, and it did not take long for the Establishment to brand him as a charlatan.

To one audience Abrams proposed, by way of example, that the curative effect of quinine on malaria is the result of radiations from the quinine molecules, which cancel out exactly the emissions from the malarial cells – an interference effect, to be exact – due to unsuspected electromagnetic radiation, rather than as a result of any chemo-pharmaceutical action. With the aid of a certain competent radio engineer, Sam Hoffman, he then built a radio wave emitter which could emit specific waves to cancel out the malignant radio waves emitted by diseased specimens. In 1922 Abrams reported his results. If he expected honest enthusiasm, he was disappointed: he was promptly condemned as a quack and charlatan both by the American Medical Association and the *British Medical Journal*.

Despite the championship of a number of eminent medical men, Abrams died two years later, killed by ignominy, with the journal *Scientific American* still vilifying his work in eighteen consecutive issues.

Meanwhile other researchers into life fields were beginning to suffer similar ignominy. Perhaps the most 'infamous' of these was Dr Wilhelm Reich.[139] He had the unfortunate habit of inventing strange words, such as 'oraccu', and talking quite openly about sex at a time when it wasn't really done. This, together with some rather nasty experiments, according to one rumour, eventually put him into prison where he spent the last few months of his life. His concept of an all-pervasive 'orgone energy' was of a field which lay outside of the electromagnetic spectrum, 'a cosmic energy that obeys functional rather than mechanical laws'. It had, he claimed, a blue colour. In order to collect this orgone energy, whose unit was for Reich the 'bion', he developed an instrument which accumulated it called an oraccu (orgone accumulator). Plants grow rapidly in this box, according to observers. It is six-sided, with all sides made of alternating layers of organic and non-organic materials. The inner wall is lined with a thin sheet of iron. In his book *The Cancer Biopathy*,[244] Reich suggested that in advanced cancer cases the orgone content of the blood had been totally consumed in the orgone's struggle against the systemic disease and the local tumour. 'This T-reaction is usually present before any symptoms of anaemia and often reveals the cancer process long before a perceptible tumour has formed.' Reich discovered that his orgone energy was readily absorbed by organic materials like wood, cotton, wool, and so on, whereas it was attracted then quickly repelled by metals. The layering of the orgone accumulator's walls thus established a flow of energy to the inside from the outside of the oraccu. The whole box is slightly reminiscent of the Ark of the Covenant whose manufacture is detailed in Exodus, the same Ark which Joshua carried for some reason round the city of Jericho. Reich believed that the red blood corpuscles carried orgone energy into the organic body in addition to oxygen. Certainly there is an iron atom right at the centre of each haemoglobin molecule, but no further explanation seems available to understand the transport mechanism.

> The orgonotic charge is also revealed in the shape of the structure of the red corpuscles. Cells with a weak charge are more or less shrunken and have a narrow blue margin which glimmers feebly. Once the organism is charged the red blood cells swell, while the blue margin intensifies and widens sometimes including the entire cell. No pathogenic microorganism can survive in the vicinity of these orgonotically highly charged red blood cells.[244]

Whatever the sinister rumours surrounding the imprisoned and maligned Reich, and however fanciful his ideas of orgone energy may have been, conceptually he is pointing to what may, in more mundane terms, be electromagnetism. One of the most recently published biographies of Reich, written by a close associate, Myron Sharaf, *Fury on Earth*, underlines this point. Furthermore, as Bill Schul and Ed Pettit say in their intriguing (and certainly more understandable) book *The Secret Power of Pyramids*,[258]

> references to the blue light or auras would seem to point to the presence of electromagnetic qualities in the energy field being generated. Observations of blue light around pyramids or reported by persons sitting or meditating within pyramids provide some evidence that the pyramid shares in the phenomena of producing identical or similar electromagnetic forces. These observations, along with the similarities between descriptions of treatment of disease and afflictions by blue light, orgone energy, and various forms of electromagnetic therapy and those reportedly produced by the pyramids would seem to point to some common denominators.

If we might digress for a moment, the origin of the word *pyramis*, if Greek, could mean 'the power of light or fire' as opposed to the word *dynamis* which was the word for the physical power of the body. A second meaning could be the bread or cake from which the sustenance is gained: only much later did the word pyramid take on the meaning of a sepulchral tomb. To anyone struggling to express the meaning of electromagnetism, *pyramis* was a pretty good attempt. But the derivation is entirely lost now in the mists of time.

Plato had no difficulty in connecting the pyramid with a basic elemental fire-power: in the Timaeus,[230] which is the only reference to Atlantis in classical literature, and from which all other descriptions ultimately derive, he suggested that the pyramid was one of the four basic building blocks of creation. Having ascribed the cube to earth, the octahedron to air, and the eikosahedron to water, he ascribes the pyramid to fire, saying: 'Logic and likelihood thus both require us to regard the pyramid as the solid figure that is the basic unit or seed of fire ... We must think of the individual units as being far too small to be visible, and only becoming visible when massed together in large numbers.' Sounds a bit like a crystalline structure with electrical properties to us! Certainly Plato was familiar with the difference between radiation and combustion: 'Next we must notice that there are several kinds of fire: the flame, the radiation from flame, which does not burn but provides the eyes with light, and the glow left in embers after flame has been quenched.' That these thoughts should be running through Plato's head after describing a legend brought out of Egypt (that of Atlantis) is intriguing. Was he repeating some of the Egyptian thinking which Solon, who first reported the Atlantis legend from Egypt to Kritias and so to Plato, had brought back with him after his visit to the priests of Sais in Egypt? Even more mystifying is that though Plato nowhere in the Kritias or the Timaeus mentions pyramids in relation to Atlantis, many subsequent writers on the subject have somehow introduced the idea of special energies and pyramids into the legend, particularly those like Cayce (pronounced Casey) whose inspiration is from hypnotic trance-like states, and not presumably from a close reading of Platonic dialogues.

In case you think he was a charlatan, ask yourself, as we have, where his inspiration could have come from. 'All strength, all healing of every nature, is the changing of vibrations from within,' said Cayce, 'the attuning of the divine within the living tissues of a body to Creative Energies. This alone is healing: it is the tuning of the atomic structure of the living cellular force to its spiritual heritage.' He said that well before the discovery of DNA.

The purpose of this digression was to allow us to point out how material structures are considered by certain researchers to collect energy, to which extent the concept of pyramid energy and the orgone-accumulated energy are similar. Both Reich and others, like Reichenbach, searched for some new energy as a result; but was that really necessary? Ions will naturally move towards any point in an organic structure,[264] and the phenomenon is demonstrated in virtually every school physics laboratory in the form of a Van der Graaf accumulator which readily produces nice blue sparks across the gap as a result of accumulated positive ions, which create differences in electrical potential. All these 'new' energies may be nothing more than boring old electricity.

To return to Reich: in his book *Cosmic Superimposition* he describes his 'Oranur Experiment', suggesting that organic bioplasma responds violently with radioactive materials, providing a by-product that is dangerous to life for a short period of time. Radioactivity was, however, reduced by its action on the bioplasma, he thought. Reich's experiments, vocabulary, and ideas are somewhat offputting to the rational observer and difficult to understand. Those who want to gain a deeper insight into the man could do no better than read Sharaf's useful and commentative biography. Whilst respecting Reich's contribution to life field research, we now leave this avenue for others who believe that some new force is involved, to tread.

Certainly, nothing is wasted: Reich's influence continues to be felt today, and from Abrams' work, for example, sprang an Association whose work continues today bringing together hundreds of practitioners of the new frontier of radionics, as the technique became known.[274] Its basic tenet is that diagnosis of illness is possible at a distance using the higher faculties of the human mind in conjunction with electronic instruments designed for the purpose of measuring disease patterns. The box itself was called by Abrams a biodynamometer, but soon got dubbed the 'Black Box', a phrase used colloquially for any mysterious electronic gadget ever since. This instrument has never been claimed as anything more than a variable resistance meter. The radionics hypothesis is that any disease gives off radiations, and that different diseases have different resistances which can be measured by reference to a healthy body.

Once a pathological condition has been identified (the instrument was known as the reflexophone) another machine called an oscilloclast is used to correct the aberrant radiation using pulsed weak electromagnetic energy, modified by the appropriate treatment rates. Tests of validity were carried out and supported the radionic pioneers' claims. More and more practitioners took up the instruments: in England such pioneers as Dr Guyon Richards, whose meticulous research work is recorded in *The Chain of Life*. He also founded the Medical Society for the Study of Radiesthesia, of which the current Radionics Association is a branch. Another radionics pioneer was George de la Warr, whose investigations[67, 68] into radionics from the electronic engineering viewpoint began in the forties. De la Warr made many improvements to the equipment and his laboratory became established as the seat of Radionics in Britain. The Association is still very active with new developments being produced, and new books on the subject being written.

In his book *Matter in the Making* Langston Day describes some of the research results which he and de la Warr obtained, and the course of development of their research. There is little doubt that the de la Warr laboratories were uncovering the first signs of morphogenetic radiation. It is unfortunate that they regarded the radiation as being 'hitherto unknown to science', rather than as simply an aspect of conventional electromagnetic radiation. De la Warr himself attached great importance to resonance in nature, as the jacket of the book points out:

> It is the ubiquitous principle of resonance between different forms of energy, which is the aspect of the unifying force that concerns Mr de la Warr. For instance, there is resonance between corresponding notes or chords in the octaves of vibrations belonging to the electromagnetic spectrum, which includes radio waves, light waves, and cosmic radiation: the thoughts and emotions of different grades appear to form octaves, and no doubt there are still higher levels of vibration.

Langston Day's book also describes the depressingly familiar events which surrounded de la Warr's famous court case in 1960. The plaintiff, a mysterious Miss Philips, claimed that de la Warr's radionics equipment was a fraud. In the expensive High Court case which followed, de la Warr eventually won a pyrrhic victory, since Miss Philips had claimed legal aid to finance her case, and de la Warr could reclaim no costs. The result of the case was that the threat of bankruptcy hung over the laboratory for at least five years afterwards.

One of de la Warr's instruments reached the zenith of incredibility: a camera which he claimed could photograph a person's thoughts. Fine material for fraud indeed! As usual the camera could be disturbed or become inactive in the presence of disbelievers, and would operate best in the hands of the laboratory's chief assistant. The three others who managed to get it to work apart from Corté (the chief assistant), were Dr Foster Cooper from St Bartholemew's Hospital, Mr F. Houghton Bentley from the Admiralty's Signals and Radar Department, and a scientist from the Royal Naval Research Laboratories. Cameras had to be specially built to suit each person (as might be expected if every living organism has its own unique wave-form). No one at that time, however, had any explanation.

Other exploits performed with de la Warr's apparatus were claimed to have discovered the missing spy Pontecorvo in Leningrad, and the uncovering of poisoning by fluoroacetates. De la Warr's work continued from 1942 to his death. Without an explanation in terms of the normal sciences, however, and partly through the necessity to protect the experiments against incursive negative organic radiations, the work has never been accepted by the Establishment. Nor are they wrong to reject it. The evidence must be replicable, and would only become so if de la Warr had controlled all the external parameters, including the influence of spectators.

In 1951 in America, Phoenixlike from his ashes, Abrams' ideas had been taken up by three other young and bright hopeful engineers from Princeton named Upton, Knuth, and Armstrong. They modified Abrams' equipment to tackle the task of pest control – an area of industry which cost farmers dear, and for a remedy to which they would pay the pesticide manufacturers of the day handsomely. Upton and his colleagues called their equipment a 'homoeotron', because it broadcast out the same (the Greek word *homoia* means 'the same') waves it received (Fig. 3.1).

Such was their initial success that their company, UKA Co., helped one large cotton-growing firm, Cortaro Management Co., to achieve a 25 per cent increase in per acre yield of cotton over the state average, and a 20 per cent increase in seed. The latter effect was puzzling until hoe hands reported an almost complete absence of snakes in the treated areas, but no effect whatever on bees, which are beneficial to pollenisation and had thereby increased the seed yield.

The most amazing thing about the UKA Co. treatment, however, and the hardest to accept, was that their device used an aerial photograph of the area to be treated in order to clear that area of the offending insects. The radionic process was thought to work by broadcasting the atomic make-up of the photographic emulsion, which they had treated with a reagent known

Fig 3.1 The Homoeotron.

to be poisonous to cotton pests! The emulsion was claimed to resonate at the same frequency as the terrain surface which it represented pictorially. (The same discovery in reverse had been made by André Bovis,[39] better known for his dehydration experiments with paper pyramids, twenty years before: Bovis also used a novel means to detect the relative freshness of different foods. He would move the food along a 'Bio-meter' – a calibrated ruler which also indicated radiation frequencies marked off in ångströms* – until his moving indicator changed direction. The spot at which the food rested at that point was claimed to be its radiation frequency.)

Between the time when Abrams reported his findings, and when the commercial applications of Upton, Knuth, and

---

* These tiny units can be confusing. An ångström unit is one ten thousand millionth of a metre (1 metre x 10^{-10}.) A nanometre is one thousand millionth of a metre (1 metre x 10^{-9}.) A micron (μm) is one millionth of a metre (1 metre x 10^{-6}.) And a millimetre is a thousandth of a metre (1 metre x 10^{-3}.)

Armstrong first appeared, a host of research works were published, many of which are briefly reviewed in *The Secret Life of Plants*,[281] (since most of them concerned plant or insect life). These works are listed below, and full publication details are given in the Bibliography.

YEAR	AUTHOR	TITLE
1922	Jean du Plessis	The Electronic Reactions of Abrams
1922	Raoul H. Francé	The Love Life of Plants
1925	George Lakhovsky	L'Origine de la vie
1926	George Washington Crile	The Bi-polar Theory of Living Processes
1929	Hans Berger	Uber das Elektrenkephalogram des Menschen
1930	Walter Russell	The Russell Genero-Radiative Concept
1934	A.G. Gurwitsch	L'Analyse mitogénétique spectrale
1934	George Grey	Radiation and Plant Research
1935	Harold S. Burr	An Electro-Dynamic Theory of Life
1936	Otto Rahn	Invisible Radiations of Organisms
1939	Ruth Drown	Theory and Technique of the Drown H.V.R. & Radiovision Instruments
1944	A.G. Gurvich	The Theory of a Biological Field
1947	E.J. Lund	Bioelectric Fields and Growth
1949	D. Whicher and G. Adams	The Living Plant and the Science of Physical and Ethereal Spaces
1951	Halliday Sutherland	Control of Life

The years between 1917 and 1936 saw the rise and the sad demise of another life field pioneer whose work was not appreciated until many years after his death. Edward Bach (pronounced Batch, not Bark) was born on 24 September 1886 at Moseley, near Birmingham in England. He died comparatively early at 50 having studied medicine in his youth, qualifying in 1912, at the same time as Einstein was sitting in a patent office developing the theory of relativity. Just as physics needed at that time a new approach to unify its recent discoveries, Bach saw that the traditional approach to medicine was lacking in insight. It was too insular, too concerned with mechanics, and it failed to recognise the more subtle holistic influences which Bach felt surely lay at the root of health and its corollary, disease.

Somewhere along the line Bach may, between his work as Casualty House Surgeon at one hospital and Assistant Bacteriologist at University College Hospital London, have come across the work of Paracelsus.

At its most basic, bacteriology searches for the physical organism which causes illness. But Bach was later to declare that such incursions were the result of illness, not the cause; very much as we have proposed in our brain-body control mechanism. During World War One his duties in charge of 400 hospital 'war beds' led him to see that certain forms of intestinal bacteria were more plentiful in the gut of the chronically ill. (We would say in our hypothesis that the patients' brains were not fully in radio control of the gut's cells.) Preparing a vaccine from these bacteria for arthritis and rheumatism he achieved some success. But in July 1917, an example of his own doctrine, he fell ill with cancer, bowed down and unhappy, and torn by the death of his first wife and his love for the woman he then married soon afterwards. A typical cancer syndrome of illness following stress as we will amplify in Chapter 8.

He struggled to free himself from the disease and succeeded in regaining his health; a triumph of mind, and the insight gained was the reward for his experience. 'Disease of the body', he wrote, 'as we know it is a result, an end product, a final stage of something much deeper. Disease originates above the physical plane.'

Bach was expressing in medical terms what Einstein had conceived for the physical sciences: that matter is energy modified, and that our material selves are modified by pernicious energies so that we fall prey to disease when our central controlling nervous system becomes too weak to maintain its disciplines. The Bach concept of disease is, like others, exactly the same as ours but couched in metaphysical rather than mechanistic terms.

In the spring of 1919, after the Great War was finally over, Bach joined the London Homoeopathic Hospital and came under the influence of that pioneer of the science, the great Hahnemann. There he began to realise the fallacy that disease is a material factor, curable only by material agents; such an approach paid no attention to the psychological aspects of illness.

At this point Bach's ideas began to crystallise: in 1930 he left London for the mountains of Wales, and then for Cromer in Norfolk, the only place in England where the sun both rises and sets over the sea. Here he practised the 'sun method' of potentising, whereby the sun's radiations are allowed to work on the individual herbs, and wrote his book *Heal Thyself*.[15]

Again the concept behind this book is similar to what we are saying about the brain's radio control over the body's cells, except that we are attempting to couch the concept in electrophysiological terms.

Bach sought natural remedies in flowers to influence not so much the physical disease as the mental state which lay behind it.

Ultimately he segregated thirty-eight mental states, and sought an equal number of herbs and flowers to correlate with them, drawn by his own spontaneous intuition. (Ra Bonewitz advocates the same approach in selecting one's personal crystal.[37]) The first twelve herbs are identified in his book *Free Thyself*. Then came the *Seven Helpers* in 1933 and 1934. He finally identified the remaining nineteen herbs just before his death in the autumn of 1936.

Bach claimed that his remedies would work objectively, without the need for any specially skilled applicator. Their wavelengths, in our terminology, can be switched on to balance the specific unbalanced signals of the brain. Harry Oldfield's instruments do it differently, and some would say less romantically, but the principle is the same, as we shall see.

This general concept of illness being a result of mental disarray, and correctable by healing wavelengths is a central theme in the alternative medicines: it applies in aromatherapy, colour therapy, biofeedback and other treatments which claim to work on the higher mental states rather than simply on the dysfunctioning cellular tissues alone.

Ultimately the same mechanisms were being brought into play with the instruments of Knuth. But despite the evidence of radio waves and their incredible message-carrying capacity, the public found the concept of the homoeotron just too much to take in. More importantly the homoeotron was a distinct threat to vested business interests.

The sad end of UKA Co. was brought about, in the summer of 1951, by their very commercial success: they had sold such a number of homoeotron contracts that insecticide salesmen were finding few buyers. In January 1952 the leading journal, *Agricultural Chemicals*, denounced them as fraudulent, and, despite their treating 1,420 acres in 1952, the officers of the US Drug Administration had been spreading stories that the process was an outright confidence trick. Their patent applications were rejected, even though they offered respectable scientific support for the hypothesis that every particle of matter has its own generic frequency. The Establishment was out to squash UKA Co. and, sure enough, the firm eventually filed for bankruptcy after some cripplingly expensive court cases.

The American Government's concern that tuned and amplified resonating devices might defraud the public was probably far less than its concern that such devices could also be applied to destroy buildings or even man just as easily as insects. A vivid account by John G. O'Neill[214] in his biography of Nikola Tesla records how Tesla not only used the principle of electrical resonance to light his laboratory with wireless light bulbs, but also carried out experiments with mechanical oscillators:

> He screwed the base of one of his small mechanical oscillators to an iron supporting pillar in the middle of his laboratory and set it into oscillation. It had been his observation that it took some time to build up its maximum speed of vibration. The longer it operated the faster the tempo it attained. He had noticed that all objects did not respond in the same way to vibrations. One of the many objects around the laboratory would suddenly go into violent vibration as it came into resonance with the fundamental vibration of the oscillator, or some harmonic of it. As the period of the oscillator changed, the first object would stop and some other object in resonance with the new rate would start vibrating. Down in Police Headquarters in Mulberry Street the 'cops' were quite familiar with strange sounds and lights coming from the Tesla laboratory. On this particular morning the cops were surprised to feel the building rumbling under their feet. Chairs moved across floors with no-one near them. ... Without waiting for the slow-pokey elevator, the cops rushed up the stairs – and as they did so they felt the building vibrate even more strongly than did Police Headquarters ... Just as the cops rushed into Tesla's laboratory to tackle – they knew not what – the vibrations stopped and they beheld a strange sight. They arrived just in time to see the tall gaunt figure of the inventor swing a heavy sledge hammer and shatter a small iron contraption mounted on the post in the middle of the room. Pandemonium gave way to a deep heavy silence.

Resonance may already have been applied more powerfully than simply to light light bulbs, or even to shake buildings.

In their mysterious account of the so-called Philadelphia Experiment,[31] where a ship was claimed to have been made invisible[56] while at sea in 1943, Charles Berlitz and William Moore came across a Navy source, who remains anonymous, whose verbatim statement of the event runs:

> I think that the conversation at this point had turned to the principles of resonance and how the intense fields which would be required for such an experiment might be achieved using this principle ...
>
> I do remember being at at least one other conference where this matter was a topic on the agenda. During this one we were trying to bring out some of the more obvious-to-us side-effects that would be created by such an experiment. Among these would be a 'boiling' of the water, ionisation of the surrounding air, and even a 'Zeemanising' of the atoms; all of which would tend to create extremely unsettled conditions. No one at this point had ever considered the possibility of interdimensional effects or mass displacement... We also felt that with proper effort some of these problems could be overcome... and that a resonant frequency could probably be found that would possibly control the visual apparent internal oscillation so that the shimmering would be at a much slower rate...
>
> I recall strongly that for a few weeks after the meeting in Albrecht's office [Albrecht is a fictitious name for the actual officer], we kept getting requests for tables having to do with resonant frequencies of light in optical ranges. These were frequently without explanation attached, but it seems likely that there was some connection here.

It might be relevant to add that the day after Tesla died (in January 1943) the FBI removed all his research papers. The Philadelphia Experiment was said to have taken place in October 1943, and Einstein the physicist had been working not, as one might have expected, on the Manhattan Project on the West Coast, but with the US Navy 'on other research' at Princeton. He had also been present at the meetings mentioned above. He had also met Tesla personally on at least one occasion.

It would not be surprising, though the US Navy have always denied it, that they actually carried out military experiments using electrical resonance during that time.

It is odd that William Moore has, since the publication of his book, 'been forced to retreat to live quietly in a remote area', and that several of the people mentioned as having been in the know about the experiment have died prematurely or disappeared.

One more vernacular account of resonance will suffice to bring home the potential dangers. Otto Rahn was a bacteriologist who had published a book[242] on *The Invisible Radiations of Organisms* in 1936. Some ten years later, he was invited to examine some equipment designed by T. Galen Hieronymus.[129] As a result he wrote to the inventor:

> Since those radiations hold the secret of life, they also hold the secret of death. At present very few people know about the possibilities, and very few know *all* the facts. It seems imperative that those few keep their knowledge to themselves, and divulge only as much as necessary to perform the immediate applications to cure disease. Your discoveries open up great possibilities, as tremendous as those of the atom bomb, and just like atomic energy, these radiations may be used for the bad as well as the good of humanity.

What had so alarmed Otto Rahn?

Hieronymus had isolated just three ears of corn, and on each one placed a corn worm. He then began to treat them with his radionic broadcaster, a machine for which he obtained Patent number 2,482,773 in 1949 in the United States and others subsequently in the United Kingdom and Canada. After three days of continuous treatment at the rate of ten minutes each hour, two of the corn worms had been reduced to just 'wet places' on the corn ears, and the third was an amorphous mass. Not unnaturally Hieronymus was shocked by the lethal potential of tuned radiation. Trying to describe the radiation he had unearthed, he speculated that a certain energy, obeying some of the laws of electricity but not all of them, some of the laws of optics but not all of them, exists. He called it eloptic energy; and it will be referred to in Chapter 5, which discusses new hypotheses of the Kirlian effect. Hieronymus and eloptic energy seem a long way from the shattered glass of Enrico Caruso.

The evidence for an energy field in living things has been a consuming interest of Harry Oldfield and myself for some years. For Sheila Ostrander and Lynn Schroder, however, it occupied only a small part of an eight-year collaboration which culminated in 1970 in the publication of their *Psychic Discoveries Behind the Iron Curtain*, a seminal work if ever there was one.[215] Their review of the work of Semyon and Valentina Kirlian took up only 34 pages in their 445-page dossier, yet it generated immense interest throughout the Western world, and scarcely any book

Fig 3.2 The phantom leaf effect. Showing the leaf before and after cutting.

on the paranormal fails to refer to it. Psychic students everywhere hoped that at last a physical phenomenon had been uncovered for that elusive non-phenomenon beloved of eminent Victorian academics like Gilbert Murray, the Human Aura.

Coming at the end of the sixties, when interest in life energy fields had been fanned by such authors as Vladimir Inyushin, Viktor Adamenko, George de la Warr, Simonton, Halacy, Cleve-

LIFE ENERGIES: THE PIONEERS

land Backster, Harvalik, Alexandr S. Presman, Andrija Puharich, Uri Geller, and Madeleine Barnothy, *Psychic Discoveries* was the prelude to more best-sellers in that new market niche like Lyall Watson's *Supernature,* which incidentally includes a section on resonance in its chapter on the physics of life. Watson mentions Garraud's infrasound machine: with this machine when two low-frequency generators are focused on a particular point two miles away they produce a resonance that can knock a building down.

The method of photography developed by the Kirlians originated when Semyon Kirlian, an electronics engineer living at Krasnodar in South Russia, was asked to collect an instrument for repair from a research institute. Whilst there he saw by chance the demonstration of a high-frequency instrument for electrotherapy. Similar machines had been designed by Nikola Tesla in the previous century (and indeed, their commercial popularity had on one occasion saved Tesla's financial bacon). Kirlian noticed that a small flash of light jumped between the electrodes and the patient's skin. Tesla had also given spectacular examples of this phenomenon, and it is surprising that Kirlian did not then immediately recognise what had already been researched in America by his fellow mid-European. At that time Tesla was still alive and generating annual sensationalist press recognition with his birthday reception at which he would invariably promise amazing new inventions, consistently claiming that he had discovered the secret of the wireless transmission of electrical power.[53, 214]

Unfortunately Tesla was 87, and no one wanted to listen to the old man's tales.

Kirlian wondered if he could 'photograph' the sparks he saw by means of a photographic plate placed between the subject and the electrode. After some painful trials Kirlian eventually developed and patented his invention,[160] which consisted of a high-frequency spark-generator, oscillating at between 75,000 and 200,000 electrical oscillations per second. The high-frequency field thus generated causes the object to radiate some sort of bio-luminescence onto the emulsion of the photographic paper. A camera wasn't necessary.[161] (How to build a Kirlian camera is described in detail in Appendix 1.)

The significant advance made by the Kirlians [168,199,201] over Tesla's work concerns their discovery of the phantom leaf effect. Figure 3.2 shows the result of photographing a living leaf from which a great part has been removed. The severed part can still be seen in energy form. The question is, could these phenomena suggest the existence of an underlying morphogenetic field onto which cellular (plant) tissue may previously or subsequently have depended? It was this question which Harry Oldfield set out to investigate, and his findings will be more fully

LIFE ENERGIES: THE PIONEERS

Fig 3.3 Nikola Tesla (centre) and Albert Einstein (front row left) during a visit to an early radio broadcasting station.

documented in the next chapter.

The Kirlians before him had startled Russian scientists when their equipment was able to distinguish, because of clear differences in their energy patterns, between diseased and healthy plant leaves. So with their pulsed high-frequency photography they had successfully prediagnosed disease. (This application is amplified in Chapter 8.)

It was Goethe in the late 1700s, who had recorded seeing flashes of light emitted from poppy flowers at sunset.[104] That minute quantities of light are produced from living organisms formed the basis of a hypothesis first put forward by Georges Lakhovsky in 1924, but only published in England in 1939.[170] Lakhovsky's paper concerned the effects of very short waves on cancer in geraniums. His major work, *L'Origine de la Vie* (1925), was sponsored by Professor d'Arsonval, a well-known biophysicist and the discoverer of diathermy (the application of electrical currents to produce heat in the inner tissues of the body), and became well known on the Continent years before it was translated into English. Lakhovsky was conspicuous for his anti-Nazi views and had to flee from France to New York, where he died in 1943, the same year as the great but now penniless Nikola Tesla (see Fig. 3.3).

In the United States a film was made featuring cases of patients treated with Lakhovsky's invention, the Multiwave Oscillator (see Fig. 3.4), but little interest evolved in Britain: in 1939 the British were occupied in a very different battle. Thus, though Lakhovsky is hailed as the first experimenter to make use of high-frequency electromagnetic waves in the domain of biology, his name, like that of Abrams, is often omitted from textbooks on life fields. Neither he nor Abrams is mentioned by Rupert Sheldrake in his *New Science of Life*,[259] nor by Lyall Watson in *Supernature*.[292] Watson's new book, *Beyond Supernature*[296] corrects the lacuna as far as Abrams is concerned – if the somewhat superficial condemnation it contains can be regarded as sufficient acknowledgement – but there is still no mention of one of the greatest pioneers in life fields, Lakhovsky himself.

The fundamental principle of Lakhovsky's system may be summed up in this axiom: 'Every living being emits radiations.' Guided by this principle, Lakhovsky offered explanations of such diverse phenomena as instinct in animals, migration in birds, health, disease, and in general all the manifestations of organic life. According to him the components of a living cell may be compared to an electrical oscillating circuit. His work was not reported by Sheila Ostrander, since she was concerned only with Russian research; but the excellent *Secret Life of Plants*, by Peter Tompkins and Christopher Bird, does do justice to his contribution. Lakhovsky even had an explanation of how cells maintain their oscillations by proposing an interesting system

LIFE ENERGIES: THE PIONEERS

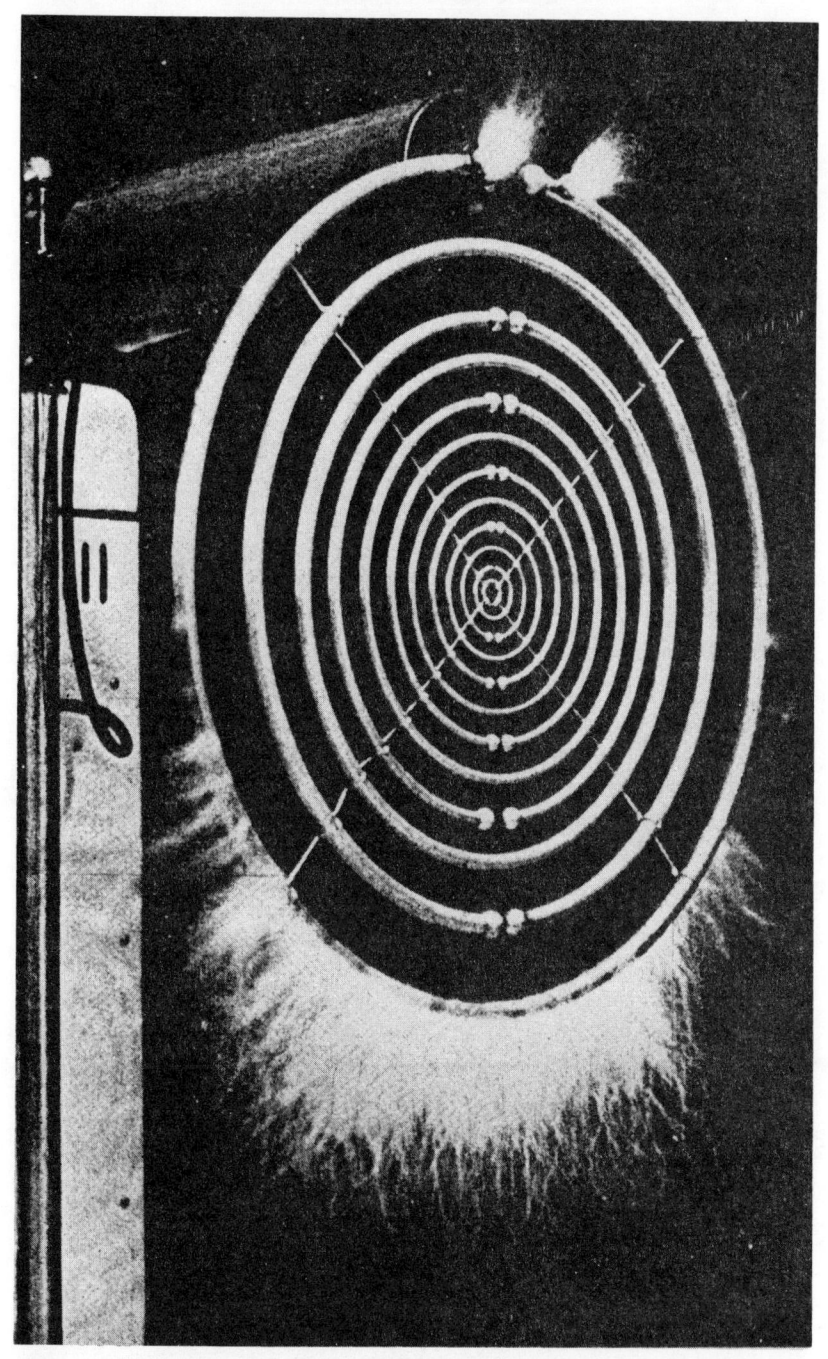

Fig 3.4 Lakhovsky's Multiple Wave Oscillator. (From The Waves That Heal, *Mark Clement, 1949)*

of 'Universion'. He considered that the 'twisted filaments' in cells (we now call them DNA macromolecules) are really minute oscillating circuits with capacity and inductance, and capable of oscillating according to a specific frequency. (See Fig. 3.5.) The living cell can thus play the part either of a transmitter or a receiver of exceedingly short radio waves, which give rise to high-frequency currents in the circuits of the cellular nucleus. He further proposed a source of the energy which would be needed to maintain the oscillations, his source being cosmic

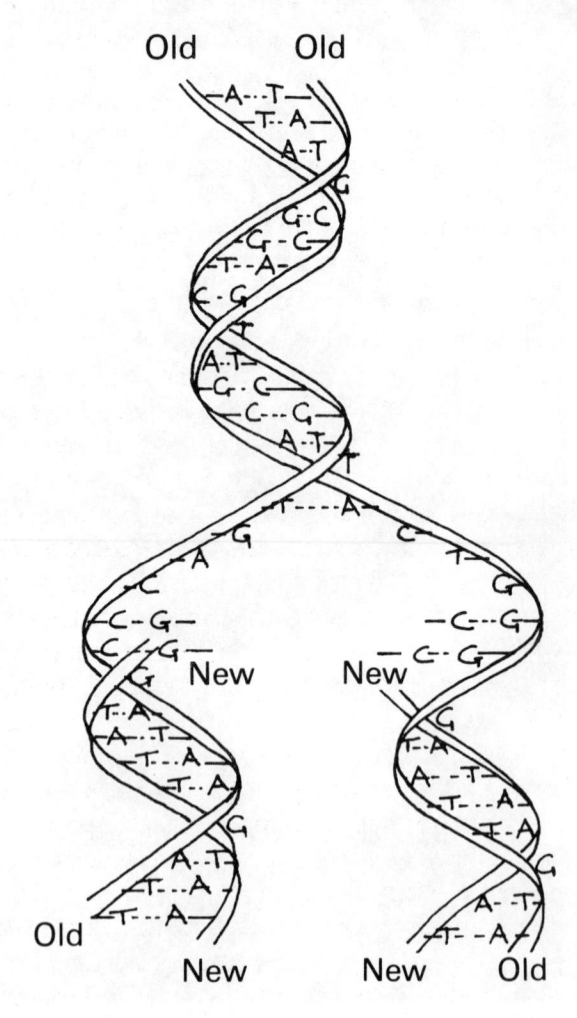

Fig 3.5 How DNA replicates. The DNA splits, and RNA chains 'new' join each 'old' strand to make up a new double helix of DNA.

radiation. According to Lakhovsky the fight between living organisms and microbes is fundamentally 'a war of radiations'.

Though we discuss these hypotheses in more detail in Chapter 5, the essence of Lakhovsky's thinking is well summarised here by his translator, Mark Clement:[55]

> During recent years observations on the part of several investigators have established the fact that most animals, including insects and birds, emit radiations while they are also sensitive to the influence of external electro-magnetic waves. These radiations emitted by all living beings, cover an indefinite range and are characterised by a multitude of different wavelengths. In the immense range of existing radiations we can only perceive the luminous octave but we know that a whole gamut of radiations exists beyond the narrow limits of the visible spectrum. The limitations of our senses prevent us from perceiving radiations of living beings and this sensory incapacity also excludes from the field of direct awareness a vast gamut of electro-magnetic waves traversing our atmosphere. Yet all these radiations and waves exist and affect all forms of life in various ways.

All this before commercial television, too!

The prognostic value of electric patterns discernible in plant cells was brought out by a contemporary of Lakhovsky, Professor E. J. Lund, who found that these change half an hour before the diffusion of hormones can be effected, and growth detected; as if the electrical pattern is a prerequisite of cellular growth.[184]

The frustrating history of life fields for the early pioneers may be summed up in the view that their claims foundered on the simple lack of electronic means to detect and perceive the radiations they believed to be emanating from living organisms. Accordingly, Mesmer's 'animal magnetism', Reichenbach's 'odyle force', George Washington Crile's 'radiogens',[62] Lemström's 'electrocultur', William Ross's 'galvanic energy', Wilhelm Reich's 'orgone energy', Ruth Drown's radiovision instruments, Albert Abrams' oscilloclast, and Upton's homoeotron were all disparaged for lack of a means to detect and make manifest the underlying radiations and their qualities in terms consistent with modern physics. Lakhovsky's fate was little different.

Clement concludes his account with a forecast that malignant tumours will one day be diagnosed at a distance on television tubes (we call them oscilloscopes nowadays) and by reference to the blood cells of the patient. Researchers are now testing the blood of AIDS carriers to prove the existence of antibodies, and even more direct tests are being developed which do not have to wait for the antibodies to establish themselves.[257]

Today, to quote a well-worn phrase, we have the technology.

Actually, the Americans may have had the technology since 1943. From time to time during this chapter we have referred to the Philadelphia Experiment. The one thing we have not discussed about it are the biological effects on some of the human beings involved, effects which appear to have been more horrendous than Otto Rahn's worst nightmares. This part of the story, branded like all the rest as fiction by the US Navy, has persisted ever since its supposed occurrence in October 1943, when a small Navy ship, the D173, was said to have been dematerialised using electromagnetic resonance. The biological by-products of the tests, it is said, caused the crew to suffer periodic dematerialisation for years afterwards, despite receiving every possible medical attention in secret institutions in response to the experiment which had gone so dreadfully wrong.

There are several circumstantial antecedents which could have led up to the attempt to camouflage a ship electromagnetically. First we have recorded the story that when Nikola Tesla died, old and penniless, in a New York hotel room on 7 January 1943, the FBI removed the research papers from the safe in his room. According to Margaret Cheney, another excellent biographer of Tesla,[53] they also took away box upon box of research documents stretching back over his entire career. Tesla had for some years been claiming all kinds of discoveries, none of which had been paid much heed in view of his advanced age. But the research he had carried out when much younger into high-frequency fields was still much ahead of his time, and indeed a *tesla* is a modern unit of magnetic field strength used even today in his honour. So his research would have been of great interest to the US military who were becoming involved in the development of atomic fission devices on the other side of the country at Los Alamos. Strangely Einstein was not much involved in the Manhattan Project: he was kicking his heels at Princeton, and was only too delighted when he was suddenly seconded into the US Navy in June 1943 to advise on novel naval explosive devices, and, according to George Gamow, a famous colleague, on anything else unusual which came up.

A large number of projects were brought to Einstein each fortnight by Gamow, one of science's more colourful characters, who came down from Washington by train to see him. It would not be impossible for some of Tesla's papers to have found their way into Gamow's briefcase. Alongside them one might also have found details of some of the amazing cures which Lakhovsky, freshly arrived from Europe after fleeing the Nazis, had been effecting by his electromagnetic multiwave oscillating instruments in several New York hospitals.

However that may be, we do glean several clues from Einstein's biographers of the period that he was in fact looking into resonance effects for the Navy: 'Einstein was intermittently employed in the Special Service Contract of the Dept. of the Navy, Washington DC as a Scientist from 31st May 1943 to 30th June 1944.' So state the records of the General Service Administration St Louis, Missouri.

Dr Francis Bitter, founder of the Magnet Laboratory at MIT, confirms that the Navy were intensely interested in the shipboard use of strong magnetic fields in the early forties, and recalls having seen 'a relatively large ship carrying a strong magnet weighing many many tons'.[36] Ronald Clark's biography of Einstein, a detailed and scholarly work,[54] mentions Einstein's connection with Gamow, saying that ideas included using a convergent detonation wave formed by combining two explosives with different propagation velocities. Plans were made for a model test at Indian Head, the Navy Proving Grounds on the Potomac River, but that the project was suddenly dropped. Finally 'Starshell', the Bureau of Ordnance publication, later confirmed that Einstein's work concerned: 'The theory of explosion, seeking to determine what laws govern the more obscure waves of detonation, why certain explosives have marked directional effect, and other highly technical theories.'

The conversation alleged by 'Albrecht' discussed how it might be possible, using resonance, to achieve the high electromagnetic field required for optical invisibility.

Whatever the military objectives of the experiment, what now concerns us is the effect it seems to have had on the crew. Somewhere, according to Berlitz, there was a newspaper report saying that the crew from the D173 came ashore after the experiment, and during a drinking session at a local bar that evening horrified waitresses by going through solid walls, becoming invisible, and generally causing a shock.

By some strange coincidence whilst Einstein was working for the US Navy on new kinds of naval mines, Francis Crick, who was to become the discoverer of the structure of DNA, was working for the Admiralty in London on exactly the same subject. By a further coincidence the first work Crick involved himself in on leaving the Admiralty was in the investigation of the effects of ultraviolet light on living cells.

During the summer of 1943 Bertrand Russell happened to be in Princeton, and spent some time with Einstein and with Wolfgang Pauli. How much Russell learned about Einstein's work is not known. It was later suggested that Einstein was horrified by the uses to which the effects could be put, and told Russell that the world was not yet ready for it. His opinion has always until now been regarded as referring to the Atomic bomb, even though he was not much involved in its development. One wonders, though, whether he might instead have been referring to the other experiment in which he had been so involved during Russell's stay in America.

In another letter, to Otto Stern, in December 1944, Einstein seems to repeat his conclusion:

> I can report no more on the matter than that we are not the first who have faced similar things. I have the impression that one must strive strenuously to be responsible. One does best not to speak about the matter for the time being, and that it would in no way help, at the present moment, to bring it to public notice. It is difficult for me to speak in such a nebulous way, but for the moment I cannot do anything else.

Hardly words about a highly secret military problem: rather something more fundamental to the concern of mankind that ought not at present to be told to the public at large. For his consultancy Einstein was paid $25 a day, perhaps an unwitting contributor to the science of life fields.

If our suspicions are correct what light can the affair throw on our study?

Leaving aside the possibility of complete teleportation, let us concentrate on the biological effects. These are described[31] allegedly by a certain Carlos Allende in a letter in 1956 to Morris Jessup, author of *The Case for the UFO*,[145] and a somewhat depressed scientist. The first description, however, comes from another member of the original crew: 'Some saw double, others began to stagger like they were drunk, and a few passed out. Some even claimed that they had passed into another world and had seen and talked to alien beings... Several had died; but the rest of us they just let go.'

And then, from Allende:

> Half the officers and crew of the ship are at present mad as hatters. They are confined to certain areas where they either 'go blank', or 'go blank and get stuck'. ' Going blank ' is not at all an unpleasant experience to healthy curious sailors. However it is when they also 'get stuck' that they call it hell incorporated. The man thusly stricken cannot move of his own volition unless two or more of those who are with him within the field go and touch him, or else he 'freezes'.
>
> If a man 'freezes' his position must be marked out carefully and then the field is cut off.

Allende then describes why, in his words, man is not yet ready for force-field work, curiously paraphrasing Einstein's letter, and then continues:

> A highly complicated piece of equipment had to be constructed in order to unfreeze those who became 'true froze' or deep freeze subjects. Usually a 'deep freeze' man goes stark raving gibbering running mad if his freeze is for more than a day in our time ...
>
> If you see a group of sailors in the act of putting their hands upon a fellow, or upon 'thin air', observe the digits and appendages of the stricken man. If they seem to waver as though in a heat mirage, go quickly and put *your* hands upon him. For that man is the very most desperate of men in the world.

Well! What are we to make of all that!

First it seems as if the effect was often replicated, and that it lasted long after the experiment had taken place. But when we compare the phenomena described here with the hypothesis which we make later in the book, there are really few surprises. Without attempting a full explanation here, let us just point out these features:

1. The symptoms included dementia, hallucination, and general confusion of brain function.
2. The extremities were most affected.
3. The patient was 'normalised' by contact with other human beings.

4. Complicated apparatus was necessary to restore the patient in severe cases.
5. A small magnetic field was likely to exacerbate the condition.
6. There was the possibility of dematerialisation or enduring burning sensations of the skin.

In a second letter the so-called Carlos Allende added that these effects were an unforeseen side effect of the experiment, that dematerialisation happened on several occasions, the patient never reappearing, and that the wearing of metallic objects such as hob-nailed boots seemed to have a particularly damaging effect.

It is of course very difficult to accept such a story at face value. However, the description fits so well with what our hypothesis, based on our Kirlian photography and phantom leaf effect experiments, that we feel justified in including it.

In a quite different sort of letter to Francis Crick and James Watson,[149] Max Delbruck said: 'I have a feeling that if your structure of the DNA molecule is true, then all hell will break loose, and theoretical biology will enter a most tumultuous phase.'

We do not think he meant his words to be so prophetic.

There was no doubt, however, following a Conference in 1975 at Asilomar to discuss the urgent restriction of experiments on recombinant DNA, that June Goodfield meant every word in her book *Playing God*[105] when she said: 'The forum of 1975 will turn out to represent the moment in history when attention finally turns away from the issue of whether or not to do the research ... which is now decided.'

What she may not have recognised at that time was that such experiments were leading to the beginning not only of chemically controlled genetics, but also the beginning of electronic medicine.

No account of the pioneers of life fields would be complete without acknowledging the contribution made over the last twenty-one years by Professor Bernard Watson of Bart's Hospital. Over the decades he has built up a powerful research unit in the Medical College of the Hospital, a superb act of administration, paralleled only by his skills in maintaining a foothold on most alternative medical electronic research work from within the Establishment. In consequence he commands a research effort which is the envy of many academic establishments; at the same time he retains that great prerequisite of discovery, a complete approachability, and willingness to listen to the most unorthodox of ideas. To most of these he can make a contribution, himself having specialised in many areas of the body. He would describe himself as a 'measurements man', but this would be too modest a description. We conclude this chapter by quoting from his recent report[290] on the work being carried out on bioelectricity in the medical electronics department of the Medical College:

> [The study of pulsed magnetic fields] is a completely new area of biological interactions which are extremely difficult to research as they involve regulatory mechanisms and also field strengths so low that they have been previously considered to have no effect. Recently our study on the immunological changes brought about by exposing human lymphocytes to pulsed magnetic fields indicates that we should be aware of the dangers of environmental electromagnetic fields caused by 50 Hz power transmissions. We intend to pursue this work in order to establish the therapeutic use and also the dangers involved.

The disturbing implication of Watson's comment is that the sea of electromagnetism in which we live may be having serious effects on our bodies' immune defences.

4
The Work Of Harry Oldfield

Harry was born in England, the son of a London bus-driver, and has since been overtaking other researchers in the more conventional sciences by his unorthodox investigations into life fields.

Even before he was 12 years old, he was known as the shrimp king at his local comprehensive school in Hammersmith. This was because he had invented a process of growing a special form of shrimp in captivity, a process quickly taken up by a fish food company which paid Harry the handsome outright royalty of £100. The company went on to make the process into a viable operation and made many thousands of pounds.

Thus was set in train a keen interest in the natural sciences. Many people today continue to benefit from Harry's more important inventions. This includes his pioneer research in the UK on the use of Kirlian photography as a medical research tool. From these beginnings he developed a three-dimensional method of scanning the body non-invasively, and a number of therapies using electromagnetic fields and crystalline structures. He is now the principal and founder of a school with students coming from many parts of the world, and his electro-crystal therapy is being taught to and practised by people round the globe.

Science had always been his first love, even as a schoolboy. It was fun, he says, but also a hard task-master, and Harry gained a good appreciation of scientific methodology – the control of variables, replication, and the importance of objective experimentation. Keen to follow the teaching profession and to specialise in scientific subjects, Harry was lucky to be accepted as a trainee teacher at the tender age of 17, proceeding afterwards to obtain his Diploma of Education. At his first teaching job, Harry found himself comfortably teaching general science to 11–13-year-olds, and biology and physics to 14–18-year-olds. At this school in his early days, Harry got the nickname of 'the Mad Prof', a name which stuck throughout his teaching career. This was probably instigated by his accidental blowing up of a school science laboratory. Harry always endeavoured to make his science interesting for his pupils! There was always stiff competition amongst the youngsters to get into the Mad Prof's science class – mainly because most of them hoped that one day he might succeed in blowing up the whole school!

His explosive reputation was increased by another incident which occurred during a third-form science class when he was supposed to be teaching the buoyancy of gases. Again, deciding to make his classes interesting and make science come to life for his young charges, he got the class to construct a hydrogen balloon, measuring some four feet in diameter. Having filled it from a small cylinder, he and his pupils proudly marched into the main school playground. But a gust of wind wrenched the balloon out of his hand. It was carried off across the playground gaining height as it went, hampered on its ascent by a short but firm knock against the Headmaster's window! The Headmaster threw open the window and looked down at the startled but innocent young faces. Harry, at this moment in time, happened not to be in the Headmaster's vision (a wise move, one might think, on Harry's part). The Headmaster's eyes now looked skywards at the magnificent but fast-vanishing balloon. 'You could only be', he said, with a smile on his face, which put the children at their ease, 'one of Mr Oldfield's science classes. When you see him, please tell the Mad Prof to keep the noise down: not all of us can have this amount of fun on a Monday morning.' Many such incidents continued to occur for some years to brighten up Monday morning.

As any other teacher might be, he was bombarded with a myriad of seemingly naïve questions from the young pupils some of which, even today, science cannot fully explain. 'In the embryo of a human being, what makes a toe a toe and not an eye?' Questions such as these led Harry to become interested, in a mildly curious way, in the general question of morphogenetic fields. The other great influence from Harry's early upbringing was his profound belief in Christianity.

Most of us can point to specific events which subsequently prove to be turning points in our lives. With Harry Oldfield it was a photograph: a Kirlian picture of the phantom leaf effect.

The accompanying article – a magazine sometime in 1976 is all he can recollect – explained roughly how to make the apparatus that had produced it, and Harry immediately put the project of doing so to his school's science club. The club was a venture which he ran two or three evenings a week for youngsters interested in science who wanted to take it further than the school curriculum allowed.

With the help of another teacher and friend, Ian McGibbon, the club had soon produced its first Kirlian photographs, and some rather unsteady attempts at the phantom leaf effect. Further refinements improved the pictures, but the energy field from which they came did not stay very long before it broke up, following, it seems, the third law of thermodynamics (entropy, where the natural state is one of chaos).

As a result of the fascinating pictures they were producing, the science club's membership increased dramatically. Everyone was interested in this amazing new way of photographing living things and people.

Ideas flowed thick and fast, and well exceeded the club's slender funds to follow them. One project which did proceed, however – and did so because it was funded by a benefactor, a Colonel McCausland, was to examine the Kirlian photographic differences between wholefoods and processed foods.

The results showed clear differences between the two. As a result, Colonel McCausland persuaded Harry to present his results to a meeting of the Health Education Council. 'The results received a good hearing, and prompted much discussion,' said Harry. 'However, at the end of the meeting a young American biochemist working here in a London hospital asked permission to speak to me in private. As it turned out, he was working on the biochemical synthesis of cancer cells and tissues. His suggestion was that I should turn my attention away from nutrition and start looking at disease. His name was Glen Rein, and it was the beginning of a long and fruitful friendship.'

Not long afterwards, Harry arrived promptly at two in the afternoon at Rein's laboratory. After a few interesting results, the two became immersed in their work. 'The next thing I knew it was two in the morning,' says Harry.

Together they tested many kinds of tissue, exploring the use of Kirlian photography across a wide range of experiments. In some of these, being short of human subjects, Glen Rein would often act as the photographic subject. Harry noticed something strange about Rein's Kirlian handprints: there would be times when he did not give out any energy for the Kirlian image to form. There seemed no logical reason for this, nor was it connected with any ailments or changed mental states. Then the common denominator was finally uncovered: Rein used radioactive tracers occasionally in his normal work. Any time that he did so, his 'Kirlian' energy level was drastically affected.

Meanwhile, the science club was also continuing with its own Kirlian researches. One day, a little girl came running up to Harry with a sloppy plate of mush – 'There's nothing in it at all,' she cried. 'The photograph was blank!' 'Well,' replied Harry,'what did you expect from a school dinner!' (School dinners, says Harry, have improved, however, since this time.)

As the work progressed the amateur team found that their Kirlian machine could not only cause objects to generate light but also sound radio energy, a discovery which eventually led to the development of body scanning instruments. After three years of such experiments, Harry gave up teaching to devote himself to full-time research, and Eileen, his wife, took on the role of financial support supplemented by a small private grant to purchase instruments, oscilloscopes and other research tools. This was in 1979. Harry's electrical engineer Jamie Pridmore gave him a good deal of unpaid support in addition.

By this time his Kirlian photography was attracting a good deal of attention in the popular press and in medical journals, and as well as giving occasional lectures Harry contributed many articles to a wide range of magazines, such as the *Observer*, *She* magazine, and the *Journal of Alternative Medicine*.

This was not, however, particularly fulfilling: even if the early diagnosis of carcinogenic tissue was possible using Kirlian techniques, this went no way towards actually treating the unfortunate patient who thereby learned of his cancer.

Harry reasoned that if energy was a pre-symptom of disease, then energy could also be applied to correct it. He found that the combination of an applied electrical field and natural crystals (to amplify its effect) were having a therapeutic effect on his subjects. What is more, his early successes were bruited abroad by subjects who had happily experienced the healing properties of his technique; and a stream of people began contacting him for treatment. Harry himself placed no advertisements. The instruments were manufactured for him by Jamie Pridmore.

Harry's interest in this complementary therapy grew, fostered by his Christian beliefs, and so he took the course in homoeopathic medicine offered by the famous Hahnemann College of Homoeopathy.

Shortly after, a distraught parent in Iceland invited him to attend his schizophrenic son. Harry's success has enabled him to help a number of people in Iceland, which he now visits each year. Lecture courses in San Francisco and Canada have also become a regular feature.

I myself came across Harry whilst researching for a TV script on the Life of Nikola Tesla, whose patents will be about 100 years old by the time this book is published. By sheer chance, I was describing to an acquaintance an article which I would very much like to have seen, when to my surprise I was told that Harry Oldfield had a copy. He was only too pleased to let me see it. In return for this favour, he asked if I could make a copy of a video for him. What video? I asked cautiously. And so I soon found myself watching three-dimensional Kirlian photography for the first time: it was unmistakably similar to the electromagnetic streamers so graphically demonstrated by Tesla a century ago.[189]

As a result of his incipient homoeopathic practice, Harry found that hopeless cancer cases were being referred to him more and more. A steady stream of people were making their way to his unpretentious Ruislip semi-detached house. To make things easier he therefore opened a weekly clinic in the London house of a grateful subject, where he now sees some twelve people a day. But this was not enough to cope with the demand. Furthermore, alternative and orthodox medical practitioners and students were keen to learn more about the electroscanning method and electrocrystal therapy which he had begun to use, based on Kirlian techniques. So Harry started holding weekend seminars, necessarily restricted to the dozen people he could fit into his drawing room. These courses were enlivened by amazing demonstrations of the crystal and Kirlian effects, videos of regeneration in human beings, practical examples of laser therapy using cold neon, and the treatment of patients on the spot as examples of electroscanning and crystal therapy in action. Only when they had completed his course would he allow them to buy his electronic instruments, fearing their misuse in the wrong hands.

The demand from other parts of the world is also growing.

Harry finds himself, often accompanied by Eileen and his son Tony, spending as much as four months each year out of Britain on lecture tours. These have included such locations as San Francisco, Canada, Mexico, Holland, Germany, and of course an annual trip to Iceland, at all of which he has lectured on electrocrystal therapy and energy field detection.

During one of his early clinics, the subject, a publisher, suggested that it would be tragic if Harry's experience with Kirlian photography and its developments and discoveries went unpublished. Even so, it has taken six years and one false start to get this book to press – as Harry would be the first to admit his own writing style was not up to the standard required!

Harry feels that invaluable though Kirlian photography has proved as a development tool, its lessons should now be applied in more sophisticated techniques. The biological mechanisms which it has exposed represent a real step forward in our understanding of how the body works, grows, repairs itself, repels disease, and reacts to crises. Without it, the evidence and impetus for a radiating morphogenetic field hypothesis would have been neglected. Like many alternative practitioners – and Harry is now a consultant to the Editorial Board of the *Alternative Journal of Medicine* – his work (never his sincerity) has been criticised. Professor Watson points out that the dictates of a medical electronics department of a hospital like Bart's cannot afford to develop the personal skills of the people they train to use their instruments:

> The machinery has got to work for us without any interpretive skills being necessary, and the answer must be in the objective print-out, cathode ray tube, waveform, or digital display – without equivocation.

Harry's view is that all violins are more or less the same, but the result of playing them will vary in the hands of a novice and a master: scanning a body for abnormal waveforms is a standard procedure which anyone can do. Adjusting the correct normalising setting of the electrocrystal therapy machine is also objective. The skill will lie only in the correct diagnosis of the disease and here he would always wish to work with orthodox medical practice. Harry does not believe that his instruments can supplant medicine, but they can, like pharmaceuticals, assist in the treatment.

In some cases they may, however, be able to do what pharmaceuticals cannot. AIDS is one such area where Harry feels that an urgent research programme, involving medical protocol, should be undertaken to investigate the use of his therapy. His experience with AIDS patients is naturally limited, but already he has seen a good remission from Kaposi's sarcoma in one of the several cases referred to him.[297] All have noticed improved vitality moreover. In the face of such a frightening disease there is no longer any room for the present schism between conventional and alternative medicine, he thinks. We desperately need to monitor the effects of our instruments on the leucocytes of AIDS patients, yet we have to rely on the goodwill of hospitals whose doctors are apathetic or hostile to our concepts.

One day during my research for this book, arriving on the sixth floor of St Mary's Hospital Medical School at the immunology department after a bewildering journey down endless corridors with rooms full of equipment, I could not help remembering that Harry's tiny laboratory is about eight foot square, jammed with all kinds of natural crystals alongside the oscilloscopes, Tesla coils, micro-computers, and a noticeboard. On the noticeboard is pinned a small note of thanks from Michael Crawford, the entertainer, a photograph of a happy smiling girl, a No Smoking sign, and a Christian prayer. The one chair in the room is for his subjects. There is no room for another.

Harry is adamant about protecting his family life, reserving the evenings and the weekends, when he is not giving courses, exclusively for the family. Eileen, his gentle Irish wife, does not pretend to understand Harry's machines, but takes care of the accounts, and supplies generous wholesome meals for visitors on courses, and liquid refreshment for waiting patients.

During the six years since he started, Harry has treated hundreds of people, and his pupils around the world have probably treated many thousands more. Nevertheless he is not quick to talk about case histories, suggesting that it is better to ask the patients whether they are cured or not. From a mass of documentation I have chosen two cases which are typical of Harry's success, which are reprinted here with the kind permission of *Alternative Medicine Today*, where they were first written up:

> Anne Whitwell was first diagnosed as having cancer in November 1984. She recalls: I had been attending the Well Woman Clinic at

the Marsden Cancer Hospital yearly since 1982 for fibro-adenosis or chronic mastitis, which apparently often presages cancer – although no one told me this at the time. Preceding diagnosis – I was 39 at the time – I had noticed a distinct energy change. I work as an illustrator and my natural vigour decreased and I often found I had to rest. I then lived near a busy road in Kilburn in London and poor air, poor eating and sleeping, tension, and a hard knock on the affected area all added up to what I was sure was cancer. On top of that I come from a family with a history of early death from cancer.

On my third annual visit to the Marsden my worst fears were confirmed. A lump was found the size of a small plum in my left breast and I was briskly informed that it 'must' be removed. In the usual passive patient role I did not protest.

The lump was found to be an adenocarcinoma or cancer of the gland tissue, and it was infiltrating, that is it was spreading locally. It was found in the inner top quadrant which the specialist said was a particularly ominous area. Worst of all though was the discovery that the cancer cells were 'poorly differentiated', which means that they are cells particularly suited to spreading to any organ or part of the body since they cannot differentiate one part from another. I knew then that my chances of survival were slim.

Despite this I was told that if I had a lumpectomy followed by radiation I had a '98 per cent chance'. I knew at once that this was not so, that I was being lied to, but I nevertheless agreed to start treatment. In retrospect I would not have had any of it. Over the years of my attendance at the Marsden I must have received about twelve X-rays on my breasts and one chest X-ray. X-rays are very powerful and I believe they seriously deplete the energies of the body and harm cells. They even make one prone to cancer I think.

At any rate shortly after my diagnosis I went into hospital for three days and was given a bone scan, which involved being given a radioactive injection and made me sick, and then still feeling ill and weak, I was given the lumpectomy, the operation to remove the lump. They sent me home for a week then, and told me to come back to start my course of radiotherapy. But I was not at all happy. Something told me to look for an alternative better than radiation. I made desperate enquiries and came to a vital decision.

I decided – against strong pressure from the hospital – to refuse radiotherapy. I knew instinctively as it were that radiation would weaken my system, damage tissue, and in any case hardly ever alters the outcome, and certainly that it would not in my case.

I have since been told that if I had had radiotherapy my thymus would have been unable to receive the healing energies it needed to re-educate the cancerous cells and my subsequent treatment might have been in vain. After my refusal I proceeded to become very ill indeed. Within two weeks of my operation, and following my decision to go it alone, I had bouts of severe weakness when I needed to rest for much of the day.

Sometimes I would experience forceful feelings of 'dark energies' surging up through my body from the bottom up. Pains would cascade everywhere, sometimes so acute that they would cause me to flinch or even shout out loud. I found out later that these are symptoms of the disease having taken a severe hold and are a sign that the cancer is at a fairly advanced stage. I was clearly dying.

But having taken the decision to take responsibility for my life in my own hands, I anxiously set out on a programme of self-improvement. I changed my diet following a visit to the British Cancer Help Centre and learned to meditate and direct healing energies round my body from the Maxwell Cade Biofeedback Centre in London. I was also greatly uplifted by the power of a healer.

But it was not nearly enough. The dark forces took a greater hold and I felt myself beginning to slip under. Then an extraordinary stroke of luck came my way.

I had been attending a cancer group held by Dr Anne Woolley-Hart the pioneer medical researcher into alternative forms of cancer treatment at St Bartholomew's Hospital. One night early in 1985 she drove me to a lecture being given at the College of Psychic Studies in London by someone called Harry Oldfield. I had never heard of him but I was really very ill by this time and I went because Anne suggested it.

He couldn't have been more sympathetic and agreed to start treating me with his new electrocrystal therapy unit. Compared with the dreadful treatment at the hospital it was simplicity and gentleness itself. My thymus, which involves the immune system, had a very low reading on the scanner Harry uses. This is apparently typical of the cancer patient. I was also found to have an equally low reading in the area of my coccyx, at the base of the spine. I went each week for an hour long session during which Harry used his quartz sistrine crystals on my thymus and laser crystal therapy on my coccyx.

These two things together were probably, I believe, the cause of my body's first collapse of energies and the resulting imbalance. My head was also low in energy according to the meter, probably due to an energy block in the neck from tensions and stress. Cathartic release would rid the system of many such blocks, but meanwhile electromagnetic inputs are a surer and quicker way of releasing blockages and restoring balance, and are essential for the person with cancer.

I started this treatment at the end of the winter of 1985, and in April I acquired my own machine and was able to start treating myself. Gradually I got better. In September four 'hot spots' appeared, three in my left breast, and one in my right and all were 'quietened' by feeding in very low energy. One morning in November – I remember it vividly – I woke up, having kept my energies in good balance daily with the machine for some weeks and I was better again. I suddenly and incredulously realised I was well.

My body with very little treatment, now maintains a good energy balance naturally, whereas before I had needed long hours on the machine every day. My pains have long gone and to this day my energy is back in abundance.*

The second case is one of multiple sclerosis, one of the most baffling diseases to medical science, and one which we discuss in more detail in Chapter 8. Mallory Ramsdale, an active and fun-loving girl of 31, was struck by multiple sclerosis in 1980, her mother having died of the same condition after many years' severe suffering. 'The first attack', she relates, 'began just as I was about to go off on holiday with my husband to America in the summer. It was nothing much at first. I just felt as if I was leaning over to the left. I thought it was the heels of my shoes worn down!' She continues:

But after only a few days in America things got worse. My legs began giving way, and within a week I could hardly stagger. My face also went numb and I had violent sickness. I was seen by two American specialists who basically did not know what it was, despite doing a great many tests. They said it was either a brain tumour, or polio, or MS – but they only mentioned MS after I told them about my mother having had MS and dying at 44. In the end they said they thought it was probably a condition known as Bell's Palsy or inflammation of the brain stem.

Back home, my own doctor put me on immediate injection for Bell's Palsy without doing any confirming checks of his own. He simply accepted what the American doctors told him. Well, it made no difference at all. I felt worse if anything. In the end they told me to rest. That was all. I was off work for four months – I am the private secretary to the Chairman of a City bank – and finally my

---

*Following 3 years of successful treatment, Anne Whitwell suffered an unforeseen setback in her illness which resulted in a fatal secondary tumour. We would like to pay tribute to Anne's bravery and to thank her family for allowing us to print her story.

condition did stabilise enough to allow me back.

That was in the November, and I was fine then until the following July. I remember because it was the time of the Royal Wedding. I woke up one morning with a tingling in my face and double vision. Then my left leg started dragging and I began dropping things. I spent two weeks at the Royal Free Hospital undergoing tests followed by further tests at the National Hospital for Nervous diseases who finally diagnosed multiple sclerosis at the end of the summer of 1981.

I was told that there was simply nothing they could do. They said: 'Go home and try and forget about it. Lead a normal life and try not to worry. If it happens again, go to your GP and he'll give you a course of pain-killing injections. I was off work three months, sitting at home at Dunstable, getting very depressed. Then my mother-in-law Dorothy stepped in and decided she would try and do something about it using spiritual healing. She is a great believer but I must admit I was highly sceptical. I thought it was all a load of nonsense. Nevertheless I agreed to give it a go and let her persuade me to see a faith healer at the spiritualists' headquarters in Belgrave Square in London.

She then says an extraordinary thing happened. I really do not know how to treat this even today – but when we got to Belgrave Square for the appointment she says she had forgotten the name of the healer we were supposed to have seen. Suddenly though, the name 'Harry Oldfield' came into her head, even though she had never heard of him before.

So she asked for Harry Oldfield, and then we were shown into a room where a surprised Harry was that night giving a lecture. He is not a spiritualist and was only renting a room there for his talk because it was one of the cheapest around, he told me later. He was very kind, and agreed to try and treat me with a revolutionary system using the low level electrical transference of healing energy from crystals which he calls 'electrocrystal therapy'.

I did not understand the method, but it seemed harmless enough, and in any case I had no one else to turn to. Harry saw me every other week for half an hour for treatment and over the next year or so I became completely better. I was able to do all the things I like doing which I could not do before. I do like having fun and I suppose I did occasionally try and burn the candle at both ends, which did not always help, but here I was able to enjoy a normal life again.

Do not ask me to explain how it worked; it just did. In fact I did have a slight relapse in 1983 when my dear grandmother died. It was quite a shock and I think it was that that did it. You do not ever cure MS, you just control it. Once it is there it is always there. It is part of the process of your body. But you can manage it.

So when I had my attack, I went straight round to see Harry and he treated me every day for half an hour. I went to him on a Tuesday, and by the Saturday I was fine again. The numbness in my face had completely gone. And I am delighted to say that was nearly three years ago and I have been fine ever since. I still go to Harry once every four to six weeks for stabilising treatment – he says it works by balancing out the energy centres, or chakras, in the human body and re-energising them – and I have my own machine at home I use about once a week for a quick top up if I get particularly tired, as I do sometimes. But to all intents and purposes I am back to leading as active and busy a life as ever. I work a twelve-hour day, commuting between Dunstable and the City, and I still like to burn the candle at both ends if I can (although it's usually followed by a couple of early nights afterwards!) I am 37 now and I've never felt better.

My own doctor thinks it's all a waste of time and money. He says it's all in my mind. He has told me : 'You know, don't you, that it's only a natural remission. You'll be worse again later.'

He can say what he likes. All I know is that I am better again and no one else was able to help me as Harry has done. I was highly sceptical of all this alternative stuff before, but not any more.

Of course, the two testimonials above are of little use in persuading medical opinion of the efficacy of Harry's machine, and they are certainly not quoted here with that object in mind. To evaluate his system requires proper medical protocol and double-blind placebo controlled trials, which will involve perhaps thousands of patients and many machines, half of which would be completely empty inside but look so like the real thing that no one could tell the difference. A small step in that direction was the use of electrocrystal therapy on people suffering from tinnitus, of which there are 200,000 in this country alone, though perhaps 7 million people in Britain experience it. A nationwide tinnitus helpline called Whistle Stop is operated by John and Jean Brown of Basildon, Essex for people who suffer from this strange ailment which causes a painful buzzing in the head and ears. Eighteen of their three hundred members received three hours treatment with the unit during six months from March 1985. Of these four felt that after treatment the tinnitus pain had not changed (though John Brown says cryptically in his write-up that in one of these cases there were other circumstances which could have contributed to this result). The remaining fourteen all felt that the treatment had reduced the tinnitus to a more acceptable level, and often stopped the pain, though the noise remained. Seven of these had such an improvement that they could scarcely hear the noise at all. The tinnitus was started off again by some trigger, like a bad headache, but the next treatment stopped it again. There was often a delay of a few days before the effects of the electrocrystal treatment were noticed to have changed the noise level; but the pain level subsided almost immediately by using the correct setting, actually during the first treatment. The machine is still in regular use by the helpline, but a number of members have since bought their own portable units. The only other methods anything like as effective, says John Brown, are relaxation techniques.

This sort of proof is more objective: it did not rely on Harry's presence, and it provided replicable evidence of a specific effect. It is sad, however, to realise that only four people in Britain are conducting full-time research into tinnitus, and none of them have carried out any clinical trials on Harry's machine. This is strange since the reason given is that the British Tinnitus Association does not believe in the efficacy of 'alternative medicines', as if electronic instruments were alternative.

If we are really uncovering a biological mechanism, then it should apply to organisms other than human beings. One of Harry's students used the electrocrystal unit on a dog named Amber which was completely deaf, listless, and was passing blood in her water. After using the equipment on her ears and stomach there appeared to be a temporary improvement in hearing, and the bleeding stopped. The dog took on a new lease of life, even though the vet said that nothing could be done for her. It is sad to record in this case, however, that the dog's hearing degenerated again in the absence of further treatment, though the bleeding was permanently cured.

What about plants? The same student put an electrocrystal unit's tube into a bowl containing a cheese plant and a miniature rose bush for half an hour when both were in poor condition: 'the cheese plant was slowly giving up, and the rose bush was in dire condition,' she records. Within two days new shoots appeared and there was a complete recovery. 'Both still thriving well' the student reported, little aware that she had just replicated the sort of experiments carried out by Maimbray in Edinburgh in 1746!

As the stories above illustrate, though Harry's reputation as a therapist is spreading, few people understand his work. One day during the preparation of this book Harry was very excited about a couple of photographs he showed me. They looked like two walking sticks upside down, one rather more emaciated than the other. 'Look, Roger, he exclaimed, 'I've managed to photograph the kundalini!' Since I had never at that point heard of a kundalini, I thought it best to nod sagely, then rush home to look it up in one of the many books I had by that time been acquiring for research. Was it some part of the anatomy? Was it an insect? Or perhaps a term from yoga?

The last guess was correct: in the yoga doctrine *prana* is considered to be the life energy (*chi* in acupuncture), and to have two major polarities which must be correctly balanced for the proper functioning of the internal organs and for good health. The two polarities are called yin and yang. Different energy levels have specific effects on the internal organs though there are said to be twelve significant levels of energy controlling different cell and tissue formations. The energy associated with the lowest centre is called kundalini, and if it is released too powerfully it can pass directly through the higher centres to the head, bypassing the body to which it normally gives vitality and exploding in the mind: the effects are considered dangerous to the stability of the sufferer. When, however, the kundalini energy is repressed the body lacks vitality. What Harry believed he had photographed was a 'before and after' picture of the kundalini to which he had applied electrocrystal therapy. The photograph was taken from a woman in her fifties who was suffering from a trapped nerve which was causing her muscle spasms. Using the transparent electrode Kirlian apparatus and an exposure of seven seconds in each case, the first picture showed the blocked or interrupted energy flow, and the second picture showed the kundalini energy flowing freely in its classic 'coiled serpent' mode.

Research still takes up a large part of Harry's time. Currently he is researching Fractal Geometric Figures. Late one afternoon whilst we were working on the book, a nearby computer suddenly jumped into life, and in large letters flashed 'Hey, I've finished!' on the screen. It startled me, since I had been by it for several hours without its giving a murmur. 'Sorry,' apologised Harry, 'but it's been working all day on a Fractal Figure; like to see it?' He pressed a key or two on the keyboard, and the screen was filled with the outline of an insect-like creature. 'Look at that,' he said, pleased. 'That was generated just from three eight-digit numbers'. Harry had been quietly investigating the possibility that morphogenetics can have a mathematically expressible counterpart. He flipped open a small notebook and wrote 'Beetle: 0.7342165, -0.12390562, 1.4673812'.

Harry's enthusiasm for scientific research has never abated. 'Many years have passed since I looked down my first microscope,' he says, 'but I will never forget that mixture of wonder and excitement when I saw my first pattern of cells, and then living single celled micro-organisms. From these single building blocks of life very complicated structures and forms can be made; the human body for example.'

The fundamental question, however, which has always arisen in Harry's mind is what organises the cell and its combination with others, to form complicated patterns and shapes? Is it just haphazard chance or something much more Divine!

Harry believes that God amongst his other very long list of talents is a mathematical genius. He has come to this view because of our work with graphical research with computers. Mathematical formulations can be plotted on graph paper giving a pictorial representation of the basic number concept. However, by hand this can be a very slow and inaccurate method, especially when the points overlap and intertwine. However, a computer can cope with this laborious process at very high speeds and it can also handle much higher complexity.

With the invaluable help of his friend and computer genius John Catchpole, he has seen the manifestation of two-dimensional graphical plots which, depending on their input formula, resemble simple crystalline structures, or single cells, plant and animal tissues, and even the animals themselves.

He believes that in nature the graph paper is three-dimensional space, the ink used to make these three-dimensional plots are the elements and compounds already formed themselves from previous mathematical formulae. 'Never a day now goes by without new patterns of life being discovered on our computer screens.' Says Harry, 'It is interesting to note, however, that if we tamper with the original formulation, a distorted or different animal or cell emerges from the plot. Could we here be looking at the very mechanisms of disease and mutation?' Harry is of the opinion that all researches into life's secrets may ultimately recognise that all creatures have been designed entirely at the Divine mathematical drawing board!

Another project is with the 'Barry Box', which prints out any wave-form made by a sound. Together with John Catchpole, he is busy translating the body's aberrant cellular signals into a graphic printout. In this way, we can clearly see the complex wave-forms of different ailments. But as Harry says, that's for another book.

As this book is being written a further chapter in Harry's career is opening. The *Journal of Alternative Medicine* has asked him to be a member of their panel in the company of others involved in subtle energies, like Julian Kenyon, Matthew Manning, and Robert Tisserand. Where this will lead is a guess at the moment, but it is certainly a further step towards the recognition of his contribution to alternative non-invasive medicine.

5
Life's Secret Mechanisms

'Sensations sweet, felt in the heart, and along the blood'

We would like to reiterate, at the head of this chapter, the well-accepted scientific principle that explanations of physical phenomena should be developed where possible in relation to existing Laws, rather than through postulating entirely new forces. In considering the Kirlian effect, though a number of ideas are described here which do rely on hypotheses not acceptable to the normal sciences, we ourselves believe that the Kirlian effect can be explained entirely by existing physical principles.

When the Kirlian effect first came to the attention of the West, a large number of spiritists and other students of the paranormal thought that it might be able at last to prove the existence of the human aura. The human aura, like the ether, is not perceivable by most people, and only sensitives claim to be able to see it, like a faint glow surrounding the head and sometimes the body of human beings. A person's propensity to have this aura was claimed to relate to their moral or spiritual standing, hence it was often depicted as surrounding saints and other morally good personages or deities. It also featured frequently in fake pictures of deceased Victorians. One might plausibly argue that the brain is giving off near ultraviolet radiation, and that some human beings' retinas can actually be stimulated by electromagnetic rays outside the normal visible ranges. Hence the lucky possessors of such refined retinal apparatus can observe this aura directly.

Actually some are not so lucky: ultraviolet radiation cannot penetrate glass, nor can it penetrate the adult human cornea. It may be able to penetrate infant corneal tissue, giving rise to the concept: 'trailing clouds of glory do we come from God who is our home', but by and large our cornea will prevent entry of ultraviolet light which might otherwise damage our sight. Ultraviolet light can, however, penetrate plastic. And since in the early days of such operations some people with cataracts had their corneas replaced by plastic corneas, there are documented cases of such persons being able to perceive ultraviolet radiation because of this. It would be interesting to see whether such people can detect ultraviolet emanations from human beings.

The electrician from St Thomas' Hospital who invented the Kilner preserving jar also invented coloured or dyed glass lenses which allow anyone, with practice, to see a glow round any human body,[156, 168] which changes in intensity or colour depending on the viewed person's emotion. The human eye, on the other hand, has to make very small movements all the time for the purpose of tracking and depth perception, both because the optic nerve exits from the eye at the fovea or 'blind spot', and because the very nature of neural stimulation is such that unless an image is refreshed its excitation will stop having an effect. If this natural eye movement is combined with a dark blue coloured retinal image (the opposite of the red colour of the retina) the image will persist on either side of the observed figure. This was discovered as early as 1878 by a rather cruel biologist called Kuhne, who flashed a light into the eyes of frogs, then switched it off, quickly killed the frogs, and pulled out their eyes before the negatives of the images had had time to fade from their retinas. For a few fleeting moments he could see the imprinted negative image of what the frogs had seen.

The manner of Kuhne's own death is not recorded.

There has been much publicity and mystical research linking Kirlian effects with the non-phenomenon of the human aura; and this, because of its association with sweeping conclusions and inadequately controlled experimentation, has made serious researchers shy away from a potentially useful research tool. For readers who wish to follow that course we recommend the little book by W. E. Butler, *How to Read the Aura*.[47] He describes the aura as follows:

> The aura is usually seen as a luminous atmosphere around all living things, including what it used to be the custom to regard as inanimate matter. Advancing knowledge begins to suggest to the scientist that even in this so-called 'dead' matter there are living forces at work, thus supporting the old Persian poet who wrote of Life as 'sleeping in the mineral, dreaming in the plant, awakening in the animal and becoming conscious of itself in man'. In many

stained glass windows we see representations of Christ and His Apostles in which the aura is portrayed as a surround of golden light. In many cases we only get the nimbus or radiance shown around the head of the figure, but in others it surrounds the whole form. The same pictorial convention is also found in some Buddhist paintings of a very early date. This may of course, be due in this case to the far-reaching influence of the early Nestorian Christian Church, which sent out its missionaries throughout the whole of the East, though to offset this it is to be noted that this same way of expressing the spirituality of the person portrayed is to be found in early Hindu and Persian art. A simple explanation of this may be that the artists who originated this conventional way of indicating the moral stature of certain people were themselves able to see this strange phenomenon which has been termed the 'aura'.

The Kirlian effect, in our view, is the result of a high-voltage corona discharge caused by pulsed high-frequency waves (which must not be confused with simple high-frequency waves), and it can therefore be explained in terms of ordinary physics: through the action of high-frequency fields, electrons are emitted from the body of an organism and this energy is dissipated in the photographic emulsion in the same way as light. An image is thus formed in the emulsion, dependent on the strength of the emitted electrons. This scientific explanation is more likely to find acceptance among physicists than any which introduces the new concept of an aura. It is of course true to say that, though a piece of music is made up of individual notes played on different instruments and conducted in a certain concert hall, such facts do not explain the art of music. And what of the composers who produce it? We are simply talking about two interpretations of the same phenomena, both of which are correct in their own right. One of the earliest quantum physical explanations of what is being photographed by Kirlian photography was offered by Dr W. A. Tiller of Stanford University.[279, 280]

> A basic idea in radionics is that each individual organism or material radiates and absorbs energy via a unique wave field which exhibits certain geometrical frequency and radiation-type characteristics. This is an extended force field that exists around all forms of matter whether animate or inanimate. A useful analogy here is the physical atom that is continually radiating electromagnetic energy in the form of waves because of its oscillating electric development and

its thermal vibrations. The more complex the materials, the more complex the wave form ...

The fundamental carrier wave is thought to be polarised with a rotating polarisation vector. ... The information concerning the glands, body systems, etc., ripples the carrier wave and seems to be associated with a specific phase modulation of the wave for a specific gland. Regions of space associated with a given phase angle of the wave constitute a three-dimensional network of points extending throughout space. To be in resonance with any one of these points is to be in resonance with the particular gland of the entity. The capability of scanning the waveform of the gland exists for the detection of any abnormalities. Likewise, if energy having the normal or healthy waveform of the gland is pumped into any of these specific network points, the gland will be driven in the normal or healthy mode. This produces a tendency for its structure to reorganise itself in close alignment with the normal structure, i.e., healing of the gland occurs. Cells born in the presence of this polarising field tend to grow in a healthier configuration, which weakens the original field of the abnormal or diseased structure and strengthens the field of the normal or healthy structure.

This hypothesis is in our view much nearer the truth: and indeed, as we shall explain later in this chapter, our own hypothesis extends this principle down to the intra-cellular level. Moreover our hypothesis, although dependent on Kirlian and other life fields research, goes far beyond it in terms of understanding how organic cellular structures are controlled and organised.

The mechanics which cause the Kirlian effect (an electroluminescent discharge from organisms) must first be understood, if the effect is to be useable for research purposes. The attitude of Kirlian researchers is that these discharges can be replicated and also that they can be interpreted, leading to the early diagnosis of disease, the evaluation of nutritional substances and better understanding of morphogenetic fields, as well as the structure and function of organic cells.

In Chapter 3 we discussed the 'phantom leaf effect' (see Fig. 3.2). Dumitrescu, whose electrographic methods (described shortly) have unearthed much data in support of the central hypothesis we are about to advance, himself discounted this effect, saying: 'If a small portion of a fresh leaf is put to one side, the stomata will close, so as to reduce water loss. By placing the leaf onto the Kirlian camera and pressing it onto one of the electrodes a number of microscopic water droplets will be squeezed out over a distance of a few millimetres. These microscopic water droplets become, when applying a voltage, centres for causing discharges on the photographic plate, therefore the cut portion also appears in the image.'

Such an explanation is not enough to convince us: an examination of Thelma Moss's photographs of the phantom leaf effect,[199, 200, 201] no less than our own, shows a distinctive outline of the original leaf, and not a secondary discharge uniquely related to any water drops which may have been squeezed out onto the plates. Dumitrescu's criticisms [76, 77] of the Kirlian apparatus as a whole, on the other hand, appear more reasonable. Having attempted for some time to use Kirlian techniques, he eventually abandoned them in favour of electrographic and electronographic methods, their principal differences from Kirlian techniques being stated as:

1. Only one pulse is used. This produces much more differentiated images than the successively overlaid Kirlian images.
2. The Kirlian apparatus can only investigate surface phenomena, not deep tissues, since its persisting high voltages may be damaging, despite low current flow. Electrography, by contrast, limits the exploration current. Ionising radiation is also reduced.

We feel that both methods are equally valid. As a result of both Kirlian and electronographic evidence and taking into account the other research on cellular tissues exposed to electromagnetic radiation, we suggest that the truth of the matter is as follows.

The electro-luminescence observed in the Kirlian effect, as we have said, is simply a corona discharge, and the quality of its brightness indicates nothing more than the conductivity of the pellicular cells (that is, cells of the skin) from which it emanates. This pellicular conductivity, however, is influenced and controlled by adjacent subcutaneous and intracorporeal cells so the effect is not strictly a surface phenomenon.

The method of influence and control by adjacent cells depends on intracellular resonance, brought about not by the chemical constituents of intracellular electrolytic fluids, but by intercellular electromagnetic radiation.

Should the transceiver functions within any cell become damaged or impaired, that cell will no longer respond to or transmit its unique resonant frequency, and other electromagnetic currents will be conducted through it irregularly. As a result, malignant tissues subjected to Kirlian or electrographic techniques will display a brighter corona discharge – higher conductivity – (or a much duller corona discharge – lower conductivity) than a cell which has not been damaged or impaired. The ability of cells to maintain their correct transceiving faculties can be impaired or damaged by radiation, viral, chemical or mechanical penetration.

The wider implications of this hypothesis embrace a morphogenetic concept in which each cell's resonant frequency helps to control the organic form of the whole organism of which it is a member.

Such a mechanism we believe operates in any organism which has not developed a brain. Plants, for example, or sponges. Or crystals.

The idea was put forward in the 1940s by Pascual Jordan[147] that like molecular structures would be attracted by resonant effects. Accordingly the phantom leaf effect is a real, replicable effect, since it reflects the phenomena of an electrical field external to the cells of the organism which is constructing the form from frequencies radiated from adjacent cells in the manner of Chladni figures. Chladni figures are an eighteenth-century discovery and the sort of patterns which you see on a drumskin if sand is poured onto it and then the drum is beaten. Or the patterns which form on a wet windscreen as a motorcoach's engine idles, causing the rain-drops to vibrate.

As a result of Kirlian and electronographic research, mainly in Romania, but also in the United States and Britain, experimental support is emerging for this hypothesis, which we call morphogenetic radiation. Nevertheless further experimentation is necessary to confirm it, and to test the predictions we make concerning their outcome.

A brief review of the evidence in support of our hypothesis is given here, which is amplified in Chapters 7 and 8.

First, Kirlian pictures can identify cancer tumours before X-rays can. Unpublished research by Kirlian and Adamenco indicated that in patients with malignant tumours there is a special form of marginal corona discharge, such discharges being especially noticed in gastric cancer. Using electronographic techniques the first images of malignant tumours by this means were obtained by Dumitrescu, Golovanov, and Celan in 1975, and they took out patent No. 82556 in Bucharest. Similar palmar discharges were found by Majajakrom in 1976, and by Shapiro in 1977. The 'bright' corona discharge relating to a malignant tumour condition is now well documented by other researchers.

Dumitrescu found not only an increase in light emission from the neoplastic (cancerous) zones, with tumours showing as the brightest area of the image, and in the case of leukaemias the whole body surface appearing intensely illuminated. A discontinuity of the luminous contour of the body and the presence of the contour of the tumour proper also are evident.

In his study of rats artificially innoculated with malignant ascites, Dumitrescu's electronographic images showed the appearance in the tumour tissue of a bright zone (appearing on the eighth day) which subsequently increased progressively in intensity and volume. Dumitrescu also investigated over 5,000 normal human beings as well as 171 who were suffering from malignant tumours in different localisations, and confirmed the localisation of the tumours by electrographic methods in 74 per cent of the cases. In soft tissues an X-ray cannot generally localise the tumour except through associated signs. (In three cases of muscle sarcoma the electrographic image showed the tumour whereas the X-ray was normal.)

Secondly, magnetic fields can modify RNA and DNA, probably by altering the angles or distances between their atomic structures. It had already been shown (L. Gross, 1964) that a small difference in magnetic field can produce physical effects: magnetic fields modify the wave function of electrons in macromolecules, producing a greater paramagnetic susceptibility, which leads to a slowdown in reaction speed, and the rate at which RNA and DNA are synthesised.

In other words, the replication of DNA macromolecules can be disturbed by the action of magnetic fields. In an interesting paper Lowenstein showed in 1974 that not only do small molecules pass through normal cells but so do electric charges, yet that this doesn't happen through tumour cells. Magnetic forces acting on membranes can affect the vital communication functions of cell membranes; and tumour cells show only weak intercellular cohesion. As early as 1970 Presman[235] was able to demonstrate that electromagnetic radiation can cause chromosomal aberrations leading to morphological and other anomalies: we are only now beginning to recognise that the pleasures of sunbathing can result in skin cancers. The apparent paradox that radiation can not only damage cellular structures but also cause the reversion of malignant cells to normal cells would also be explained by our hypothesis, since in such cases the unique frequency of the cell may have been restored. Madeleine Barnothy in 1964 acted as general editor of a book *Biological Effects of Magnetic Fields*,[22] and included the suggestion that magnetic fields act to alter genetic codes by interfering with proton spin, and by modifying wave functions. Furthermore in 1962, according to a paper by D. Kim S. Yang (see ref. 77) of the Department of Physics, Ohio State University, a researcher called Darfman was able to show that DNA has high magnetic anisotropy, which simply means that DNA is very sensitive to magnetic fields.

One significant fact which emerged from Yang's important paper gives a crucial piece of evidence supporting our general hypothesis.

A researcher called Balitsky[18] was investigating the early detection of carcinomas in 1973. He was using rabbits which had been infected with a particular cancer called the Pierce-Brown carcinoma. He discovered that he could predict the onset of the carcinoma by a specific anomaly in the EEG recording. In other words, he was able to show a direct correlation between cancerous cells and the waves which emanate from an animal's brain. An equally important experiment had been carried out by another researcher, Riviere, in 1965: he applied a magnetic field in conjunction with microwaves at a particular frequency for twenty minutes at a time over a period of one month, the subjects this time being rats. The magnetic fields were 300 to 620 ϕe, and the wavelengths were between 3 and 80 cm. The results were staggering. Tumours and their metastases regressed and in some cases were eliminated – all by radiation at the right frequencies. Kenyon suggests that 'malignancy may be caused by a disturbance in the self-regulating mechanisms of the body, these mechanisms being most probably electromagnetic in nature.'

Though Kenyon goes no further than this, he has put into words the underlying basis of our own thinking.

The concept is that magnetic fields can act therapeutically by facilitating the communication between aberrant cells and adjacent normal cells, which can thereby bring about a return to normality. There are a number of alternative medical practitioners who report improvements in patients treated with various magnetic devices. Other experimental results from magnetic field studies include the discovery that DNA molecules align themselves perpendicularly to magnetic fields, that pregnant rats can gain 20 per cent in weight, while chicks are observed to develop morphological anomalies which last for thirty generations afterwards, a proof that the genetic code has been altered, all by magnetic or electromagnetic means.

Maybe the somewhat incredible practice of Albert Abrams in aligning his patient along the north-south axis before tapping his abdomen was not quite so crazy!

However that may be, the experimental results above are not inconsistent with a hypothesis that cancerous cells can be 'engineered' or brought back to normality by external wave transmissions of specific frequencies. The same hypothesis would, within the realms of existing physical laws, explain the mechanism whereby Upton's 'homoeotron' might eradicate insects by interfering with their DNA molecules and introducing a new and pernicious wave-form via the pesticide wavelengths broadcast simultaneously. Gurwitsch's experiments where dying onion kernels affected adjacent living onion growth rates could be another example of the same mechanism at work. It would explain how Hieronymus' apparatus was able to destroy corn worms, or even ultimately how organic matter might be dematerialised entirely.

We are made of nothing but patterns of resonant energy! As Einstein cannot have failed to realise, if in his famous formula

$$E = mc^2, \text{ then } m = E/c^2$$

which means that not only is all energy (E) merely matter (m) multiplied by light, but that all matter is simply energy modified by electromagnetic wave-forms (c^2 in the formula means the squared speed of light, light being an electromagnetic wave-form).

As Dumitrescu puts it:[77]

> The question of malignant tumours themselves acting as a radiation source becomes a possibility. This behaviour suggests the possibility of the existence of biological radiation in the ultraviolet light region which is more intense in the areas of neoplasma. These

observations allow us to revert to the hypotheses made by Gurwitsch forty years ago.

What Kirlian apparatus can do is to assist in the investigation of surface cellular electrical conductivity. It also offers support for the general hypothesis of morphogenetic fields of the kind put forward by Rupert Sheldrake. It is unfortunate that Sheldrake omits all mention of the Kirlian and Dumitrescu work, and at no time proposes that organic regulation can be carried out by an artificially constructed wave-form.

The idea of morphogenetic radiation is not inconsistent with Dreich's entelechy idea,[73] a concept in which 'something about living organisms remains whole even though parts of the physical whole are removed'. Our hypothesis would also explain the results of K. R. Lashley's many years of fruitless research during the twenties looking for a part of the brain, which he called the En-gram, wherein memory was housed.[174]

Lashley carried out many experiments where part of a rat's cerebral cortex was removed. After this the rat was encouraged to learn its way through a maze. Surprisingly Lashley found that no matter which part of the cortex was removed, the rat's ability to learn was not impaired by it except when the lesion approached 50 per cent of the total.

His consequent theory of cerebral Mass Action was supported by Wilder Penfield,[221] and summarised by Morgan and Stellar in 1950, in their classic work, *Physiological Psychology*[197] as follows:

> The fact is that neither the learning nor the retention of a maze habit is localised in any one area of the cortex. Instead, the degree of retardation in learning or loss of memory following cortical lesions is proportional to the amount, and not the place, of the cortical lesion. This fact (called cerebral Mass Action) has been demonstrated over and over again. There can be no question about it. The only question is, What does it mean?

Doubtless the poor rats didn't give a damn!

We offer our hypothesis with confidence not only since it is consistent with experimental evidence, but also because it uses no new principles. It completely replaces the sort of hypothesis only too common in this field, an example of which might be that put forward by Sir Alister Hardy, the zoologist, of a 'psychic subconscious species blueprint'. With morphogenetic radiation comes the flexibility to handle the old heredity-versus-environment controversy, and the whole mechanism of morphological evolution.

In developing a mechanical model transceiver, Dumitrescu produces a diagram which looks similar to the DNA macromolecule (Fig. 5.1). The unfolding of the DNA double helix within its di-pole-like chromosome could be triggered by, and itself trigger, electromagnetic transmissions: the detachment and recombination of individual hydrogen bonds may induce resonant signals in adjacent cells as the DNA reduplicates. The strength of these signals may be impaired or improved by interfering external radiations which may in turn retard or advance the growth rate of the cell cluster, or even the entire organism.

The electrified myrtle shrubs of Maimbray may have grown faster because of this radiative mechanism.

Maimbray's results incidentally were replicated more or less completely by Dr Larry Murr,[205] who artificially simulated in his laboratory the electrical effects of thunderstorms and rainy weather. After years of work in his microclimate, significant increases in plant growth could be established by certain levels of voltage, and damaged by others.

The sort of mechanism we propose would explain the results of work reported by Soviet botanists, where a corn stalk was planted in a glass container near to properly watered companions: the stalk somehow stayed alive for weeks and grew nor-

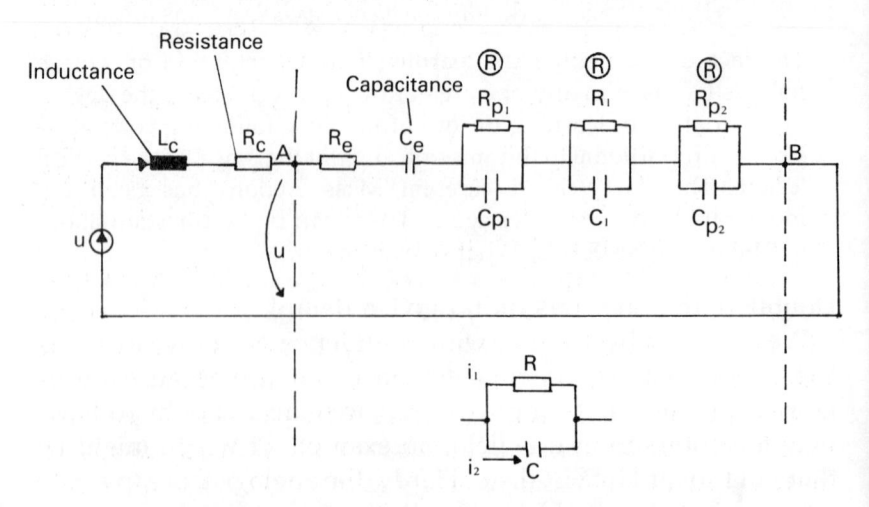

Fig 5.1 Schematic diagram of DNA as an electrical resonating circuit. (Source: Dumitrescu)

mally. In some way, report Tompkins and Bird in *The Secret Life of Plants*,[281] water was transferred from the healthy plants to the 'prisoner' in the jar. Our mechanism would appear to work in the same sort of way that Hans Jenny was able to create the so-called Chladni figures, three-dimensional patterns in inert materials, by means of his 'tonoscope'.[144]

Even more understandable in terms of morphogenetic radiation is the experimental work carried out by S. P. Schurin and his colleagues from the Institute of Automation and Electrometry at Novosibirsk, USSR in 1972. They placed identical tissue cultures in two hermetically sealed (that means the lid is fused on to make it air-tight) vessels, separated by a wall of glass. Into one vessel they had introduced a lethal virus, which killed the culture inside. The other tissue was unaffected. But when the experiment was repeated, this time substituting a sheet of quartz crystal for the glass, the second tissue culture was also destroyed. The viruses could not have penetrated the barrier, but their morphogenetic radiations could have. (Remember how ultraviolet radiation doesn't pass through glass.) The researchers reported increased radiation from the virus as it attacked the culture it was about to kill.

Schurin is quoted by Tompkins and Bird as saying:

> We are convinced that the radiation is capable of giving the first warning about the beginning of malignant regeneration, and of revealing the presence of particular viruses. At the present time the early identification of many ailments, for instance the numerous forms of hepatitis, presents major difficulties.

This statement was made, of course, before the present worldwide concern about AIDS (the Acquired Immune Deficiency Syndrome whose virus has now by common agreement been designated HIV – human immunodeficient virus), which is now reaching pandemic proportions.

Ultimately our hypothesis of morphogenetic radiation would predict that cerebral 'brain-waves' of various kinds act as complex signals controlling cellular activity, without recourse to the habitual neural pathways of the central and peripheral nervous systems, which are solely concerned with events at a supra-cellular level. Frankly, neural pathways and their mechanisms are far too slow to handle the co-ordination of the millions of cells which are dying, growing or perhaps changing in our bodies all the time.

It was Linus Pauling in the 1920s who first pointed out[217] that at the heart of the covalent hydrogen bond was resonance. John Gribbin sums this up in his lucid book *In Search of the Double Helix* as follows:

> Even hydrogen can be thought of as making ionic bonds. If one atom gave up its electron to the other, we would have a molecule H+H-; if the exchange went the other way we would have H-H+. The covalent sharing of the two electrons can be thought of as very rapid switching between these two states, with first one atom then the other laying claim to both electrons, and the two atoms being held together by the electrostatic forces. This idea of oscillating between two states, or resonance, was at the heart of Pauling's work in the late 1920s, the work which put the theory of covalent bonding on a secure mathematical footing within the framework of quantum theory. As far as the molecular biologist is concerned, the covalent bond is *the* bond.

A picture is emerging of an individual DNA macromolecule as a specific 'signature tune' – each note being made up of a triplet – set out along a biological music sheet, ready to be played (or unfolded) like a cello: its four bases represent the four strings, on which the four fingers can play a specific tune in any sequence of sixty-four notes, each different from the others (Fig. 5.2).

Each 'note' would have its own resonant frequency, determined by the speed of oscillation of the covalent H-bond, and this oscillation will vary dependent on the nature of the bases to which it is linked. The length of the cello string will be determined by the hydrogen bonds which hold the helix at its correct pitch.

Any of these bonds can be fractured by resonance from outside the organism in the form of ultraviolet radiation; normally, however, the tune is played by the brain. *Und welche Geiger hat uns in der Hand?* 'And which violinist is playing this tune on us?', as Rainer Maria Rilke demanded to know.

Within the signature tune there are three stop codons but only one RNA start codon (adenine-uracil-guanine), which instructs the process of replication to start. Furthermore not all DNA has two helices: it could be possible that single-stranded DNA is a read-only or a write-only system. There is also circular DNA to think about, and the radio significance of pleated sheet forms of macromolecular structure. We guess that RNA does

LIFE'S SECRET MECHANISMS

first position	second position				third position
	U	C	A	G	
U	Phe	Ser	Tyr	Cys	U
	Phe	Ser	Tyr	Cys	C
	Leu	Ser	Stop	Stop	A
	Leu	Ser	Stop	Trp	G
C	Leu	Pro	His	Arg	U
	Leu	Pro	His	Arg	C
	Leu	Pro	Gln	Arg	A
	Leu	Pro	Gln	Arg	G
A	Ile	Thr	Asn	Ser	U
	Ile	Thr	Asn	Ser	C
	Ile	Thr	Lys	Arg	A
	Met start	Thr	Lys	Arg	G
G	Val	Ala	Asp	Gly	U
	Val	Ala	Asp	Gly	C
	Val	Ala	Glu	Gly	A
	Val	Ala	Glu	Gly	G

To read the genetic code in terms of amino acids the bases have to be taken in triplets. This table enables you to translate any such codon into its appropriate amino acid – for example, the triplet AGU translates as Ser. Three different triplets translate as 'stop'; only one unique instruction indicates the start of a genetic message. The shaded areas = Essential Amino Acids.

Fig 5.2 The genetic code. (From In Search of the Double Helix *John Gribbin, 1985).*

not have a transceiving capability. It may not only be an external resonating force which encourages the breakdown of a hydrogen bond but also a particular enzyme may be able to accomplish the same result chemically. But when it *is* sequentially broken down the double helix unwinds and replicates. And it will only unwind and replicate if the notes are played in the right order. Playing just a part of the 'tune' will only unwind part of the helix.

Chemotherapy, actually, could just as easily be working the same way: the introduction of a pharmaceutical (which will have its own individual 'tune') may correct cellular disorder by reimposing its own harmonies on malignant substances, organic or inorganic. (Abrams illustrated this by the effect of quinine on malaria: the wave-form for quinine cancelled out exactly the wave-form of malaria in one amazing lecture room demonstration he gave.) But the hope which we express is that, once these mechanisms are charted, we will be able to substitute for chemotherapy an electronically generated sequence of resonances which will do the same job.

The instruments which are being developed from the original Kirlian techniques could form the basis of twenty-first-century medicine. We discuss this further in Chapter 8.

Unfortunately, also implicit in the hypothesis of morphogenetic radiation lies the spectre of electronically induced disease, some possibilities of which will be considered in Chapter 7.

Kirlian patterns do not have the random chaotic characteristics of electrical discharges generated on their own, such as one might see emanating from a high-frequency coil, but the well-ordered and reflected pattern of a living thing. We use the word 'reflected' deliberately because the field one sees in a Kirlian picture is an artificially induced field of electricity which in turn produces an image on a photographic plate by the action of a corona discharge. The field is earthed through the object, and the object's emanations are recorded onto film by direct contact or by transparent electrodes (see Appendix 1). It is the way this discharge behaves as it passes through different kinds of object which is the clue to its analysis: for instance in an inanimate object such as a coin, a steady stable pattern is seen. In a living object, however, it is in a constant but ordered state of flux. If the living object dies, an immediate change in the discharge pattern is seen. So we are perceiving, by means of the corona discharge, a reflected pattern of the life energy of the object: we are looking as into a mirror at an image which is not itself the mirror.

The hypothesis that organisms are living oscillators of electromagnetic wave-forms is supported by what is known as the Russell effect.[251] This is where living objects have taken their own pictures by being laid on unexposed sensitive films with moisture screens interposed. The exposures were for long periods, hours or even days; and the effects have been replicated by a number of researchers. No artificially induced fields were used, so the effect is a totally natural one.

This technique has certain disadvantages: a live object fluctuates for many natural reasons from second to second, so because of the long time-factor one is seeing a series of energy changes. It does, however, support the view that minute electromagnetic radiations emanate from living things. We have already indicated in Chapter 3 many examples where radiations are emitted as a function of life, and Lakhovsky was postulating as early as 1924 that living things are natural oscillators of electromagnetic waves. His view was reinforced by Herb Froelich, a British physicist, who proposed that living cells were in a constant state of oscillation. The idea was taken up by Herbert Pohl, Director of the Cancer Research Laboratory in Stillwater, Oklahoma. He reasoned that where there are radio fields there are also electrical fields. Using barium titanite, a fine powder which is very sensitive to electricity, he found that this 'tracer chemical' was attracted to cells, showing that these were radio beacons of a very low magnitude, which could then be detected by photomultipliers capable of registering light particles as small as a single photon.

Living things are enveloped in a sea of electromagnetic energy, of various depths, sometimes calm, and sometimes, when disease has struck, turbulent and dangerous. In Kirlian photography lies the possibility of monitoring this everchanging seascape, provided we follow the precautions which enable useable results to emerge.

As a result of this awareness, Inyushin, a Russian physicist, has suggested that, whilst matter can exist either as a solid, a liquid, or a gas, there is a fourth state of matter which can occur called a plasma, very similar in substance to the material of the sun.[141, 142] The energy plasma of the sun, however, varies from hundreds of thousands to millions of degrees in temperature, and no such state of matter could exist on earth. According to this scientist a similar substance, which he calls bioplasma, *can* exist and it is this plasma which is made visible by Kirlian photography. All living things – plants, animals, human beings – not only have a physical body made of atoms and molecules, but also a counterpart body of energy. Inyushin described his experiments with Kirlian apparatus into this bioplasmic field force in 1968.

He even described the impact of emotions on animal bioplasma as follows: 'Rabbits, when alarmed, showed radical changes in bioplasma radiation [on Kirlian apparatus]. A condensed bioplasma was generated. The radiations given off by the bioplasma were dark with intense flares of a purplish colour.' Inyushin went further, suggesting that Kirlian techniques could also be applied to parapsychology to determine the psychic state of a subject.

One researcher (Varsemov) linked the Kirlian effects to acupuncture, others (Raikov and Ademenko) to hypnotic states and, in one of the most startling experiments on the radiative effects of living tissues, Dr Alexander Studitsky at the Institute of Animal Morphology in Moscow minced up muscle tissue and placed it into a specially made incision in the body of a rat: the body grew from this an entirely new muscle! (We have not overlooked the potential application of our concept in allogenic skin grafting, which is the subject of much medical research at present.)

For a more detailed review of Inyushin's research, readers are directed towards Ostrander and Schroder's *Psychic Discoveries*.[215]

Viewers of a Central television programme put out by Channel Four in 1984 were amazed to see an example of a finger, which had been amputated at the tip, regrow some three-eighths of an inch in two years, and that the new fingerprints were exactly the same as before. This type of recovery happened only if the electric potential flowing into the wound was left unchanged. Sewing the finger up appeared to have changed its potential and, in such cases, reported by Professor Bernard Watson of St Bartholomew's Hospital, though the fingers healed they did not regrow.

Whilst we recognise the validity of the phenomena he found, we do not think there is any reason to invent a new kind of field force to account for it, when existing physical laws can explain what is happening. There is certainly an interpenetrating electromagnetic field associated with living organisms, simply because the very components of cells are chemical salts and acids acting like electrolytes, and they thus carry electrical

LIFE'S SECRET MECHANISMS

charges. Around each cell is a fatty lipid layer which acts like an insulator for most of the time against the less ordered events occurring outside the cell. This layer sets up a potential difference in electrical terms (Fig. 5.3). This means that electricity from inside the cells naturally wants to flow to the outside to eliminate the potential difference in charge inside and outside the cell. This movement can be detected in individual cells and tissues, and needs no more esoteric explanation than the laws of chemistry already provide. The question is, do intra-cellular current-flows also radiate messages to other cells?

Certainly living organisms cannot function without electricity, though this may be on a different scale: remember that

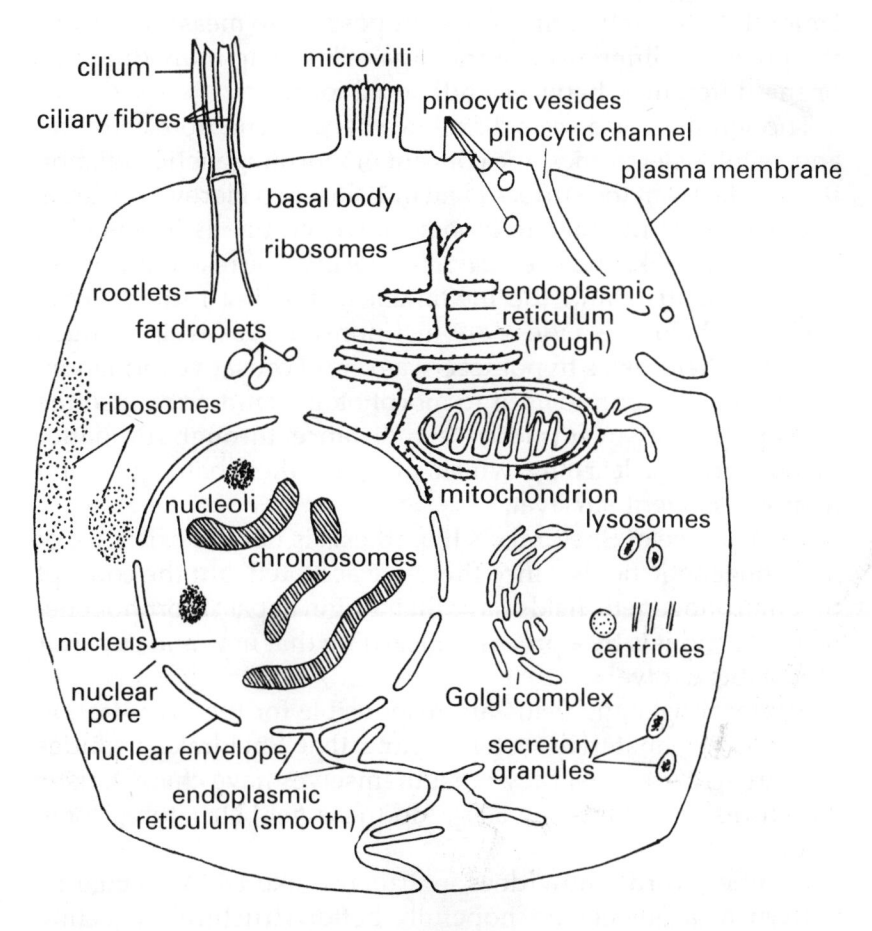

Fig 5.3 A typical organic cell. The DNA is tightly coiled inside the chromosomes.

Luigi Galvani discovered in 1780 how excised nerve muscle preparations from frogs' legs would contract and jump after electrical stimulation.[96] Furthermore, when electrical imbalances exceed certain tolerances, death by electrocution results. But with Kirlian photography we are seeing an amplification of much weaker effects in living things and also the potential differences in conductive inanimate objects.

'The mechanical, optically recognisable morphology of an organism', said Ernst Florey [88] in his detailed review of bioelectricity (Chapter 16 of his *Introduction to Animal Physiology*), 'therefore has an electric counterpart: an electric morphology which can be detected with electrostatic and electronic recording devices.' He goes on to describe the electric circuitry of cells, lamenting that at that time it was impossible to measure directly the potential differences of the organelles of an individual cell, or the differences between individual ions.

Though there is a scale difference between neuro-electronics and cellular electronics, the concept of morphogenetic radiation was not far from the surface even in 1966 when Florey's textbook appeared. For the idea to bloom, however, one is indebted to Rupert Sheldrake, whose *New Science of Life*[259] arrested the attention of scientists and the media alike, drawing forth reviews such as 'Sheldrake's ideas are just nonsense' as well as much acclaim. Sheldrake's hypothesis was one of causative formation, and it did not confine itself to morphology, embracing also the concept that organisms learn 'at a distance' through resonance the patterns of learning which progress their behaviour and their consequent survival.

The essence of Sheldrake's hypothesis is not the existence of morphogenetic fields, since these are accepted, but the concept that morphogenetic fields have their origin in past morphogenetic fields and it is by a process of learning that new and superior organisms evolve.

'If morphogenetic fields are responsible for the organisation and form of material systems [note that Sheldrake includes non-organic systems] they must themselves have characteristic structures. So where', he asks, 'do these field structures come from?'

In other words, how does a structure like DNA change its pattern to a newer and hopefully better structure? Rejecting purely mechanistic explanations, Sheldrake also examines vitalist and organismic solutions and identifies their inadequacies. He proposes instead the idea that the morphogenetic fields themselves play a causal role in the development and maintenance of systems at all levels of complexity.

He develops the concept of morphic resonance, an influence which may not, he suggests, be limited in time and space, but reflect both past and future fields:

> Morphic resonance is analogous to energetic resonance in a further respect: it takes place between vibrating systems. Atoms, molecules, crystals, organelles, cells, tissues, organs and organisms are all made up of parts in ceaseless oscillation, and all have their own characteristic patterns of vibration and internal rhythm; the morphic units are dynamic, not static. Morphic resonance takes place through morphogenetic fields, and indeed gives rise to their characteristic structures.

The thought occurs to us that if we were to retranslate Plato's Theory of Ideas into similar terminology, the theory being essentially that if human beings can attain an idea of excellence, then this attainment might take the form of a crystalline device's vibrations being intelligibly received by the organic receptive mechanism of the brain. One observation we have noticed in using the electrocrystal instrument is that the presence of a nearby human being seems to assist a patient to return to normality. It is as if the crystals are picking up the nearby human signals and amplifying them for the benefit of the aberrant cells of the patient. One example of this was in the case of a lady with multiple sclerosis. Harry was going off on one of his tours, so could not treat her. He suggested that she make use of the machine being used by the tinnitus helpline organisation which happened to be near her home. When she used the machine at their premises, in the company of one of the officers, there were the usual beneficial effects. But later when she got her own machine, and used it on her own, the effects were not so marked. (Although there are many patients working happily on their own electrocrystal therapy generators.) We can see how such a mechanism might operate. Another parallel example lies in the already quoted Philadelphia Experiment: the electromagnetised crew desperately needed the help of others to touch them so as to prevent their dematerialisation: the human 'normal' radiation was clearly a beneficial influence in preventing runaway aberrance.

We do not necessarily wholly agree with Sheldrake's hypothesis, which he supports with numerous examples, since the existence of Kirlian fields (which are clearly energetic in nature) may have underlying non-energetic fields of turbulence – a blueprint onto which a material form may attach itself. Kirlian research neither supports his hypothesis nor denies it. Kirlian photography is useful only as a tool to measure the intensity of a morphogenetic field, and the current state of research is such that it can make little contribution to the causality of that field, except in terms of conventional physical chemistry.

There is one thing we *can* say. On a simply mechanistic view, the proximity of two morphogenetic fields (in terms of frequency and similarity of wave-form, that is) must influence each other and cause subsequent structural changes. Accordingly, we see no reason for postulating any further causative factor, and would be more interested in the spatial and temporal horizons of the fields we are investigating: Do they attenuate with distance? Do they weaken with time? What happens during the period of decay? Again, we suspect that there are no new principles to be discovered.

If that is our view, then how do we explain learning at a distance, the example quoted by Sheldrake being that of crystals suddenly growing maverick varieties (inorganic), and a tendency for rats of succeeding generations to learn a task more quickly, even if they were not the progeny of ancestors who had learned the task (organic)? The latter experiment[5] was carried out by W. E. Agar at Melbourne in 1954. In terms of organic structures we believe that an organism, even a relatively simple one, with all its cells in resonance, can send out a much more powerful signal than is generally appreciated. This might eventually form the basis of an explanation of such diverse phenomena as 'love at first sight', telepathy between family members, and crystal formation via seed crystals. (Lakhovsky has some interesting experimental results with moths which throw light on this possibility. It would be nice to develop this hypothesis, that morphogenetic radiation can transmit complex information between organisms over long distances, but there is no space to develop the idea in this book.)

Even so the phantom leaf effect in Kirlian photography begins to throw some light on the problem, in that the phantom is technically outside the radiating organism. To replicate the phantom leaf effect needs certain conditions, suggesting that we can learn something about the factors necessary to establish a strong morphogenetic signal, and hence eventually set up experiments to test such parameters as its signal strength over distance, time of decay, and so on.

First a highly active electrical field is important, with easily ionisable electrolytes in a balanced ionic state. We found for example that plants fed on chemical fertilisers virtually never exhibited the phantom leaf effect. With organic fertilisers a better balance of electrolytes may be established. Plants also experience seasonal and circadian changes which may in turn influence the phantom leaf effect. For example, during the peak growing season, mitosis (cell divison) is at its speediest, while water and carbon dioxide are being converted by sunlight into sugars (photosynthesis). Pollution-free environments also assist in obtaining the effect. Next there are certain prerequisite electrical parameters: voltage and frequency of pulse can have important influences on the strength of the effect.

With the exception of high altitude Alpine growing plants, for some reason in some plants a low barometric pressure will not produce any phantom effects. At present we have only succeeded in identifying a few of the necessary conditions, and there may well be others which we have not isolated. In summary, however, the effect seems to offer oportunities for investigating morphogenetic fields. Sheldrake does not mention Kirlian photography in his book (which may of course be because he feels the technique, which has proved so difficult for researchers, is beneath analytical attention). To that extent morphic resonance is not a theory of the Kirlian effect *per se*. The relevance of Sheldrake's hypothesis to the Kirlian phenomenon is nevertheless obvious, and it offers opportunities for the diligent researcher to advance both constructs.

Before ending this chapter, we would like to suggest a hypothesis explaining how pulsed high frequency can accomplish such effects as the phantom leaf effect. Our views may stimulate debate on this phenomenon, since we have not yet come across any similar hypothesis in the literature.

A pulsed high-frequency transmitter can be compared to a water tap with a bowl of water beneath it. If the tap is turned on fully, the water below will start to swirl round the bowl and cause a waveless whirlpool-like effect. If, however, we *almost* turn the tap off, so that it drips separate water drops onto the surface of the water in the bowl, after the whirlpool has subsided the drips will send out waves continuously across the surface as they hit the water. These waves will be subject to all the rules of wave mechanics,[58] such as harmonics, resonance, interference, and so on; and though we cannot vary the height of the tap from the bowl (without moving the bowl), we *are* able, by turning the tap gently, to control the speed of the drips, and hence the frequency of the waves.

Pulsing a high-frequency wave is the same: the pulse frequency can allow the waves' harmonics to have their maximum effect, because the gap between successive waves allows each wave to express itself without interference from succeeding waves (Fig. 5.4). The highest harmonic possible theoretically will be infinite. Harmonics cannot develop from steady continuous high frequency devoid of pulses, since there would be no

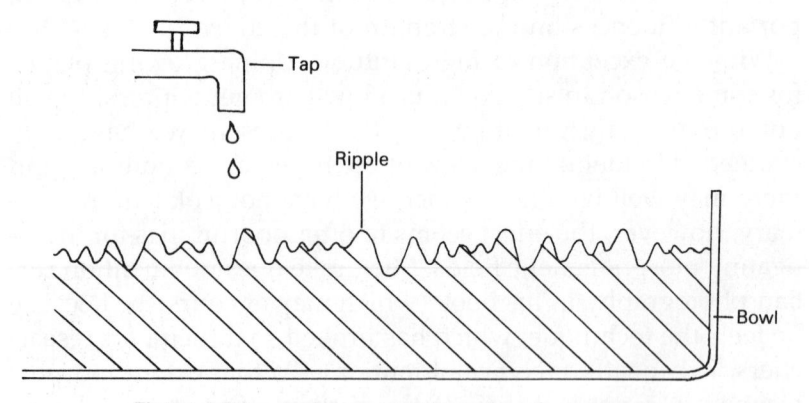

Fig 5.4 i. Waves pulsing across the surface of water in a bowl.

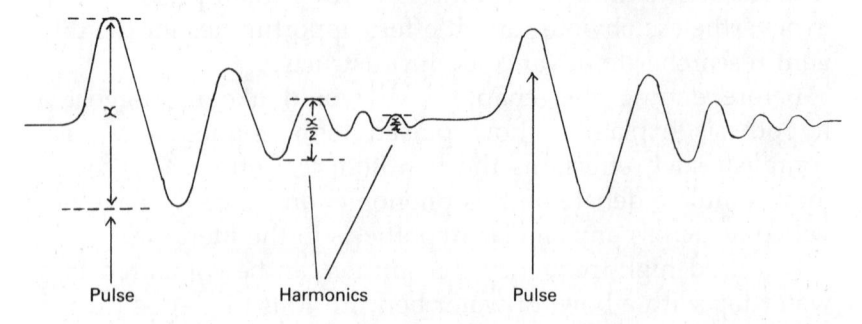

Fig 5.4 ii. The formation of harmonics in a pulsed wave.

gap in which they can do so. And by altering the space of the gap we can control the harmonics generated. If we multiply frequency in Hz (1Hz = one cycle per second) by number of pulses per second we can see that large numbers of harmonics can be achieved, even on the simple assumption that only one harmonic is produced in each gap.

Example

One whole wave at say 50 KHz (taking a fifty-thousandth of a second to complete itself) with a gap between it and the next pulse of say a one-two-hundred-and-fifty-thousandth of a second, would be able to generate a wave of only one-fifty-thousandth multiplied by one-two-hundred-and-fifty-thousandths squared:

$$(50{,}000 \times 2.5 \times 10^{10} = 12.5 \times 10^{14})$$

Harmonic frequency = 12.5×10.14 Hz.

In the example above the harmonic frequency would be in the ultraviolet light frequency range. Radio waves are about 10^6 Hz which is much lower than that. Interestingly, both ultraviolet radiation and Kirlian apparatus during prolonged exposure cause reversible lesions in the retinas of animals, and the bacteriocidal qualities of ultraviolet radiation are well known.

Jane Waters of the Alternative Centre, London, has had many years' experience in the treatment of psoriasis, 'a dreadful skin disease which strikes without respect to age or race. More than 80 million people suffer from it round the world, with perhaps over one million in the UK alone.'

In her Centre's paper on psoriasis[101] Waters admits there is no known cure, but draws attention to the way in which ultraviolet light in the range 315 nm to 280 nm (the so-called ultraviolet B range), simulates almost all the beneficial biological effects following exposure to sunlight and also has a beneficial effect on psoriasis. Waters found that eliminating wavelengths less than 296 nm, may improve the effect. Using a monochromatic UVB machine at 300 nm, 304 nm, and 313 nm she found that psoriasis which had quickly returned to sites previously exposed to 'broad band' UVB cleared for eight weeks on average. Moreover, UVA in the 320 to 400 nm wavelengths seemed to be effective in clearing psoriasis from small exposure sites, but UVB was effective in doses 1,000 times less. The Selective Ultraviolet Phototherapy (SUP) treatment accordingly emits a continuous spectrum of 270 nm to 400 nm with a peak at 313 nm. Long-term side-effects include a wrinkling of the skin and some malignancy. Even so, patients need 5-10 years of continuous treatment to reach danger levels. Normally patients will be clear of lesions (with five treatments per week) in less than two months.

A number of other features noted in psoriasis patients support our hypothesis: stress for example, has a notable effect. This we would explain by the lack of, or rather the reduction of, the brain's radiative cellular control as a result of stress patterns which have either absorbed energy or are casting an interference pattern. Again we postulate only normal physical concepts to explain the mechanism.

We now believe that the Kirlian effect acts by its radiation of harmonics in the ultraviolet frequency range. Moreover the mechanism by which ultraviolet radiations can kill bacteria is, we think, a destruction of the intracellular covalent hydrogen bonds of the bacterium, so that it can no longer broadcast its frequency to adjacent organic cells. We think that cells broadcast via the resonance of their DNA paired bases' hydrogen bonds, and transmit morphogenetic information to adjacent cells. The Kirlian phantom leaf effect is, therefore, produced by intensifying, rather than destroying, the relevant specific frequencies, and that these are reproduced by downward harmonics in the visible light frequency range, and captured on photographic film. If the correct frequency is broadcast by a large number of cells it becomes a strong signal which binds the whole cellular structure of an organism together. It embodies a morphogenetic field. The implications of this extension of our radiated morphogenetic hypothesis are as follows:

1. That the radiation apparatus of an organic cell can be damaged by an incorrect frequency. This would explain how skin cancers and bacteriocidal action is caused by ultraviolet radiation.
2. That a cell's radiation apparatus can also be repaired by rebroadcasting the correct frequency. This would explain why lesions can be detected by Kirlian photography and

lesions caused by ultraviolet radiation are reversible: the remaining cells in the organism reprogramme the damaged cell in the latter case, and make manifest its shape in the former.
3. That the purine and possibly the pyrimidine bonds of damaged cells broadcast a different frequency from the rest of the organism, which progressively affects the adjacent cells. This would explain how malignant tissue progressively affects adjacent cells, and how neoplasms (new tumours) can also appear non-adjacently.

One practical example of how our postulated cellular radiation apparatus works is the phenomenon whereby certain essential amino acids cannot be manufactured by human organisms, but only by plants. We know that purine and pyrimidine paired bases are connected by hydrogen bonds covalently, and that these pairs are arranged sequentially in triplet codons along the DNA macromolecule, each codon defining a specific amino acid.

The frequency of the resonance of a hydrogen bond is calculated as follows. Let us assume that two hydrogen atoms, each consisting of one nucleus with one electron spinning around it, come into resonance when the path of their electrons touches. At this point the electrons begin to spin round a figure of eight circuit embracing both nuclei, and do so in pairs, thus sharing the two nuclei between them. Conceptually the two atoms are now bound together by the path of their twinned electrons. Some theorists would prefer to think of a cloud of electrons rather than discrete particles, but the upshot is the same if the cloud's forces are resolved into one energetic pathway.

The distance which the pair of electrons travel round the nuclei is effectively one circumference outwards and one circumference on the return journey.

From the distance between the H atoms and the speed of the joined electrons the frequency of their journey, that is the number of journeys they can complete in one second, can be calculated. The distance the electron travels between H+ and H− is between π times. 2.78Å and π times 3.40Å, depending on whether the molecule is dry or wet. The speed of an electron in the first H shell is 2014km/sec. Therefore the frequency at which the H-bond resonates is:

(A) The Dry State: (2.78A apart):

2.014×10^6 m. divided by $2 \times \pi 2.78 \times 10^{-10}$ m. times per second

which is

11.53×10^{14} times per second or Hertz.

(B) The Wet State (3.4A apart):

2.014×10^6 divided by $2 \times \pi 3.4 \times 10^{-10}$ m. times per second

which is

9.43×10^{14} times per second or Hertz.

These frequencies, it will be observed, are in the low ultraviolet radiation range, which accords with our hypothesis (Fig. 5.5).

Certain triplet codons (the 'essential amino acids'), however, cannot be manufactured in the human organism, but have to be ingested by foods created only by plants. An interesting feature of all the so-called 'essential amino acids' is that, with one important exception, they all include the uracil purine nucleotide. Now uracil is not found in DNA, only in RNA. So DNA

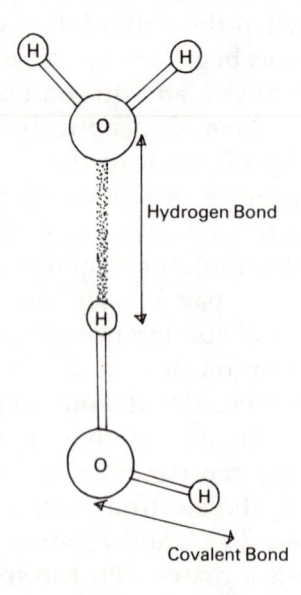

Fig 5.5 The hydrogen bond. Two water (H_2O) molecules illustrate the difference between a co-valent and a non-valent bond.

cannot broadcast any triplet which includes it. This would be predicted according to our hypothesis.

The eight essential amino acids and their triplets are shown in Table 5.1.

AMINO ACID	TRIPLET CODON			KEY
Isoleucine	AUU	AUC	CUG	U= Uracil
Leucine	UUG	UUA	CUU	A= Adenine
	CUC	CUA	CUG	G= Guanine
Valine	GUU	GUC	GUA	C= Cytosine
Phenylalanine	UUU	UUC		
Methionine	AUG			
Threonine	ACU	ACC	ACA	ACG
Tryptophan	UGG			

and the exception, which proves the rule:

Lysine AAA AAG

(Histidine is only found in infants.)

Very well. But how can our hypothesis explain why DNA, which is known to have adenine bases in it, cannot seem to broadcast the specific frequency of its hydrogen bond, paired always with the purine thymine? (The table above is for RNA. The DNA equivalent AAA generates UUU, which is phenylalanine. Excess phenylalanine is the agent responsible for mental retardation in cases of phenylketonuria, a point mutation.)

Well, first the hydrogen bond between adenine and thymine is much weaker than the others, only two bonds against three, or as John Gribbin put it in his book *In Search of the Double Helix*, a two-pin plug instead of a three-pin plug (Fig 5.6).[111] Secondly adenine plays a very special role in cellular affairs: as ATP (emitted by the mitochondria) it binds to two other phosphates and delivers energy round the body to the muscles; its weak bonds come in very handy here, because they break so easily it has no trouble at all in dropping its energy packets where they are needed. So it may be that DNA is broadcasting AAA and AAG but that the signal-noise ratio is too low for it to be heard, or that it can only emit a feeble signal.

Most interesting of all is the finding that lysine, the amino-acid formed from adenine, plays a special role in the production of antibodies, and helps to reduce herpes and related syndromes.

Fig 5.6 i. The bonding of adenine and thymine: only two bonds instead of three as with cytosine and guanine. See how similar they appear once the bonding has taken place.

LIFE'S SECRET MECHANISMS

Fig 5.6 ii. How the bases are attached to their sugar-phosphate strands.

Have we stumbled on the reason why AIDS victims lose their T- and B-lymphocytes, thus becoming vulnerable to opportunistic diseases? If our guess is correct we should be able to produce lysine synthetically either in vitro or in vivo, by broadcasting its frequency to the human body or to a mixture of chemicals including methane, ammonia, water vapour, and hydrogen with ultraviolet radiation of the correct frequency.

A similar experiment with ultraviolet irradiated chemicals was actually successfully carried out in 1953 by Stanley Miller, and since then by many others. Commenting on Miller's experiment in his book *Life Itself*, Francis Crick[60] points out with unwitting foresight that:

> The results are too complex to summarise here, except for one striking fact. If the mixture of gases contains appreciable amounts of oxygen, then small molecules related to the molecules present in living systems are not found. If gaseous oxygen is absent, such small molecules are produced, provided the mixture of gases contains nitrogen and carbon in some form or other. Some gas mixtures produce a bigger variety of amino acids than others, especially if H^2 is not present.

Radiation of waves at cellular frequencies, we believe, is how the Kirlian photography can produce the phantom leaf effect. If we are right, this opens an entirely new epoch: the age of electronic medicine is at hand.

We have put forward our hypothesis to explain wide tracts of experience in a few small principles. It remains to test this hypothesis and to give it mathematical form.

Before concluding this chapter it is important to relate its principal hypothesis, which we hope is couched in terms understandable by biologists and physicists, to the somewhat scattered and apparently unrelated tenets of the so-called alternative medical practices which have recently received such disparagement in a British Medical Association report.

One of the earliest alternative medicines, in turn owing its origin to the theories of Paracelsus, is homoeopathy, of which Samuel Hahnemann is generally acknowledged to be the modern founder. His work *Organon of the Art of Healing* was published[116] as early as 1810. The word homoeopathy comes from the Greek word *homoios* meaning similar, and the Doctrine of Similars is based on the precept that by applying a small quantity of a noxious substance to a sick body which induces (in a healthy body) the same symptoms as the disease, then the disease will be cured. A mad notion at first sight! In practice the homoeopathist will use a very very diluted amount of, say, yellow jasmine (which makes a healthy person display all the symptoms of influenza) to cure someone who has influenza. The homoeopathic approach was based on empirical research: it came about by trial and error with different substances. And it worked. But Hahnemann was in some difficulty in explaining the mechanism by which it works, and this made and still makes acceptance of the concept difficult for most people, especially those engaged in conventional (or 'allopathic' as homoeopathists call it) medicine. George Vithoulkas in 1979 gave a useful explanation of homoeopathy in electromagnetic terms:[285] after mentioning Kirlian photography as a means of exposing life fields, he wrote:

Electromagnetic fields are characterised by the phenomenon of vibration. As electrons race around atomic nuclei, they first move in one direction then another, as viewed by an external observer. This oscillation back and forth occurs at a specific frequency which is determined by the type of sub-atomic particle and its level of energy. For our purposes however the significant point is that everything exists in a state of vibration, and every electromagnetic field is characterised by vibration rates (or frequencies) which can be measured. The human organism is no exception. To grossly oversimplify a highly complex situation one can visualise an individual human being as existing at a particular vibrational frequency which may change dynamically every second depending on the mental state of the person, internal or external stresses, illness, etc. The electromagnetic field is very likely the 'vital force' that Hahnemann referred to.

Once a morbific stimulus has affected the electromagnetic field of a person, things may progress in two ways. If the person's constitutional state is quite strong and the harmful stimulus weak, the electromagnetic field changes vibration rate only slightly and only for a short time. The individual is not aware that anything has happened at all.

But if the stimulus is powerful enough to overwhelm the vital force, the electromagnetic field undergoes a greater change in vibration rate, and effects are eventually felt by the individual. ...The symptoms of a disease are nothing but reactions trying to rid the organism of harmful influences which are merely the material manifestations of earlier disturbances on a dynamic electromagnetic level. ...

> As all substances possess characteristic electromagnetic fields, the task of the homeopath is to find that substance whose vibration rate most closely matches that of the patient during illness. ...When the vibration rates are matched, a phenomenon occurs which is very well known to physicists and engineers as 'resonance'.

Well, there's the mechanism all right. And beautifully expressed by Vithoulkas too. But why should only a very small amount of curative substance be required? Vithoulkas explains that only small quantities of normalising vibrating substances are required to affect the whole organism because the phenomenon known as Brownian Motion will see to its propagation through the whole body at nigh the speed of light. The phenomenon of Brownian Motion is that all molecules are in a constant and random state of movement. Therefore even the addition of one single atom will influence the whole pond, so to speak, into which it drops. In an inert substance the whole substance will act as if it were one molecule of any active substance it contains. Electricity flows down wires by the same mechanism. So even the smallest particle of the correct frequency will have a remedial effect on a dysfunctioning body, no doubt assisted as far as possible by the body's own resonant cells. The relationship of homoeopathy to our hypothesis can now be clearly seen.

All that was lacking in the homoeopathic argument was the linking of these effects to the radio transmissions between brain and cell in the normal organism, thus giving it a structural and anatomical basis.

Aromatherapy works in precisely the same way:[236] the effect of a small quantity of an essential oil rubbed onto the surface of the skin can be clearly detected in the urine within hours. The whole science of urology is founded on the same basic concept in reverse, though urologists would probably limit their expectations and their explanations to chemical ones.

Acupuncture is also related totally to our hypothesis in that it attempts to stimulate non-neural electromagnetic pathways not in the brain but in the more accessible parts of an organism, its body. Yoga, relaxation tapes, and even sensory deprivation techniques work in a different part of our proposed system, aiming to lower the noise or energy fields which are draining the signal of its energy for transmission: if the stress in the brain is reduced, then there is more energy left to send out normalising signals. Colour therapy does the same job using the various frequencies of light to calm or excite the life fields, and impose order on our wayward entropic cells.

To some extent all these alternative therapies succeed and thus attract their devotees. But it does not take much discernment to realise that there are serious difficulties in their specific application, and that controlling the specific frequencies for each individual by means of chemical substances however diluted demands enormous experience and patience. The tools of the alternative therapist's trade are subtle and cannot ever compare with the kind of fine tuning possible with modern electronic frequency tuning devices, which have been honed by the public demand for high quality radio reception and high fidelity recording techniques. To some extent all the alternative therapies suffer from the fixity of the wave-forms they impose, and much research has yet to take place in order to identify the specifics necessary to normalise aberrant influences. With electromagnetic detection systems the task is much simpler. The advantage of an electromagnetic instrument is also that it is closely controllable, replicable, and its effects can be fully and immediately monitored. We have not mentioned all the alternative medical practices now available, but the principle we have offered can quickly be applied to them with a little thought: reflexology, where the foot is studied to identify disease, can now be seen in the context of the place on the body furthest from the brain, where abnormal influences will first manifest. Toning, the use of the body's own sound to induce therapy, and indeed any music whether practised in monasteries or concert halls, is simply toning at one stage removed, and music therapy generally can now be understood as the reimposition of calming wave-forms. The whole concept is well discussed by Mrs Keyes in her book *Toning, the Creative Power of the Voice*.[155]

In short many of the alternative therapies make use of their underlying mechanisms to normalise the body's wave-forms, and as we will soon propose, a similar process happens when we eat our daily bread.

But it isn't only the therapeutic application of Radiated Morphogenetic Fields seen in alternative medical practices which can provide examples of the mechanism at work.

There is also dowsing.

Dowsing is an accepted technique for finding water, oil, dead bodies, lost jewellery, and archaeological sites. The word comes from *deus*, meaning a god or holy spirit, and dowsing (the use of the divining rod) is often regarded as teleradiaesthesia, a form of telepathy practised by sensing distant objects with 'the Mind'. Even experienced dowsers like Scott Elliott confess they just do not know how it works. (We ourselves have no construct for the mind: we only know the brain.)

Henry de Francé in his useful little book *The Elements of Dowsing* provides a potted history of the French development of dowsing, mentioning that an English engineer of German origin, Diederich Wessel Linden, first connected dowsing with electricity as early as 1750. The theme was picked up by De Thouvenel who wrote a 'Mémoire Physique et médicinal, montrant des rapports évidents entre les phénoménes de la Baguette Divinatoire, du Magnétisme, et de l'Electricité (A Physical and Medical Treatise showing clear connections between the phenomena of the Divining Rod, Magnetism, and Electricity).

In discussing dowsing, let there be no mistake: it works. Anyone can do it, some better than others. There are thousands of replicated examples of successful dowsing: oil companies use professional dowsers all the time. The two principal methods are the Method of Fields and the Method of Samples, both of which were being practised in the seventeenth century and are probably much earlier than that. Some argue that certain rods in the hand of an Egyptian scratched on a 3700 BC temple plaque are divining rods. A footnote in the *Life of Proclus* by Marinus talks about the Chaldean practice of strophalomancy, the use of rotating tops for the purpose of divination as part of the Orphic tradition. The same book mentions that 'he had experimented with the divinatory power of the tripod'. Some sort of prophesying instrument we presume, of the fifth century AD or before. The truth is no one knows how old dowsing is.

'The Method of Fields assumes that every object is surrounded by a field,' says Le Vicomte Henry de Francé, 'that is to say a space in which its influence is felt. Every field is characterised by its vertical and horizontal dimensions, as well as by its 'direction', as shown by a beam of radiation acting at an angle to the meridian which is peculiar to the object. Sounds familiar. In other words this field could be identified by a receiving system designed to accept bi-polar information – like the brain.

De Francé continues:

Studying the results of the Method of Fields, at first on metal conductors and then on the reaction bands found by dowsers on the ground [Mr Maby] ascertained that these reactions, examined with electrometers, magnetometers, milliampere meters and ionisation counters corresponded to corpuscular and wave effects. There is then an agreement between the claims of the dowser and the statements of the physicist.

The Method of Samples is based on the following experiment: place on a ground or table two objects, alike or different, at a smaller distance from one another than the combined extent of their horizontal fields. If the objects are alike, you will observe that the pendulum adjusted over the first object continues to gyrate over the whole space which separates it from the second object and even over the whole surface of the latter. It can then be said that harmony or accord exists between the two objects and the first is said to be a sample of the second. ... You will also find harmony or affinity between the body and a food that suits it. You can strengthen this accord by putting the two objects in line with the sun or with a magnet, or by placing them on a meridian (N.S. line).

This sounds suspiciously like the technique discovered by Abrams. De Francé recommends beginners to practise on objects which are magnified or electrified, saying that there is no doubt that the nature of what is perceived in dowsing is the outstanding magnetic, electric, calorific or radioactive physical properties.

We do not have space here to develop the theme, but even from this first glance it will be evident to the reader that dowsing is a mechanism wholly in line with our central hypothesis of Radiated Morphogenesis.

6
Electrocrystal Therapy: Diagnosis and Treatment

This chapter is divided into two parts. In the first part we discuss the diagnosis of disease using an instrument which has been developed from the ideas contained in the Kirlian photographic method. In the second part we describe the use of pulsed high-frequency electrical currents, amplified by natural quartz crystals, to treat disease, developed by Harry Oldfield.

Diagnosis by ESM

We have called our method of measuring energetic emanations from organisms the electro-scanning method (ESM). This can also incorporate analysis at audio frequencies, or analysis on an oscilloscope. The method has evolved from Kirlian photography as an alternative analytical tool to the photographic effect. It has the advantage that it can be used in complete daylight and can handle three-dimensional objects. We introduce it here because it is an independent method which backs up what we are seeing in the Kirlian picture. ESM not only has computer compatibility but also offers a means of permanently recording scans of objects and living things onto magnetic tape. We noticed in the very early days of our research that an object energised in the Kirlian field, if well tuned in to its harmonic resonant frequency, gave off radio waves and an audible sound. So to put it simply, we lowered the voltage, increased the accuracy of the fine tuning, and sent the resulting vibration over the whole person or object. With an accurate sensor tuned into the normal level of this field, abnormal or cyclic changes in this reference field could be detected. It did indeed seem to mimic the field effect of the Kirlian method, even though, because of the lowered voltage, there was no visible corona discharge. Procedures are used which do not involve touching the subject, to lessen the risk of artefacts (which sometimes arise with the photographic method if the precautions described in Appendix 1 are not taken). Transparent and/or magnifying electrodes can get over this problem, when the light is recorded directly with a conventional camera on open shutter.

These electrodes, sealed within conductive electrolytes, were passed over different parts of the body, evincing glowing pinpoints of light, some steady, some flickering. These points of activity seem to correlate with the relative health of the individual. After a friend of Harry's, who was familiar with the points used in acupuncture, had seen these displays, he stated that he believed we were seeing acupuncture points in their living state. Since acupuncture points are available for reference in many textbooks we could, after a little practice, map them on transparent plastic overlays placed on the volunteers. They corresponded quite accurately with most of the charts. There were, however, inconsistencies in some of the observations from individual to individual. Some points seemed inactive, while others, when health was off-balance, became highly visible!

Whilst we do not have time here to argue the case for or against the validity of acupuncture as a therapeutic method, it is interesting that we actually observed these points with our instruments. Again large tracts of experience are being reduced to a simple principle: our hypothesis begins to explain the mechanism of how acupuncture works, and suggests that it is a system exploiting the places where resonances emerge from the human body.

We also observed effects on these points before and after needle insertion: the activity of the point in most cases was 'calmed down' after the acupuncture. Initially when we first saw the points we thought they were active sweat glands. However, when we raised the temperature of the observation darkroom to a level which caused profuse perspiration, no increase in these spots was noted. Some of them even disappeared. We also dabbed volunteers with salt spots at specially marked places on their skin to see if we could make our own artificial acupuncture points. We didn't succeed. We found out later that other famous researchers in the USSR and America had made similar observations and had duly noted them.

In acupuncture textbooks, flows of energy all over the body along lines called meridians are described with which the acupuncture points are somehow connected. Unfortunately, we were unable to detect such channels. However, we would like to emphasise that we were making surface observations only. Perhaps these channels occur much deeper down, the observed points of activity being only where these meridians reach the surface. It would be logical to presume that somehow these meridians might be manipulated from trigger points on the surface, by needles inserted into the points. (Sometimes acupuncture needles, incidentally, have to be inserted quite deeply.)

So much by way of introduction to the ESM method.

Let us now examine this development from Kirlian photography more closely, and its relevance to the diagnosis of disease. When we look at a photograph, we are seeing a two dimensional representation of a three-dimensional world. In the same way when we see a Kirlian picture or make an observation through a flat transparent electrode, we are seeing only in two dimensions, because the electrical force field is only generated from a two-dimensional electrode. But the object we are observing the energy from, be it a hand or leaf, is a *three-dimensional* form. So the energy we are seeing in a standard Kirlian print lacks another dimensional component.

We are pleased to report that with special apparatus we have now succeeded in reproducing the Kirlian effect in three dimensions (Fig. 6.1). However, please remember that when photographed in an ordinary sense, we are still seeing the energy of the specimen in two dimensions. Even though a video recording

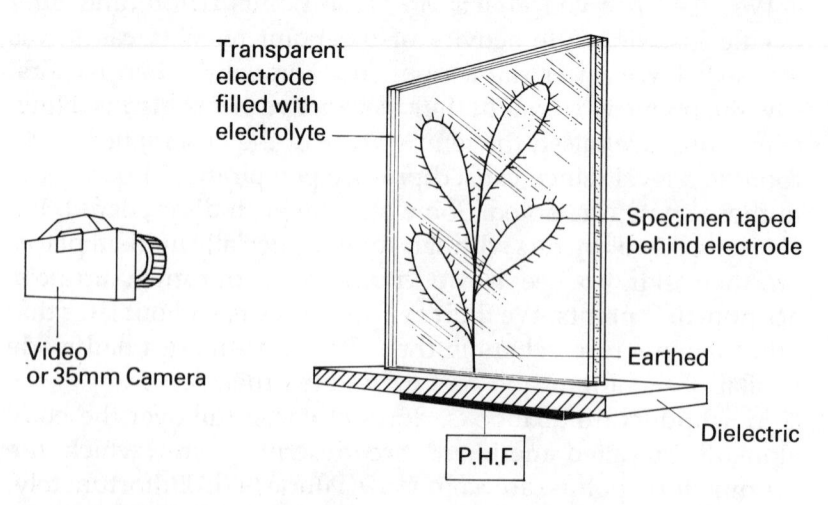

Fig 6.1 Schematic diagram of 3D Kirlian apparatus. Note that there is no film between the dielectric and the specimen, since it is in the ordinary camera.

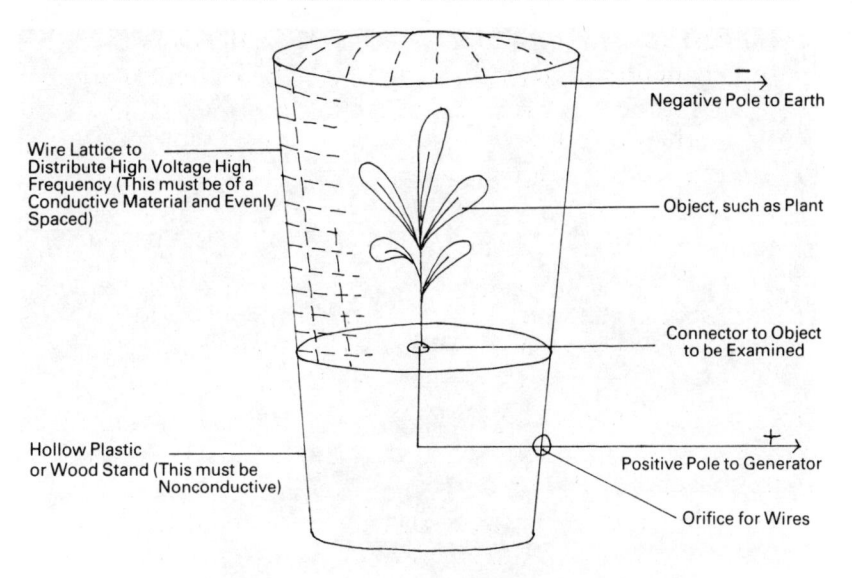

Fig 6.2 Diagram of basic set up for taking 3D Kirlian pictures. The polarity can be reversed in which case the frame is wired to the generator and the specimen is earthed.

with image intensifiers might prove a good means of making records in the future, the 3D effect can only be observed directly.

The method used to produce 3D Kirlian pictures demands a higher voltage than that used in the ordinary Kirlian process: it can be achieved by using larger coils, for greater induction, or by increasing the voltage to the primary section of the coil, in an ordinary Kirlian apparatus. It must be pointed out, however, that in the latter method there is a risk of overheating, and the burning out of equipment!

Tesla had the same problem!

Now, if you recall, with the making of 'ordinary' Kirlian pictures, we have a positive plate that loses electrons and a negative specimen (earthed) which gains electrons. In our 3D system, this process is reversed; the specimen itself becoming the positive pole and the surrounding mesh curtain the negative or earthed pole of the field (Fig. 6.2). This system can, of course, be reversed in polarity, but the object under test seems to give more information in the former case, except in two-dimensional studies; and, although our apparatus has the means to reverse the polarity with a different wiring arrangement so that the specimen becomes the positive pole, it does not always yield

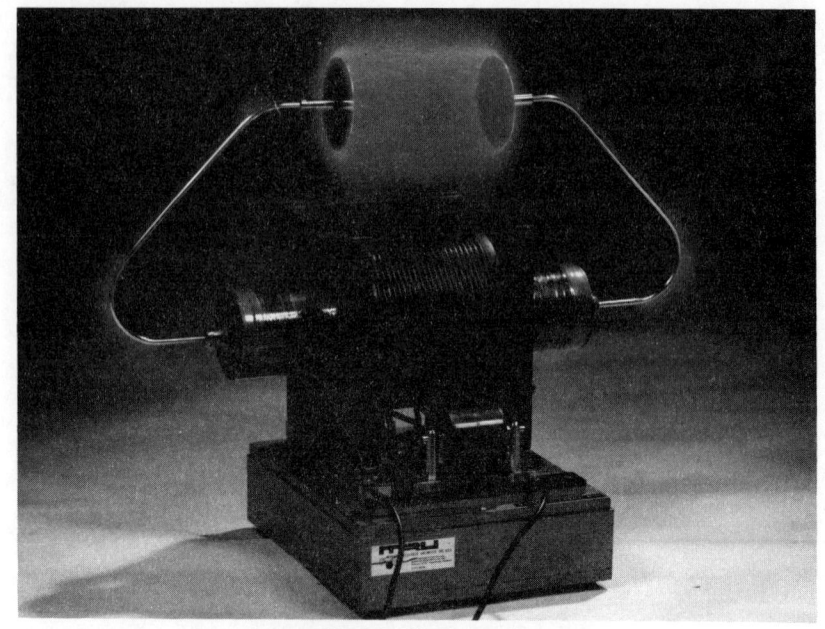

Fig 6.3 The Tesla coil.

additional information, often less. It seems that with the higher voltages involved and, we believe, higher resultant harmonics, different aspects of the field are at work.

Experiments have been conducted in which high-voltage, high-frequency fields have been placed around people to obtain 3D-type effects. Volunteers for these experiments have found the feelings this equipment generated somewhat disconcerting. 'Being plunged into a live ants' nest' was one description! Also very little, or in some cases, no visible light was seen from the subject. This is probably because the volume of a human body absorbs much more energy generated from the apparatus and requires higher voltages and higher frequencies before electroluminescence occurs. Even larger coils can be used, with the object on top of the coil discharging into the air.

We cannot claim this as an original idea: Tesla did it at the beginning of this century (Fig 6.3)!

He did not, however, ever claim that the electrically generated field was, by its patterning, saying something about the cellular condition of the body, and was thus reflecting much more subtle forces. Tesla's demonstration was simply to show the safety of this type of electrical field, and to quell rumours put about by Edison of the danger of alternating current. By a subterfuge Edison arranged that the first criminal to die by electrocution was killed by means of alternating, not direct, current.[53, 148]

We have achieved good results in the 3D method with small objects, medium-sized plants, crystals and mineral specimens (Fig. 6.4).

You will see that we have two working systems of 3D Kirlian energy monitoring. One uses a large induction coil generating a 10 cm spark gap, when a medium primary voltage of energy is used. If we work on the rough rule of thumb when measuring high voltage, that every millimetre of spark produces an energy of approximately 1,000 volts, then this coil can generate (for medium to long periods) 100,000 volts. The current, however, is very low indeed. The smaller 3D system can generate approximately a 4 cm spark gap and, therefore, has a voltage of approximately 40,000 volts, which is the minimum requirement for most small 3D visible studies.

All experiments must be conducted under strict darkroom conditions with no safelight. Any incidental stray light will in-

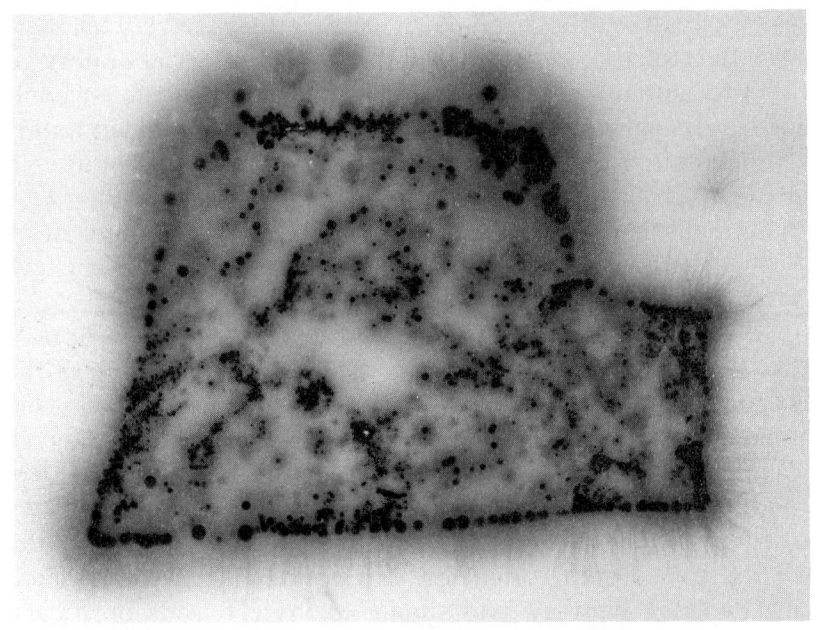

Fig 6.4 3D Kirlian photograph of a mineral sample.

terfere with the visual effect. The apparatus must be placed on non-metallic surfaces and no metal must be worn by the experimenter – wrist watches, bracelets, etc. This is in case the researcher accidentally earths the energy through himself or herself by touching or brushing against the negative, earth return screen, surrounding the object. It is also advisable to conduct the experiments on a foam-backed carpet and away from earthed objects such as radiators. If shorts do occur, and if the short is through an object with a small surface area, then a high-frequency burn is possible, which is very unpleasant rather than dangerous. **Even so, people with known nervous or heart disorders are not advised to experiment on such apparatus. Incidentally, when direct observations are being made with the apparatus, and no protective glass magnifier or plate is being used between object and eyes, there is a risk of retinal lesions with ultraviolet light.** This can easily be overcome by observing the field through ordinary glass lenses (not plastic) which stops most ultraviolet radiation. Another alternative is a securely mounted glass pane in front of the apparatus.

We hope that after reading about these safety factors, you have not been entirely put off the research!

No one was more conscious of the dangers of high-voltage electricity than the great Nikola Tesla. Tesla was a very tall man, well over six foot in height. When working in his laboratory on high-tension apparatus he would don enormous rubber boots with soles six inches deep. Once a cleaner who came in to tidy the laboratory one evening found him still at work, and went into a dead faint at the sight of such a giant looming over her.

Seriously though, one can never have too many safety rules: it needs only one accident to deter people from what we believe potentially is a useful research tool.

If we familiarise ourselves with figures A.1 and A.3 in Appendix 1, we can refresh our minds on the physical set-up of the apparatus. We have a special generator delivering a pulsed frequency and primary voltage to the primary input of the coil. This creates, in the secondary part of the coil, a field of very high voltage and frequency which collapses and expands according to the pulse repetition rate. The high-tension section of the coil is then connected to a conductive, well-insulated high-voltage delivery lead similar to the HT leads on a car's coil. This lead is as short as possible to avoid loss of power and

ELECTROCRYSTAL THERAPY: DIAGNOSIS AND TREATMENT

shunt capacitance effects, which could cause artefacts from fluctuations in the field. The specimen is secured in an upright position with the HT lead in close contact with the same. The negative earthed screen is then either wired up to the neutral terminal or earthed by a separate path. Great care must be taken to see that the thin wire mesh screen is shaped either evenly into a dome or a cylindrical form. In the smaller version of the three-dimensional device, there is no screen but a metal cylinder, painted black, is placed inside to stop reflections, with a cover consisting of a magnifying lens. The specimen in either system, mesh or cylinder, is placed in the middle of the apparatus. If the object is uneven, try to shape the mesh for more even spacing or move the cylinder around until there is even distribution of the field and no direct shorting by contact or by the positive specimen moving with the vibration of the field. If this is achieved, a clear field will appear around the specimen which can be varied by the pulse repetition control knob. We find that different specimens energise at different pulse rates, suggesting that with sophisticated equipment the specific resonant frequency of any object can be uncovered. (This may be a new and important discovery.) The rough rule of thumb seems to be the less conductive the object, e.g. a mineral specimen, the higher the rate. However, always use the minimum rate for initial observations, just in case the specimen is overcharged and direct shorting to the electrodes occurs. The aim for most occasions is to cause the least possible disturbance to the specimen.

We now discuss our electroscanning method (ESM). This too is a three-dimensional energy field detection system. Some seven years ago we discovered that specimens in the Kirlian field not only gave off light which could be captured on film, but emitted radio and sound energy as well. This apparatus, the Bentham-Oldfield scanner, can also produce good results with no input voltages.

The method is as follows: a glass electrode filled with saline solution (common salt will do) is attached to a high-voltage, high frequency generator. Our Kirlian cameras include this feature and our range of electrocrystal therapy units (mentioned shortly) can all be converted into ESM diagnostic units. The subject holds the electrode in his or her hand and stands upright in a relaxed manner. A detector is used to test the field; these detectors can be oscilloscopes, sound level meters or frequency monitors. But, whatever method is used, we are looking for magnitude and phase shifting of the reference field which the generator sends into and around the subject. The field itself is pulsed from the generator along the delivery wire into the tube. A secondary field effect is set up in the subject by induction. The field can also be tuned to a stable (control) spot on the subject by a frequency tuning system in the apparatus.

We use a control spot on the subject which has never been injured and where there are no skin eruptions. We then tune the field to a stable reading on our equipment. Once this has been achieved and checked against another control spot on the subject, scanning can begin. It is important to have this second check on another spot known by the subject or the clinician to be stable. Try the two ear lobes: unless your subject is a boxer or rugger player, or has pierced ears, these are likely to be intact. The two spots should be of the same amplitude and in phase with one another. We can now compare signals away from these control areas on other parts of the subject's body. If the amplitude stays more or less the same and in phase with the reference signal then, since it is behaving like the control

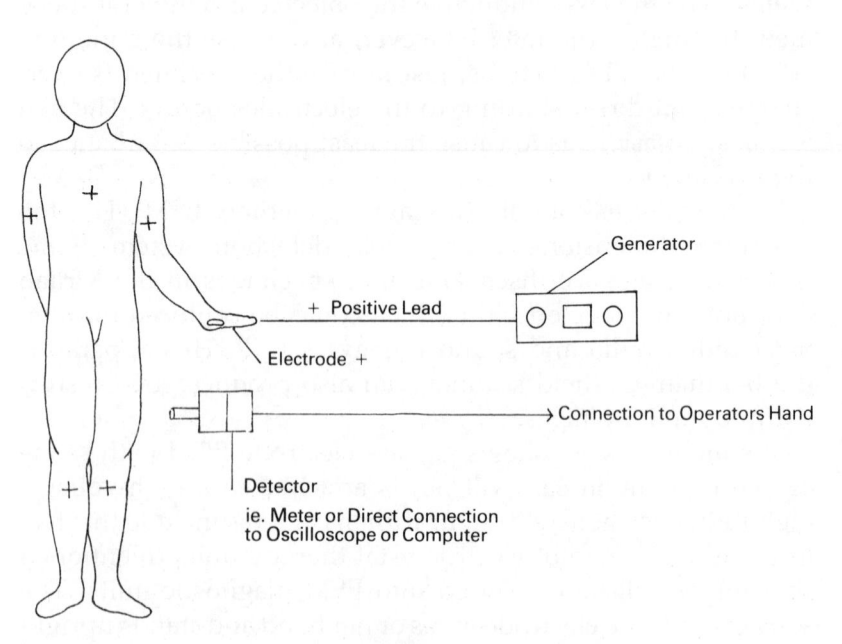

Fig 6.5 Basic set-up for electro-scanning.

area, we regard it as normal. If, however, there are changes, then this area comes under suspicion. It does, however, depend on the degree of change: conclusions must not be drawn too soon and comparisons are periodically made during the scan to the control sites in case of signal drift. If, after all these checks, the reference signal still changes beyond tolerance levels, then some clinical abnormality might be the cause of the change. Careful analysis suggests that the greatest change or distortion is the amplitude change in the field. On a decibel scale, changes range from one or two decibels to ten and beyond! If we were able to see this field change with the naked eye, we would see evenly distributed fields around the body on healthy sites and concave and convex fields where there were disturbances past and present (Fig. 6.5).

Let us examine now the components from which this field of reference is constructed. First and foremost we have a pulsing electrical field, which induces harmonic oscillations in the object or subject being studied. These set up a resonating field of energy around the subject composed of electromagnetic waves and a small proportion of sound pressure waves. (We have estimated the percentage field distribution of sound to EM field to be approximately 30 to 70 per cent.) The field is composed of many different frequencies and harmonics stabilised and sent into the subject in pulses. This pulse train can range from just several thousand pulses to as high as 100,000 pulses a second in some individual cases. Just as in Kirlian photography, these pulses must not be confused with individual frequencies but should be compared to, say, a choir of voices, broadcasting and stopping at intervals. Between intervals there is a harmonic oscillation and, before this has had time to die away, another burst of energy is pulsed and so the whole process is repeated.

We believe that during the scanning and detection process, if the medium of transmission (e.g. human tissue) is in good order, then this composite signal is transmitted faithfully. However, where the physical and/or energy field of the body is disturbed, the reference field resonates in a different way. This causes a fall or an increase in amplitude as the field is absorbed or reflected at any one moment. The reference field can also experience phase effects, which themselves can wobble or shift in and out of step with the original induced signal. There are also occasions where individual frequency bands are absorbed

Fig 6.6 Kirlian apparatus set up at the Rollright stones. (Devereux)

by the suspect site, and this can be observed with a spectrum analyser.

These effects have not only been observed in living fields but also in megalithic stone circles (Fig. 6.6).[69]

This was an ESM scan carried out at the time of a summer solstice (the day the sun stops rising a little further each day along the horizon, and starts in the other direction). These megaliths behave like any other inanimate object at most times and do not change the reference signal, except under certain unusual circumstances and cyclic events! These stone sites, incidentally, contain a very high percentage of quartz. The crystals we use in electrocrystal therapy are of course also quartz.

We would now like to concentrate further on a set-up for human subjects and ESM. However, this is not meant to hinder the imagination of any researcher who might wish to test our equipment on something a little different. For example in *Medical News Weekly*, December 1981 (17/22 Vol. 13, No. 48) can be seen a strange object in Harry's hand – an unusual subject for ESM scanning and Kirlian photography (Fig. 6.7)!

ELECTROCRYSTAL THERAPY: DIAGNOSIS AND TREATMENT

MEDICAL NEWS

Thursday, December 17/24, 1981
Volume 13 Number 48

WEEKLY

Charting a lobster's corona in a Hounslow backyard

Fig 6.7 Harry Oldfield and lobster!

When dealing with human subjects, we recommend that they remove their footwear or, if possible, stand on a rubber car mat or insulated floor surface (e.g. foam-backed carpet). Do not put them near filing cabinets or central heating radiators, etc., since

ARM Normal

Filtered

stomach pathological site

Unfiltered

Noise Ratio filtered equipment

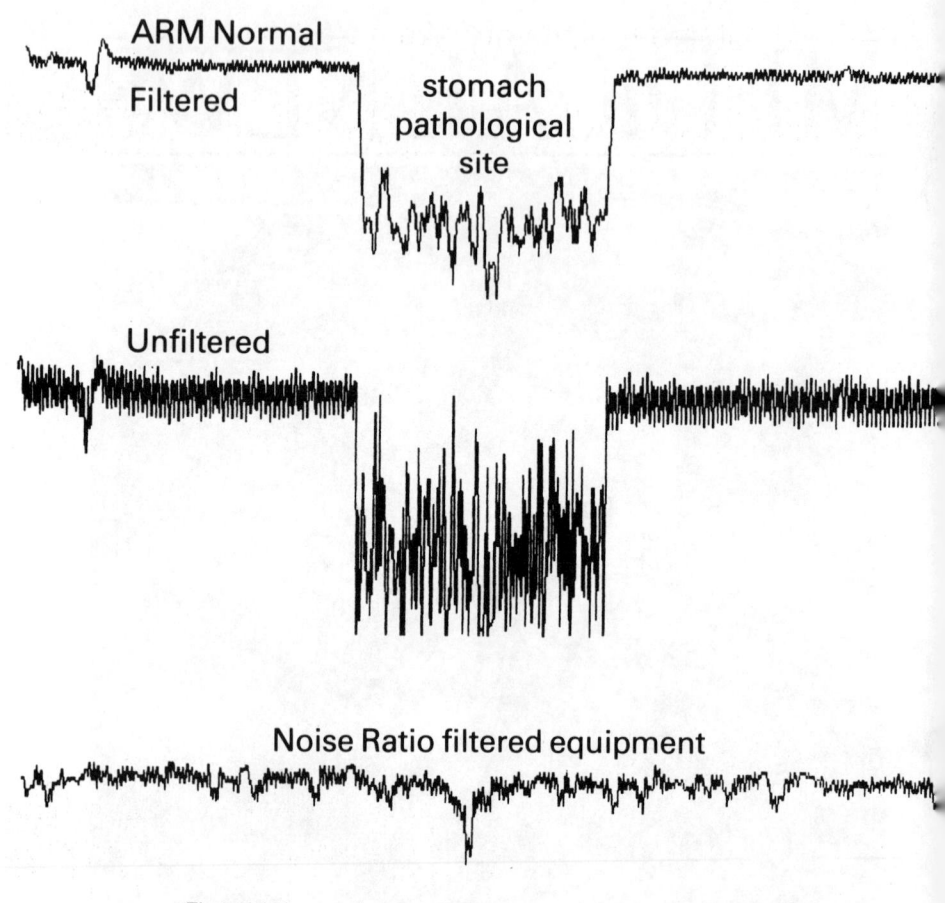

Fig 6.8 (Above and opposite) Scans produced by the ESM equipment.

this might affect the readings. Take off any large metal jewellery, belt buckles, etc., as this also can distort the field. The field will always try to find the quickest or the least resistant way to earth.

Once all these things have been done, switch on the apparatus and tune in the field on a normal part of the body, e.g. the forearm (Fig. 6.8.) If the field is stable, holding the detector at an even distance from the body (about 2" to 3"), make A/B comparisons between this site and another normal site on the body. If they give the same readings within a variation of approximately one to two decibels (sound level meter), or a 1 cm sq. grid deviation of amplitude on an oscilloscope, then you can proceed to look at other parts of the body. These small

ELECTROCRYSTAL THERAPY: DIAGNOSIS AND TREATMENT

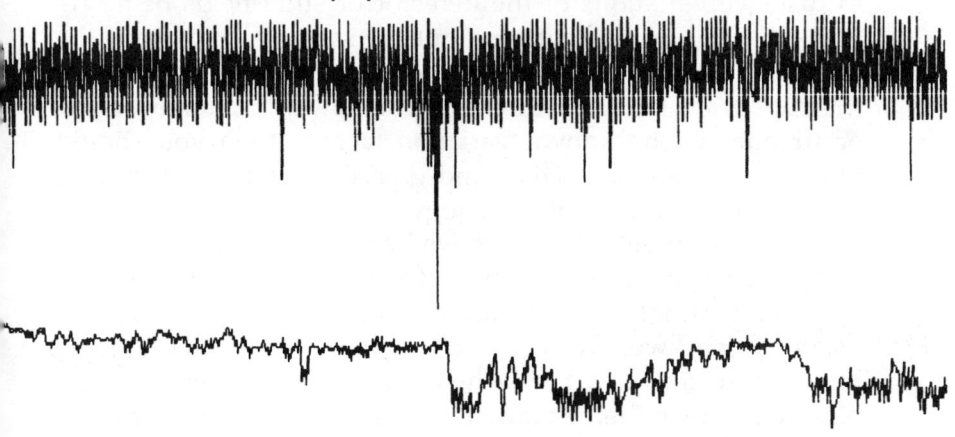

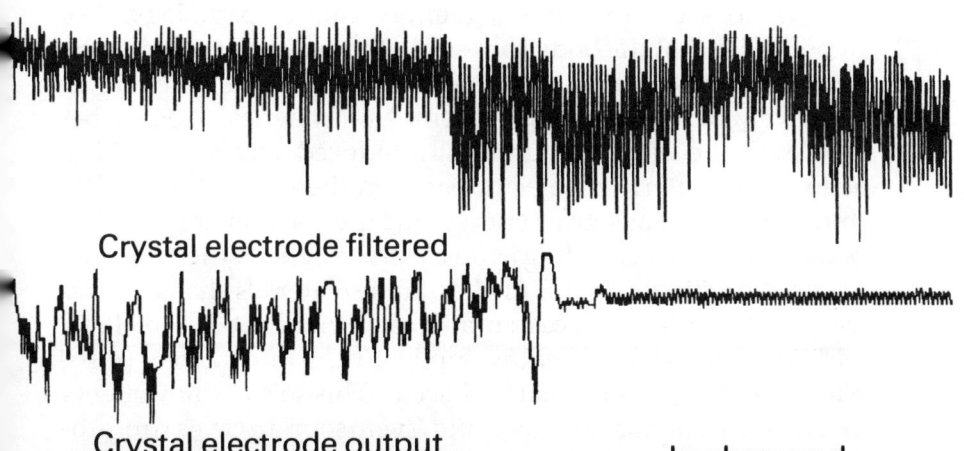

Unfiltered equipment without electrodes

Crystal electrode filtered

Crystal electrode output

background

deviations between normal sites on the body can be put down to distance variations of the detector or stray fields being reflected off the person carrying out the scan. (Always have the detector at arm's length and do not touch the subject because this causes artefacts in the field.) If you now find changes which occur outside the known variation factors, then you should note this change on a chart and gradually build up a map of possible areas of clinical pathology.

All very well but what have we been able to detect?

We are seeing a field change of energy and not necessarily a physical pathological condition in the body itself. Using the above system, we have been able to detect sites ranging from old fracture sites to a headache active at the moment of scanning! Obviously there is much more research to do in order to improve diagnostic accuracy. *At the present time and state of development it is a valuable addition to, but does not take the place of, conventional medical diagnosis.* In due course, however, we are optimistic that further refinements will allow greater confidence to be placed in the method, and that more sophisticated instruments will emerge.

How does the instrument identify clinical pathology? We hypothesise that the body (physical), the nervous system of the body, and the radiated morphogenetic field of the body are all effectively part of the same system. No mysteries! We also believe that the electro-magnetically induced reference field is acting as an interface detector between these cell clusters. We think that the 'collective' energy and physical material of the person under scan is acting as an electro-magnetostrictive transducer. We will explain this further. Some materials change physically in size when placed in a constant magnetic field. If an additional alternating field is applied, then fluctuations (resonances) in the physical material occur. This sets up movements in the surrounding medium, and even sound waves are produced. In physics the effect can be produced by a polarising magnet, and an alternating field is produced by passing a varying current through a coil placed around a magnetostrictive device. We think the body or, more accurately, its cells are acting as the stable polarised magnet so to speak, each cell acting as a discrete domain. The reference field, which is also produced from a coil, is induced into and around this natural field of the body. It might even explain the percentage of sound

ELECTROCRYSTAL THERAPY: DIAGNOSIS AND TREATMENT

TOP VIEW

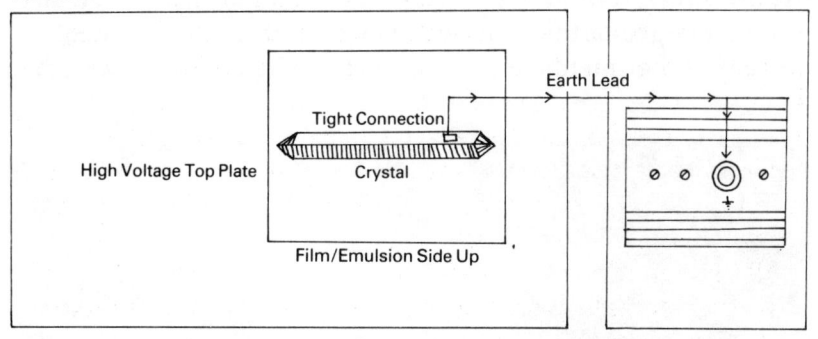

Fig 6.9 Using the electrocrystal therapy apparatus to take Kirlian pictures of crystals and other objects. The crystal is placed on the top of the apparatus.

we are able to detect coming from the body. The field is stable where the cells are in phase with one another (a healthy state), but where there is clinical pathology then there is a phase shift in one or more of the cell clusters, which can then be detected in the induced reference field. There are probably other hypotheses of equal validity, and we welcome other views of the phenomena we have uncovered.

In developing diagnostic techniques it was important to explore the relationship between inorganic and organic matter and how they are differently affected by Kirlian photography, and by their own interaction. We did this by photographing crystals and living organisms simultaneously. The techniques described and the pictures shown here were all carried out using Kirlian cameras. Though it is a small digression, we include a brief description because of its importance in understanding how we developed our diagnostic techniques.

The problem facing the experimenter who wishes to take Kirlian photographs of crystals is the problem of low conductivity. If the crystals are of copper, iron, or conductive metallic origin, silver, gold, etc., few problems will be encountered with the Kirlian method. However, if the crystals are of quartz or fluorite, etc., much longer exposure times are required because of the high resistance (in the electrical sense) of the object. This does not mean that the results are less interesting or spectacular, as can be seen from the photographs. All these types of crystals not only need longer exposure times, e.g. sixty seconds for a two-to-three-inch quartz crystal, but, in some cases, they also require a larger earthing electrode for clearer results (Fig. 6.9).

Many experiments were conducted where quartz crystals

Fig 6.10 Crystal affecting a living field of a rose leaf.

were influenced by exterior field energy effects. These included stimulation by laser, sound, and human systems. Also shown here is the photographic evidence for the effect of crystals on living fields (Fig. 6.10).

In such an experiment a living leaf was photographed with a quartz crystal. After an interval of several minutes a second picture was taken and the resultant increase in the energy field of both objects can be clearly seen.

When control pictures of both objects were taken separately, no increase was observed.

In other experiments with volunteers we examined the effect on the corona of fingertips holding crystals. Again we discerned a clear increase in the corona discharge of the finger. This effect was increased even further with the introduction of electrocrystal therapy: energy fields which were previously high and distorted are calmed down and balanced normally. This is the subject matter of the next section.

Electrocrystal Therapy Treatment

In case you think that what we are about to propose seems far-fetched, we start this section by relating details of the work which at the time of writing (1988) is being carried out by Dr George Guilbault at the University of New Orleans.[112]

He uses quartz crystals, like those used in wrist watches, coated with antibodies. Under a small electrical current the crystals start to oscillate at a frequency determined by the coating of antibodies.

The antibodies used by Guilbault identify the pesticide parathion. If exposed to air contaminated with even the minutest amounts of parathion the molecules 'grab hold' of the pesticide molecules and the crystal oscillations are upset. This change is then measured.

The system is highly specific: even closely related molecules like those of the pesticide marathion do not produce the same response in the crystals.

Even more in line with our morphogenetic radiation hypothesis are the results being obtained by researchers in Glasgow and Warwick. A pair of electrodes is bridged by an organic polymer. The polymer's electrical properties change according to the vapour which passes over it. The responses of one polymer are linked, but by putting several sensors together, each made with a different polymer, the researchers hope to build up a unique 'fingerprint' of the vapour.

It is only a small step from this to the identifying, in electronic wave-form terms, of a specific DNA macromolecule, and re-broadcasting that wave-form amplified to the organism in order to bring back into line mutant cells. It is this concept which lies at the root of electrocrystal therapy.

Most mineral specimens can be electrically activated, especially the quartz crystal lattice. There is no doubt in Harry Oldfield's mind now, after the many hundreds of cases which have passed through his hands, that crystals, gem stones, and many other minerals have intrinsic healing properties. The characteristics of the stones come into three groups:

1. Stimulators, e.g. garnets, rubies;
2. Balancers, e.g. emeralds, jade;
3. Tranquillisers e.g. amethyst, sapphire

There is also a fourth group which we call amplifiers. These are first and foremost quartz crystals which greatly increase the effectiveness of the healing aspects of minerals, and these crystals themselves can be greatly increased by pulsed high-frequency electricity because of the harmonics they generate. This method we have called electrocrystal therapy.

The minerals, gems and/or crystals are placed in a sealed glass tube filled with brine solution. This is so that the specimens are surrounded by a conductive electrolyte, which means that any imperfections in the formation of the stones do not disturb the uniformity of the electromagnetic field to be induced. The stones are now electrically stimulated at various pulse repetition rates. The minerals can be stimulated or attenuated by various different pulses (Fig. 6.11). Whilst pulsed high frequency can be effective on its own, when combined with the stones, the spectrum of healing increases to startling proportions, and we have treated disorders ranging from migraines to multiple sclerosis, with a noticeably good success rate. However, we accept that though all these disorders have only been beneficially treated, it is still much too early to be making any claims of complete cure, since many cases need long-term monitoring to see if symptoms return, perhaps many years later. There is also the possibility of natural remission, or suggestion on the

ELECTROCRYSTAL THERAPY: DIAGNOSIS AND TREATMENT

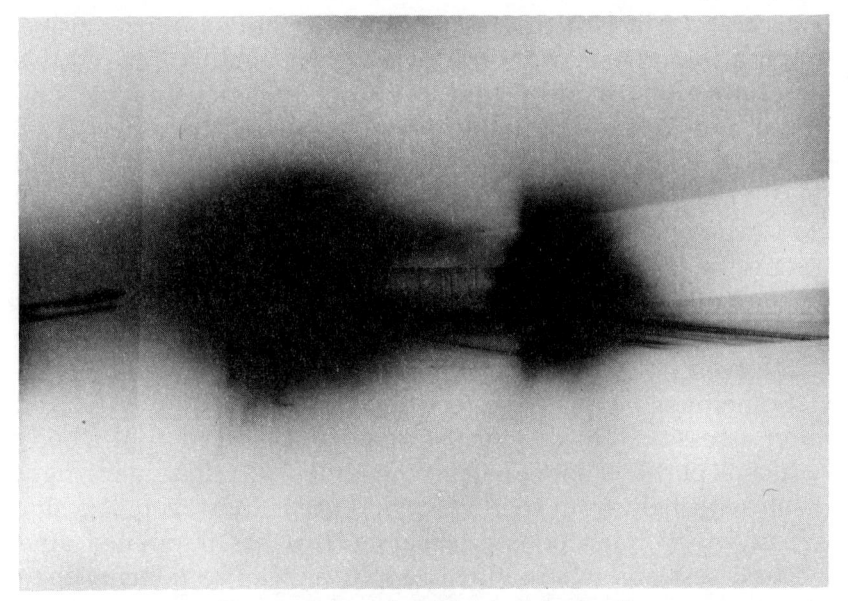

Fig 6.11 A mineral sample being stimulated.

part of the therapist. All these factors must be considered even if, as with this therapy, we are getting excellent results. We are only too willing to take part in the necessary clinical trials which should be placebo-controlled double-blind trials with full medical protocol, since only in this way can our method be evaluated. All we can do ourselves is to recite cases and results or testimonials. Some of these are given in Chapter 4 and other results from earlier equipment of the same generic type are scattered throughout this book.

We have not only turned our attention to people but also to animals, including cats, dogs, and horses. The power of suggestion from the therapist can be ruled out here, and that is also the case with very young children, babies, and the foetus.

The method used in almost every case is that the glass tube filled with quartz crystals and saline solution is laid against the affected area or placed against a trigger point or chakra. The tube of crystals is fixed in place with a velcro strap and the instrument is switched on. Even though the thick glass tube is a superb insulator, a secondary field effect is set up by electromagnetic induction. We believe that when this happens, the electrical field passing through the various stones picks up the particular healing vibration of that stone, so in effect the electrical component is acting as an amplifier and/or carrier wave. Such a hypothesis cannot at this present time be proved; we can only monitor and record its effects on various people, animals, and diseases. Another way of showing the effect is by actually removing the stones from the tube. The induced field is still the same, but the effects are greatly attenuated, possibly because some of the harmonics are missing. The presence, it seems, of the crystals helps to maximise the beneficial effects. We are often asked if there are any adverse medical symptoms brought on as a direct result of the therapy, but so far there have been no recorded adverse effects due to this therapy.

Sometimes people have reported being tired or over-relaxed after a session, but this we see as a natural reaction of a body which is perhaps not in balance needing a resting stage to right itself with help from the therapy. There is, however, one side effect which most people welcome: this has happened after several sessions where older people, as well as noticing their illness decreasing in intensity, have also noticed an increase in their own vitality which covers both physical and mental processes.

Another effect has been where people have come with one type of disorder and have reported afterwards that not only was this alleviated but other conditions too, which had not been mentioned.

A similar feature is found with hypnotherapy. The truth of the matter is that if the body is brought back into balance by our treatment, then other pathological conditions brought about by imbalance will also be assisted. It is not quackery, just the operation of a biological mechanism. This kind of result convinces us not only of the value of the therapy but of its holistic results. In the early days Harry only treated patients symptomatically, and found not only that physical well-being resulted, but also that their mental and psychic stability improved. He was pleasantly surprised. Perhaps he should not have been, knowing that crystals and gemstones had been used in a holistic manner in man's ancient history and even in man's more recent history in the Far East and India. Legends of their use have also been traced back to ancient Egypt and further back to the legendary Atlantis, the only classical account of which, incidentally, being in the dialogues of Plato called *Timaeus* and *Critias*,[230] which suggests: 'When the mind is too big for the body its energy shakes [vibrates] the whole frame and fills it with inner disorders' – an explanation remarkably close to our own concept of stress and its effect on organic cells in disease. The account in the *Timaeus* does not, however, anywhere mention the curative use of precious stones.

These ancient people did not just wear gemstones for decorative reasons, but for therapeutic reasons and mental power. Amethysts, for example, were said to prevent the wearer from becoming too drunk (*methus* being Greek for wine). Moreover the Greek word for adornment was 'cosmos', from which our own word *cosmetic* comes; but in Greek it also meant the world or universe; we also have the word 'cosmology', and the adornment was considered to help the wearer to get in tune with the world about him. The ancients looked on crystals especially with the same affection with which we would regard a well-trained intelligent dog! The quartz crystal has the power to amplify and modify cerebral radiations: it is in effect acting as a kind of thought amplifier and/or focusing channel. A thought in the brain has a quantum of energy associated with it and, though it is very weak, this quantum of energy is also a signal.

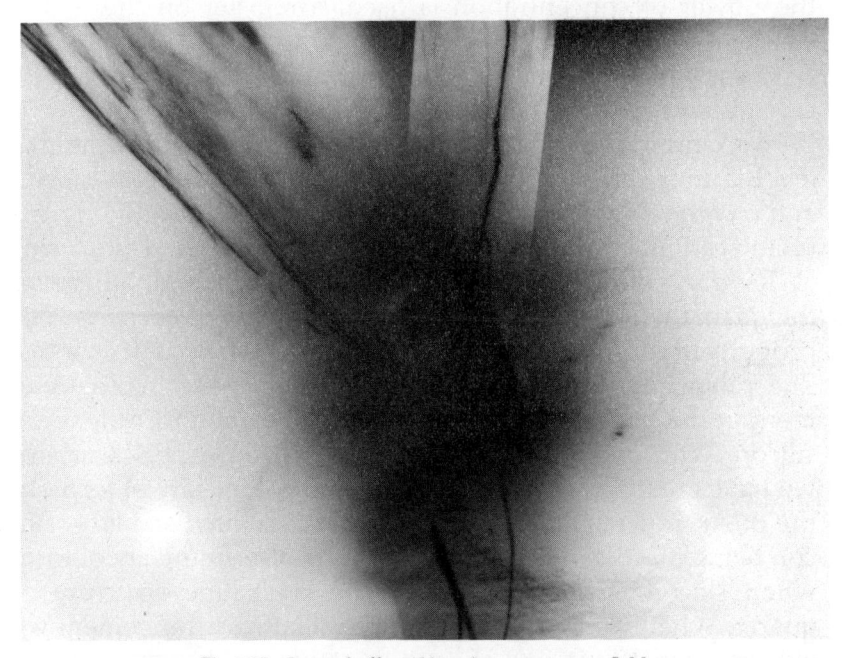

Fig 6.12 Crystal affected by a human energy field.

The principle of any amplifier is to turn a weak signal into a strong signal for a particular purpose. This seems to be how a crystal works, and our equipment can demonstrate this process in action, based on existing electrical detection techniques. We tap into the crystal lattice, in an electrical sense, and measure both material and induced currents of activity. All crystals have a base frequency with this apparatus but, when influenced by human energy fields, the crystals react in a way which can be detected by instruments (Fig. 6.12).

The first methods of measurement are high impedance/resistance measurements with very low conductive minerals, e.g. quartz, and low impedance measurements using bridges of high conducting crystals like iron pyrites crystal. The second method of measurement is the natural uninduced activity of electrical forces within the crystal, which is carried out by the conversion of existing EEG and EMG equipment. This method, however, is more expensive and can be more prone to artefacts caused by handling and electrostatic fields, etc.

With the first method, when a finger taps or hits the stone with a mechanical force, nothing registers on this equipment. However, if a hand is brought into the field of the crystal and the power of concentration is used, a register on the dial is clearly seen.

This is particularly true of quartz crystals. What makes quartz crystals so special?

To examine this question we must first look at the atomic level: a unit cell of quartz is made up of the elements silicon and oxygen. Now, if we look at the environment of life forms (plants, animals and human beings) the element these life forms all have in common is the element carbon. Indeed, all life on this planet which science recognises as organic is based on this property of carbon – its ability to receive or give up unit charges. The valency number of carbon is four, and the only other element in the periodic table that can match carbon for valency is silicon. With one of these sister elements so to speak (carbon) we have great activity and diversity and complexity of form. In the other, however (silicon) we have represented stability (silicon being inactive to the naked eye) and also simplicity of form when silicon is incorporated in the crystalline structure of quartz. When we look at a giant crystal lattice arrangement we are seeing matter in one of its most stable and balanced states.

Just imagine a knife edge balance also in a state of stability and equilibrium. What happens if this balance comes into contact with outside forces? Obviously the balance is disturbed and a measurement can be taken. This is exactly what has been happening with our crystal experiments: we measure the tiny imbalances which occur when the stability of the crystal's natural frequency is disturbed.

In our experiments with crystals what upsets the internal lattice balance are energies of many types. These are either electromagnetic (e.g. quartz watches), or psycho-physical (e.g. detectable by impedance and natural electrical emissions from the crystal lattice). We have deliberately left out mechanical stimulation, piezo-electric effects, and thermic effects on crystals. This is because there are many technical books and papers written in much greater detail than we have time and space for here, or capability to do so.

Electromagnetic imbalance can be induced in crystals by the electrocrystal therapy method (already introduced) and by the laser light method. This is where a cold helium neon laser is used to release energy from the crystal network. This is achieved by the direct contact of crystal to the skin, and by projection methods (Fig. 6.13), where coherent laser light is passed through the crystals producing interference patterns. It is these patterns that are played onto the patient's body.

Laser stands for 'light amplification by stimulated emission of radiation'. The laser has also been described as a quantum device, since its action can be explained by means of theories of quantum mechanics. The laser generates a special pencil-thin coherent form of light. In our case it is monochromatic (red light) because of the element used in its generation which is neon. Radiant light energy is propagated in the form of electromagnetic waves. Light of a particular controlled frequency is described as monochromatic light. It is light of this nature with every particle of its particular light (call them phota if you must) beating in resonance, which makes a laser apparatus function.

Since all of these 'phota' are in step with one another, they tend not to spread out like an ordinary beam of light. It would be much better for the non-physics-minded reader to think of this as a single thin ray of light which does not spread out. Now when such a light source is shone through a crystal, the

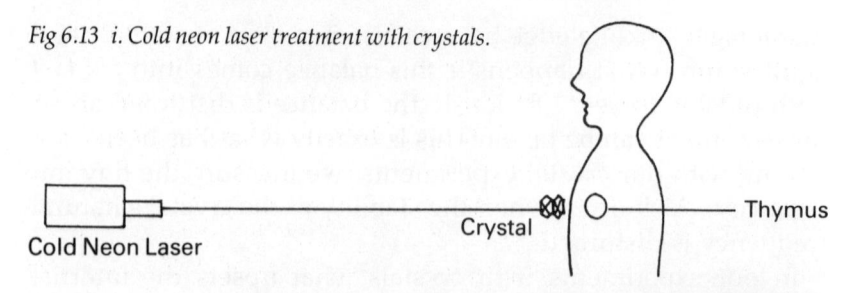

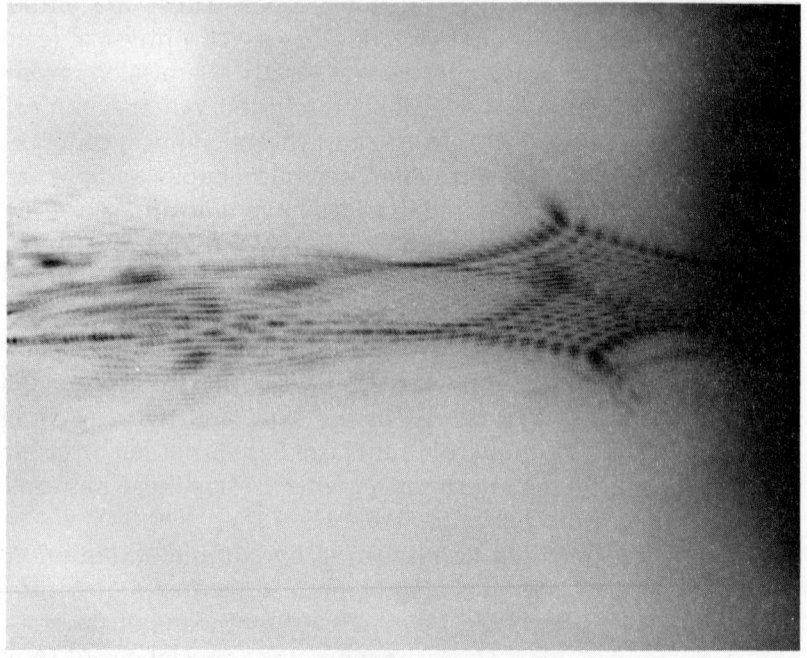

Fig 6.13 i. Cold neon laser treatment with crystals.

Fig 6.13 ii. Plate produced using neon laser treatment.

light undergoes refraction and sometimes reflection off imperfect lattices and inclusions, etc. However, unlike ordinary light, which after this process would spread out or diverge, the laser light passing through may be refracted or reflected but the light, although split into individual beams, remains coherent. Therefore, any split light forms an interesting pattern due to the individual structure of the crystal itself. Remember that the equilibrium of the crystal is also disturbed. When this pattern is played on a part of the body which responds and vibrates sympathetically with the healing aspect of the crystal, interesting therapeutic results are seen. Now as these split beams travel away from the crystal they fan out or diverge to a certain small degree without the information of the pattern being lost. This can be very helpful not only for projecting onto a screen for demonstration purposes but also for projection over the whole area of the person being treated.

This method, however, has both advantages and drawbacks over the classic electrocrystal therapy method: the laser method has to be used in darkness as other divergent light beams of higher intensity spoil the effect. Furthermore, the apparatus is expensive, although our equipment is cheaper than most commercial lasers available. By contrast the advantages are speed of operation: no leads to attach, nor physical contact with the patient.

Roughly speaking, we have found the laser method overall a more intense form of crystal healing.

Interestingly, just as Lakhovsky found when using his multi-wave oscillator in New York hospitals in the early 1940s, and cases of which we refer to in Chapter 8, certain individual patients found that nothing helped them until they experienced our treatment. In fact it seems to be the lot of the so-called 'alternative' practitioner that he or she is only sought out when all other methods have been tried and found wanting. Unfortunately some of the very methods used by the so-called orthodox medical practitioners, like major surgery, the use of cell-destroying chemotherapy, or heavy and repeated irradiation, or narcotic or addictive drugs, leave us with little to work on by the time the desperate patient comes to the door.

The next aspect of crystals and their energies we examine is the development of a system where sound is generated from crystals. This process uses highly tuned electromagnetic waves to excite individual crystals to such a high level that they begin to emit audible sound waves; each crystal seems to have a loud individual note at which it resonates. The rule seems to be that the larger the crystal, the lower the frequency and the smaller the crystal, the higher the frequency. However, one might argue, apart from an interesting noise, what sort of use can be obtained from such an exercise? I suppose we could say that pure research for its own sake needs no justification as long as it is interesting. However, we have found that this is both interesting and practical. We believe we have now a working system for a new form of crystal therapy. The sound itself seems to have a therapeutic effect on any who hear it, depending on the therapeutic attributes of the crystal being used. Even deaf people, or people with hearing difficulties, have received benefit, proving that the harmonic vibrations which have been set up are bringing about the effect in the body, and not simply the physical sound at audible frequencies.

The advantages of this method are, first, that the treatment is non-invasive and, secondly, that a variety of crystals with different properties can be used and, thirdly, that groups of people can be treated at once. We have even found that gloomy living and working environments have changed when crystal sounds have been generated into them. This last statement is, of course, a subjective statement but, when we are dealing with subtle energies such as these, I think that some subjectivity may be included. Only time and more research on people and places will give any positive answers to this new variation on crystal therapy, which is an extension to the well-known soothing effects of good music, all of which necessarily produce harmonic frequencies.

We now go on to yet another variation; the very exciting discovery that the subtle energy workings of a crystal can be observed by use of a hologram technique: early experiments have shown that when a hologram of a crystal is made (a 3D light image made with a laser) it still has an energy link with the solid material crystal. The method we used was to wire a crystal to a high impedance device and then 'influence' the hologram image. The results have shown that large impedance changes have occurred during these experiments. Such 'influences' employed were sunlight, human hands on the hologram and even thought direction! Not only does this border on mind/matter experiments, but shows a definite physical bond between a 3D light image created from the hologram method and the physical object in itself, which can be disturbed by brain-induced vibrations. It would not be inconsistent with our hypothesis that brainwave induced effects can be created in hologrammatic form.

It is probable that most physicists will be taking a somewhat sceptical view of any claims for a communicative connection between inorganic quartz crystals and organic matter, despite the similar valency of the silicon in the crystal and the carbon in the organism (not to mention the research work of Sir Jagadis

C. Bose[38]). They will be even more sceptical of any suggestion that crystals can be used for healing purposes, in the absence of any explanation within the parameters of the normal sciences.

Quite right too! So let us now attempt an explanation which stays within the accepted boundaries of conventional physics.

Let us start by asking, What is a crystal? We use here the explanation given by Ra Bonewitz.[37] A crystal is an inorganic solid (or sometimes liquid) whose atoms are held rigidly in place in a very distinct and repeatable pattern. It is important to understand that the atoms of a crystal are bonded very regularly together in two different ways:

1. Ionic bonds: here the loss of an electron by one atom yields a positive ion, and gaining an electron by one atom yields a negative ion.

2. Covalent bonds (the most common type of crystal bond). In this type of bonding the outer shells of two atoms are not completely filled with eight electrons, although the atom is in electrical balance. The two atoms, therefore, decide to 'share' their outermost electrons, obeying the electrons' preference for travelling in pairs, and always having four pairs of electrons in a shell.

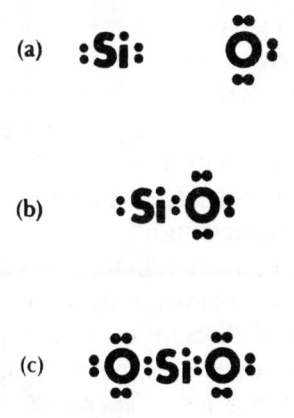

(a) :Si: Ö:

(b) :Si:Ö:

(c) :Ö:Si:Ö:

Fig 6.14 The formation of a silicon oxide molecule, the building block of a quartz crystal.

The silicon atom has attached its four electrons to two oxygen atoms, becoming very stable. The chemical formula for quartz is SiO_2.

In this way crystals set themselves up (as they cool from gas and liquid) in beautifully regular polyhedral forms. In fact they are the purest forms of solid, which is why they have such smooth and symmetrical faces. Inside them the atoms are held in place in regular arrays to form a lattice, and are very hard, because all the electrons are sitting in regular pairs. Any impurity in the crystal will have an enormous effect on all the atoms of the crystal, like a white snooker ball striking a perfect triangle of red snooker balls. The atoms are packed hexagonally or cubically depending on their nature (gold is cubic, for example) and if one fires X-rays at a crystal the atoms diffract to reveal regular patterns which reveal its internal construction. This makes possible a means of identifying precisely what type of crystal was being X-rayed, as a result of a classification system constructed by James White Dana in the nineteenth century. For an excellent description of the many kinds and shapes of crystals read Ra Bonewitz's book *Cosmic Crystals*.[37]

We wish to confine ourselves here to the ordinary quartz crystal, which is one of the simplest and most common, with various varieties like rock quartz, amethyst, and rose quartz.

When we tap a crystal gently with a hammer, it gives off some of its electrons, under the pressure of the hammer blow. This generates a form of electricity called piezo-electricity (from a Greek word meaning to strike) – and its spark is often used to relight domestic gas boilers when the pilot light goes out. Even if a single ion somehow gets entrapped in the crystal lattice it disturbs the immensely regular pattern within. We can show this by passing a current through the crystal and measuring its resistance on a meter called an ohmeter. Ohmeters can be very sensitive. Not surprisingly, if you hold a crystal in your hand the frequency of your own macromolecules, which as we have seen resonate a complex wave-form, can imprint itself into the otherwise regular oscillations of the crystal lattice. So the crystal's electrons will move in regular fashion vibrating exactly as your own macro-molecules. *The crystal is copying your own specific wave-form!*

The energy absorbed in this way by a crystal is transformed into another manifestation of that energy: if you heat a crystal you get electrical energy. If you squeeze it you get light. If you introduce a certain impurity you get a particular visible wavelength (colour). And as we have seen, even the subtle changes in the coating of a crystal can be used to detect the very small changes in frequency caused by linking an antibody to a specific pesticide like malathion.

Crystals are even used to measure changes in radio wavelengths and can receive and amplify complicated waveforms emanating from radio-transmitters hundreds of miles away.

Given these phenomena, it should come as no surprise that crystals are very sensitive indeed to the subtlest of energies.

Crystals can also work in reverse, themselves amplifying specific harmonics. And in this lies the basis of electrocrystal therapy. Given the premise that disease is caused by a cell or group of cells going 'off tune', then the action of a crystal is to receive the correct 'healthy' signal and rebroadcast it, so that the specific 'normal' wavelength can be pushed back into the healthy cell, and thus carry out a retuning function.

All very well, but have we any evidence for this? It is not enough for us to say that crystal energies are sensed by intuition alone, however true that may be. We will have to offer replicable evidence.

Ra Bonewitz records that placing crystals over the chakra points causes a distinct reaction in brainwave patterns, which can be measured by EEG equipment. That's more like it! In fact it would be predicted by our hypothesis. We haven't carried out that particular experiment ourselves; but a striking and much simpler example of how a crystal can modify harmful wave-forms is often demonstrated by Harry, using an ordinary TV set. The set is turned on, and its emanations can be clearly picked up on his electroscanner, with the needle being powerfully deflected from its proper balanced position. Then Harry places 'Big Bertha' – an enormous white quartz crystal – on top of the set. Within seconds of his doing so the electroscanner needle jumps back to normal, as the crystal absorbs the radiation. When Harry takes Big Bertha away the needle moves wildly off balance again. There is little doubt in our minds that TV sets can give off electromagnetic radiations. We do not know whether they are harmful or not, despite many experiments on the possibly bad effects of cathode ray tubes on pregnant women and others, since no clear evidence has been forthcoming. We suspect that any effects will only be apparent after many years of build-up, but it is a private concern of ours now that we have seen the clear effects that TV sets have on crystals. Perhaps every TV set should have a prophylactic crystal built into it until the matter is resolved, or we might just get another, this time electronic, thalidomide to deal with. This time, however, the effects would be enormous and millions of people would be affected. Indeed the huge electromagnetic radiations propagated by all kinds of electricity transmission lines, radio and TV broadcasts, underground trains, even domestic electric wiring systems, could well be having a deleterious effect on our delicate brains and impairing their ability to control our bodies' cells, as we have already said.

It is only now becoming clear that electrical power lines can cause serious emotive changes such as depression or even suicide. Robert Becker has quoted many such instances,[26] and the possibility exists that US and Russian transmitters have been beaming powerful low-frequency waves at each other for years, which can be picked up clearly on our domestic radio sets in Britain. The Russian programme is called 'Operation Woodpecker', and it radiates at about 10 Hz – the frequency of normal alpha rhythms in the brain. Perhaps one future use of crystals may be to counteract such influences.

Bones are themselves crystalline. The effect of using crystals on bones seems, according to Bonewitz, to be a matter of 'deprogramming from the bone tissue its unharmonious programming which has been as a result of the trauma of the injury'.

Sheldrake[259] mentions an interesting phenomenon which illustrates the power of crystals to communicate information, which incidentally underlines that it is not always 'harmless' information which is transmitted.

Having recognised that crystals are organisms in their own right, despite being inorganic in structure, and that they too have morphogenetic fields, he illustrates this by the phenomenon that the introduction of a 'seed' crystal into a saturated salt solution greatly enhances the growth of crystalline structures. Under our hypothesis the radiations emanating from the molecular resonance of the covalent bonds in the seed crystal will encourage the binding of more molecules to the crystal: the morphogenetic field of a crystal is technically infinite, whereas that of an organic structure is not.

'Chemists who have synthesised entirely new chemicals', says Sheldrake, 'often have great difficulty in getting those substances to crystallise for the first time. But as time goes on these substances tend to crystallise with greater and greater ease.' He quotes from Holden and Singer's textbook *Crystals and Crystal Growing*, an extreme example of this:

> About ten years ago a company was operating a factory which grew large single crystals of ethylene diamine tartrate from solution in water. From this plant it shipped the crystals many miles to another which cut and polished them for industrial use. A year after the factory opened, the crystals in the growing tanks began to grow badly; crystals of something else adhered to them – something which grew even more rapidly. The affliction soon spread to the other factory: the cut and polished crystals acquired the malady on their surfaces. ...
>
> The wanted material was *anhydrous* ethylene diamine tartrate, and the unwanted material turned out to be the *monohydrate* of that substance. During three years of research and development, and another year of manufacture, no seed of the monohydrate had formed. After that they seemed to be everywhere.

The tenth-century Persian physician Ali Abbas[1] who wrote in his *Perfect Book of the Art of Medicine* that magnetism will cure both gout and cerebral spasms, encountered little opposition to his views. He was part of the Establishment, and his advice was acted on successfully.

We do not expect the same acceptance level for our own theory: we conclude this difficult chapter well aware of the scepticism it must arouse. After all, what we are suggesting ultimately is that it is possible to replace chemotherapy by morphogenetic radiation to restore normality to the morphogenetic fields of all life forms by non-invasive electronic means. Chapter 7 continues the argument by providing practical evidence that this actually does happen.

7
Nutrition: Pictures of Health

To penetrate the mysteries of raw energy, biochemists and nutritionists will need to acknowledge that the healing powers implicit in raw foods are greater than the sum of their parts as measured in terms of nutrients and calories.

Leslie and Susannah Kenton
Raw Energy, 1984.

People instinctively know that raw foods like salads, fresh apples, and fruit juices are good for them. What they may not know is that they are literally radiating themselves with goodness. Lakhovsky's hypothesis (1924) leads almost inevitably to the conclusion that all ingestion of raw food is ultimately radiating the ingesting organism, provided that no time lag allows the 'radiation' to drain away meantime: each cell of the raw apple, glass of carrot juice, or lettuce leaf, is oscillating. Kirlian photographs, by measuring the intensity of the corona discharge, can tell how long it takes for these oscillations to die away. So ingesting raw food will strengthen the existing oscillations of the ingesting organism in a way which cooked foods do not. Though the interaction is not yet well understood, there is plenty of experimental evidence to confirm that raw food is better for us than cooked food.

'An apple a day keeps the doctor away.'

Let us look briefly at the wealth of experimental evidence which supports this view.

Werner Kollath was a professor at the University of Rostock a little before World War Two. When rearing animals on a diet of processed foods almost entirely devoid of vitamins and minerals, he saw that they grew fairly well until adulthood when they started showing all the symptoms of human beings in the industrialised countries, such as dental decay, constipation, toxic colons, loss of calcium, and so on.[162] No amount of vitamins was able to reverse this condition. Except fresh foods with green leaves and fresh vegetables, that is. Other researchers working in Stockholm and Munich got the same results. Unfortunately, the industrialised countries have still not fully woken up to the benefits of raw foods, and it might be cynical, but one wonders to what extent the powerful food manufacturing corporations are really interested in spreading the gospel, when it would mean a completely new attitude to processing, and preserving and distributing food today, and the dismantling of existing methods.

Widespread public awareness of the immense benefits of raw food as opposed to processed food might well cause the public to desert their supermarkets and return to the local farm for their weekly shop. It might even bring them round to thinking that it may not be such a good idea to wait a week before buying again. The sad fact is that we are in this country all now locked in to a food distribution system which is almost impossible to change, yet which is inherently bad for our nutrition!

In fact, whatever governments may claim to the contrary, the average health of the British citizen is no better today than it was at the turn of the century. Mortality statistics have only changed through the lower numbers of infant mortalities and longevity of the aged, not through the better health of the living population itself.

Cooking raw food before eating it is now known to impair its nutritive effect, but few explanations of why this should be have yet emerged: Lakhovsky's hypothesis provides an answer. The benefit may be the result of the cellular micro-currents which radiate at specific frequencies, and these radiations may be what the ingesting organism needs to sustain its electrical activity as well as any purely chemical exchanges. Roger Williams, a highly respected American nutritional biologist, claimed in 1973 that cellular malnutrition is at the root of ten times the number of diseases as clinically defined deficiencies.[304] By this he means such diseases as allergies, arthritis, athero-sclerosis, coronary thrombosis, emotional disorder, insomnia, peridontal disorders, and disorders of the immune system. 'If we are to overcome the current crisis in Western medicine', he says, 'we must find ways of tackling malnutrition at the cellular level. That means altering the focus of our effort away from treating the symptoms of illness and looking for outside causes.'

What prophetic words! As we saw in Chapter 5, one of the most significant experiments to support Lakhovsky's cellular oscillation hypothesis came from a Russian biologist, S. P. Schurin, and two colleagues from the Institute of Automation and Electrometry who placed identical tissue cultures in two hermetically sealed vessels separated by a wall of quartz, then introduced a lethal virus in one of the chambers which not only killed the colony of cells within, but also its next door neighbours, even though there was no way in which the virus could have penetrated the second chamber. Their further researches suggested that ultraviolet radiation from the afflicted cells was radiating fatal information to the second colony of cells which passed through the crystal lattice.

The same sort of theory was put forward in the 1930s by Gurwitsch, another Russian researcher, whose ideas were laughed at for forty years. (We have mentioned Gurwitsch before.)

Alexander Gurwitsch must have been fond of onions. He noticed that cells in the tips of onion roots seemed to be dividing at a definite rhythm, and wondered whether the source of this unexplained physical energy might not be coming from nearby cells. To test the idea he mounted one root tip in a thin glass tube and pointed it at the exposed part of another onion root tip. The rest of the root tip he covered with glass. After three hours, the exposed root tip had divided 25 per cent more than the protected area. The rays he called 'Mitogenic rays', and was promptly ridiculed by his peers for the further suggestion that these rays were powerful, and even shorter than ultraviolet in the electromagnetic spectrum, that is, with a wavelength of around 10 nm long or less.[114,115]

Gurwitsch's work is dealt with more fully elsewhere, but other scientists suggesting that raw food has its own special properties were also initially greeted with total disbelief and ridicule.

Max Gerson, Max Bircher-Benner and Weston Price were all ostracised by their colleagues for putting forward views too early for their time.[35, 99, 237]

Max Gerson, a German doctor, suffered cruelly from migraine headaches. At that time, and still today, migraine is thought difficult, if not impossible, to cure. At best one may have to wait until one's forties or fifties before migraines will disappear. But Gerson started experimenting with his own diet to see if he could alleviate what was not only for him, but also for his family, so debilitating a malady that he was often forced to lie in a darkened room for days. He found that eating fresh fruits, apples particularly, would make the migraines go. Other patients discovered the same relief. But more mystifying than this was the effect on one patient suffering from lupus lesions, a kind of tuberculosis of the skin. At the time there was simply no cure for lupus. Yet, on the fresh fruit diet, the lesions healed. Other hopeful lupus lesion patients were also healed. But Gerson was almost too frightened to put his hypothesis before the medical world. And moreover he had no explanation for it, without which the fresh fruit remedy was unlikely to find acceptance by the profession. But the cures continued – he even cured Albert Schweitzer's wife of severe lung tuberculosis. All the time it seemed sheer quackery that one way of eating could cure so many unrelated diseases. Eventually, in 1958, his work with cancer patients was published: *A Cancer Therapy: Results of Fifty Cases*.[99] In it Gerson suggests that the starting point of all illness is the potassium/sodium balance. If this goes awry, then the potassium in raw foods is needed to correct the deficiency and thus improves cellular respiration, which in turn mobilises the white cells in their fight against invading cancers. Even today there are many who cannot accept Gerson's ideas because they do not accept his explanation of the underlying mechanism.

Max Bircher-Benner was equally ridiculed by his fellow Swiss physicians when he followed the teachings of Pythagoras and the Essenes in trying a raw food diet to cure his own jaundice. His clinic, set up in Zurich in 1897, still functions as one of the most highly respected healing centres in the world. Though Bircher-Benner was amongst the earliest of the proponents of holistic medicine, the lack of an acceptable explanation for the way in which fresh raw food actually does its work undoubtedly limited his acceptance by colleagues in the medical profession.[35]

A final example of professional ostracism is the case of the American dentist, Weston A. Price. He travelled into lonely regions of the globe researching dental and bone development of peoples in such remote areas as the Loetschental Valley in the Swiss Alps, and in 1945 published his results in a book [237] which concluded that a primitive diet of fresh and largely uncooked foods, devoid of chemical fertilisers, promoted a high level of health. In the population of the Loetschental Valley there had never been one case of tuberculosis, and they had no need of a dentist, since no one had ever had tooth decay.

When Price returned from his travels to announce his findings he was promptly laughed down.

Gradually, however, physicians all over the world have come to realise that raw foods have clearly beneficial powers of healing which their cooked counterparts lack; but few have been able to explain why.

Take for example the story of a Danish doctor, Kristine Nolfi. She one day was horrified to discover that she had breast cancer. Sustained with a diet of raw foods she was able to fight off the disease and eventually, despite the opprobrium of her fellow doctors, gave up using drugs altogether and founded and ran the Humlegaarden clinic in Denmark based on this form of healing until she died in 1957.[208]

Dr Norman W. Walker in the same way suffered badly from neuritis. He tried raw juices and found them effective: he was still alive at the age of 107 in 1984, having written many books on how the use of fresh juices maintains health.[284]

Examples of similar proponents of fresh foods amongst doctors are almost too numerous to mention, just as theories of their mechanism are few.

Ann Wigmore was in her fifties and very ill when she discovered the benefits of fresh food. As a naturopath she travels the world lecturing about her findings in her seventies, some twenty years after the onset of her illness, the founder of the famous Hippocrates Health Institute in Boston.[303]

It was unfortunate that Arnold Ehret died accidentally in 1922. Otherwise his contribution to a dietary approach to disease might have had great impact. Ehret suffered from heart disease, kidney trouble, and Bright's disease until a diet of fresh food cured him. He then developed the Mucusless Diet to prevent what he called the 'internal pollution of the colon' at a fraction of the cost of previous treatments.[81]

It seems that not only are proteins 'denatured' by the heat of processing, but that foods chemically fertilised and then processed with chemical additives can cause damage which lingers on for as long as four generations. An American physician, Francis M. Pottenger, carried out experiments with the adrenal glands of cats. He noticed that when fed on scraps of raw meat the animals were much healthier. For ten years thereafter he conducted some of the most rigorously controlled dietary experiments, spanning several generations of animals.[234]

Pottenger's cat colony would have caused any mouse an immediate coronary! There were 900 of them. Those of his cats which were fed on cooked meat, pasteurised milk and cod liver oil developed a high incidence of allergies, skeletal deformities and sickness. As the generations passed they developed weaker, smaller litters with lower birth weights. Another group of his cats was fed on the same diet, but this time the meat was raw and the milk unpasteurised. These animals were healthier, and so were their offspring: Pottenger finally found that it takes four generations of cat to correct naturally the inherited damage induced by eating cooked foods.

The striking thing about all these naturopathic treatments, and one which probably causes most disbelief in their efficacy, is the very wide and varied types of disease or illness which they claim to cure. Without a general theory of how such approaches work the naturopath can do no more but get quietly on with his other work, and as a result the adoption of such techniques is only slow: we are still largely in a drug-oriented therapy society, where curative chemotherapy rather than a more diagnostic preventive approach is the norm. Again one is not surprised that the huge international drug companies are disparaging of electrical treatments for disease, since they would thereby lose massive markets for their pharmaceutical products. In any case many drugs are themselves culled from naturally occurring plants whose essence has been extracted. Even the action of pharmaceuticals of this type may be electronic rather than chemical in nature.

In 1950 Dr Masanore Kuratsune, head of the Medical Department of the Japanese Kyushu University, tried a most dangerous experiment. He administered to himself and his pregnant wife the same diet as that given to Japanese prisoners of war: a mere 729–826 calories daily per 11 stones of weight. This is nearly one-third of the daily recommended number of calories. The actual food would have been brown rice, vegetables, and a little dried fruit. The difference was that the two 'prisoners' ate the diet raw. Both continued in good health until they switched to the identical diet, but this time cooked. Then suddenly all the symptoms of the illness and disease found in Japanese war camps appeared: oedema, vitamin deficiencies, and collapse.

Similar effects were found by Sir Robert McCarrison in India with experiments on monkeys, which developed colitis when fed on their usual diet, but in cooked form. In Switzerland parallel work by O. Stiner on real guinea pigs produced a host of diseases when the diet was cooked.

Given this background, what is the cause of the problem?

Everyone knows that vitamins are destroyed by heat, and that proteins are similarly 'denatured', that is their molecular structure is altered. Lakhovsky argued that what has actually happened is that the oscillating circuit has been physically destroyed within the cell.

A further clue that he may be right comes from studies by Hans Eppinger, chief doctor at the First Medical Clinic of Vienna University.[84] He and his colleagues investigated why uncooked foods successfully treat resistant diseases such as heart disease, hypertension, kidney and blood diseases, alcoholism and arthritis (a more diverse set of illnesses one could scarcely find). They found that uncooked foods affect the body at a cellular level in many important ways: particularly, they raise microelectric potentials throughout the body. This in turn assists what is called the 'selective capacity' of the cell: its ability to distinguish between friend and foe in nutrition terms. The stronger the micro-electric tensions, the more intense the ability to repel noxious substances and to attract useful ones becomes. The process may be essentially electric in nature just as an electromagnet attracts and repels iron only when its current is switched on. Absence of these potentials occurs when the organism is dead. Weakness occurs through a lack of ingestion of fresh foods. Cancerous cells all have a sort of mucus which surrounds them, preventing white blood cells from entering and overcoming the cellular dysfunction. Indeed one of the greatest problems obstructing cancer treatment is how to break through this mucous barrier. Whereas the barrier has been considered chemically, the possibility exists that it acts more like an electrical field insulator, or Faraday cage.

Interestingly, raw foods with high redux potentials – that is they have a high tendency to acquire and lose electrons from other molecules – seem to have a more beneficial effect than low-redux raw foods, according to Dr John Douglass in Los Angeles.[71] He also noticed from talking to patients in the Kaiser-Permanente Medical Center there, that after several weeks on a high-raw diet the patients felt more sensitive to external stimuli, and found cigarettes and alcohol 'distasteful'.

It was the contention of Hans Neiper in his address to the Royal Society of Medicine in 1980 that pancreatic enzymes break down the mucous envelope surrounding a cell enabling the body's immune system to invade the cell.[206] The way in which it does this is not fully understood, but a morphogenetic radiation resonant approach seems to make sense, and we have already discussed the mechanisms in Chapter 5. Dr Henning Karstrom of Sweden points out[150] that even though you get all fifty known nutrients in your diet – i.e. vitamins, minerals, fatty acids and so on – health will suffer unless large quantities of uncooked and unprocessed foods are included. Even when only applied externally, raw foods have a pronounced beneficial effect, which again suggests an electrical rather than a chemical process is at work: the essential oils and aromatic compounds we put in our bathwater can relieve irritation, muscular spasm and even toothache. A whole new therapy, aromatherapy, has arisen which exploits this principle, one of its leading exponents being Shirley Price, trained by Eve Taylor who has been practising the therapy for fifteen years or more.

Bioflavonoids, known for their disease-preventing role, are also electrically unstable: the rutin bioflavonoid in small doses actually alters the electrical rhythm of brainwaves, clearly suggesting an electric effect.

Actually, all this is not really surprising when one remembers that plants are 'alive' solely due to the action of sunlight, an electromagnetic wave phenomenon, which is used by chlorophyll to photosynthesise solar radiations. There is a close relationship between chlorophyll and haemoglobin: chlorophyll actually assists in the control of anaemia. That is why we are recommended to eat spinach when anaemic. Bircher-Benner suggests that the quality of 'aliveness' derives from photosynthesis and that a special form of energy passes from the plant to the body directly derived from the sun. If so it must almost certainly be electromagnetic in nature and may also, like other electromagnetic waves, transfer energy by radiation rather than by chemical action.

We commonly talk of electric currents being 'alive'. If Lakhovsky was right, then all raw food is alive by reason of its electrical energy. Indeed more and more nutrition experts are beginning to realise that the measurement of foods by calories alone is not good enough. Professor Israel Brekhman, the famous Russian biochemist, prefers to think of foods as being full of structural information,[40] and that raw foods contain more structural information than cooked foods, since the act of cooking destroys the information. There is, he suggests, a synergistic action by some plant-based substances which act generally, not specifically. The same quality is true of electricity; and the specific resonant frequency of a complex wave-form is 'information' at its highest level.

In their book *Raw Energy*[152] the Kentons identify the possibility of an electromagnetic solution to the mystery of raw food energy, citing Szent Gyorgyi's *Introduction to Submolecular Biology* (1960). Way back in the 1920s E. J. Lund demonstrated[184] that plants emit electromagnetic waves and generate tiny electric currents which organise their growth. Robert Becker, whose work on the influence of electromagnetic fields on human beings is now world famous,[26] believes that the next great advance in bio-medicine will be the way in which electromagnetic forces influence living organisms. From the world of botany it has now been established that bud formation is heralded by changes in electromagnetic radiation long before there is any change at the cellular level. Human ovulation can also be predicted accurately by monitoring changes in the electrical potentials of the body. The evidence continues to pile up.

If the central hypothesis contained in this book is correct, then the application of electromagnetic waves to living organisms directly can promote health, and the application of waves of the wrong frequency can destroy it.

This is the principle of Lakhovsky's Multi-Wave Oscillator, of Dr Voll's Vegatest, MORA therapy, and of Harry Oldfield's Electrocrystal Therapy.

The implication of all four, taken logically, is that we are all ultimately dependent on electromagnetic radiation – and more specifically the radiation of light – for our sustenance. Here is how plants act as a stepping stone by which we get light into our bodies. This energy subsequently assists each cell to receive and generate its specific resonant frequency and in this way maintain its form and health.

We would like to quote from Tompkins and Bird[281] another of their illuminating passages:

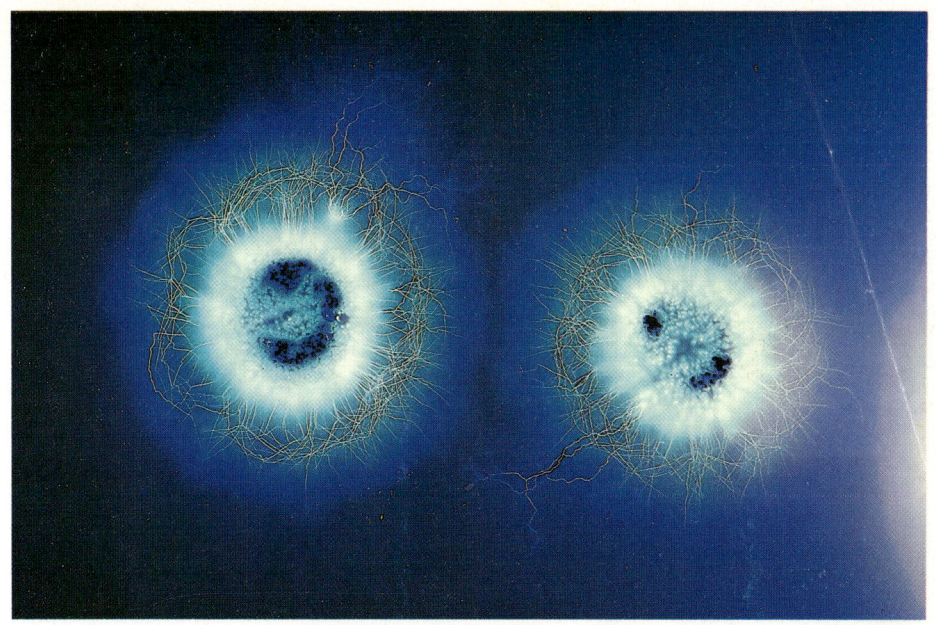

Fig 7.1   The Kirlian field of oranges.

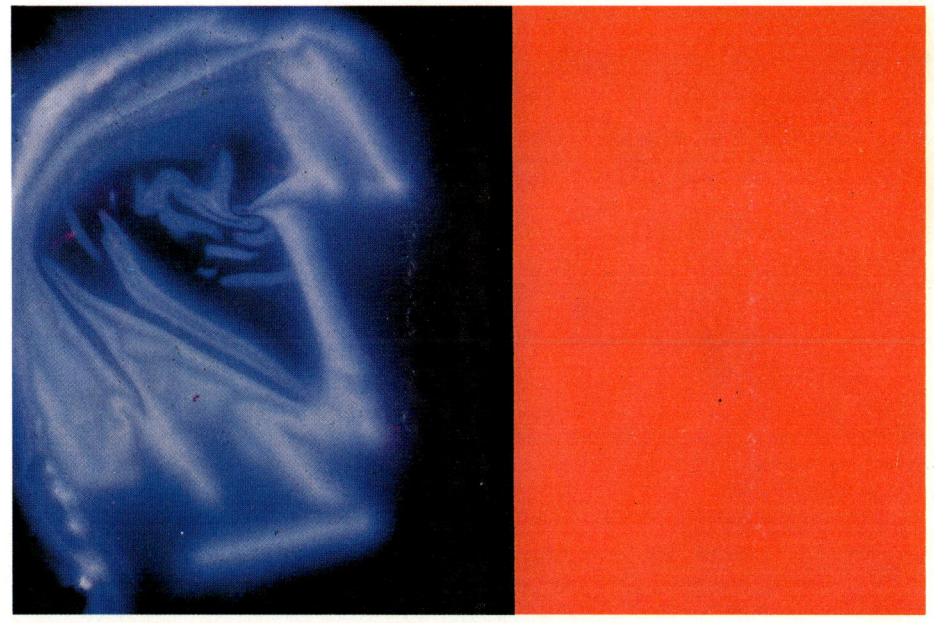

Fig 7.2   The Kirlian field of milk.

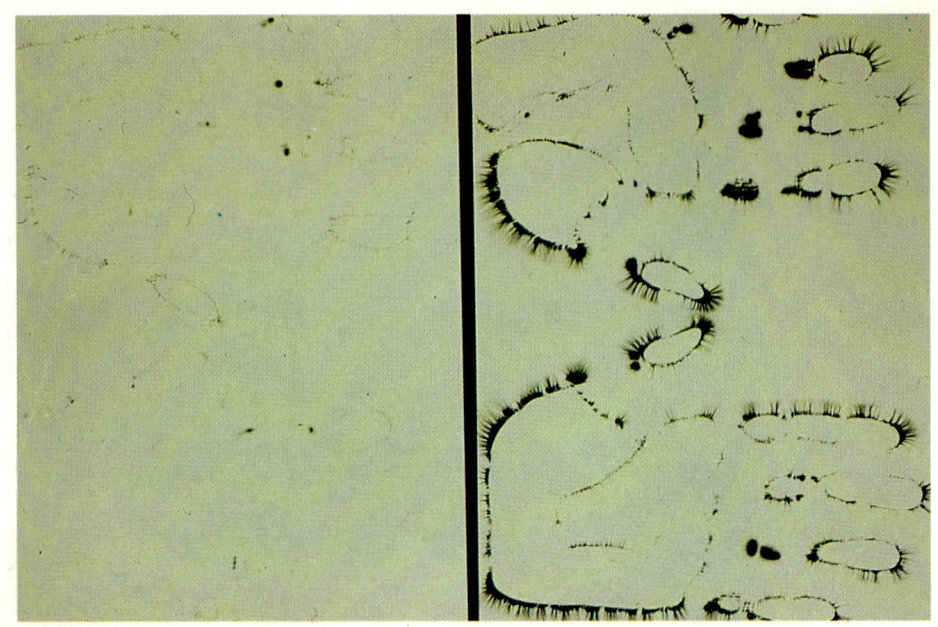

Fig 7.3 (left)   The Kirlian field of a subject on a 'junk food' diet.   Fig 7.4 (right)   The Kirlian field of a subject on a wholefood diet.

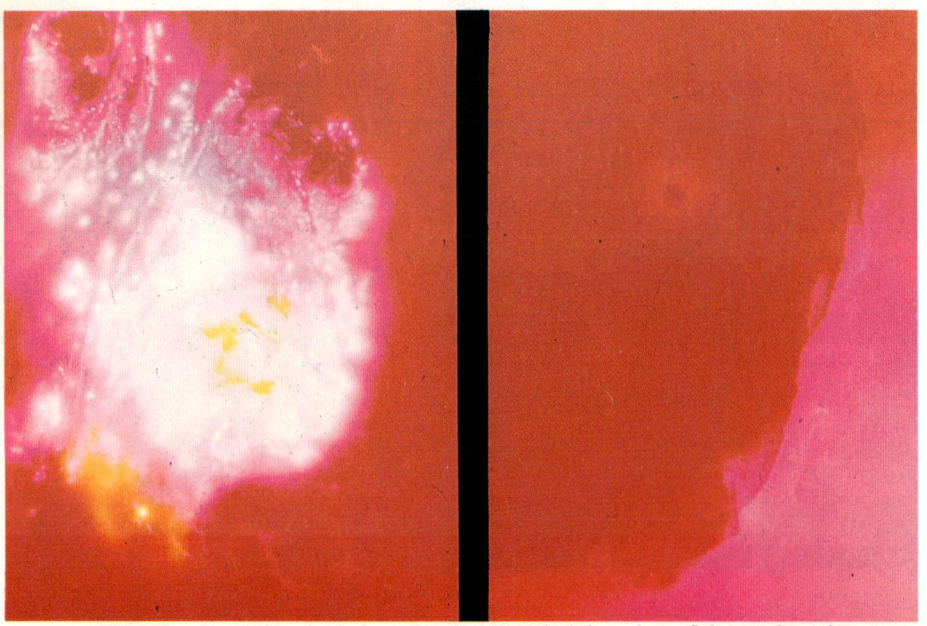

Fig. 7.5   The Kirlian field of cereals. Muesli on the left, and cornflakes on the right.

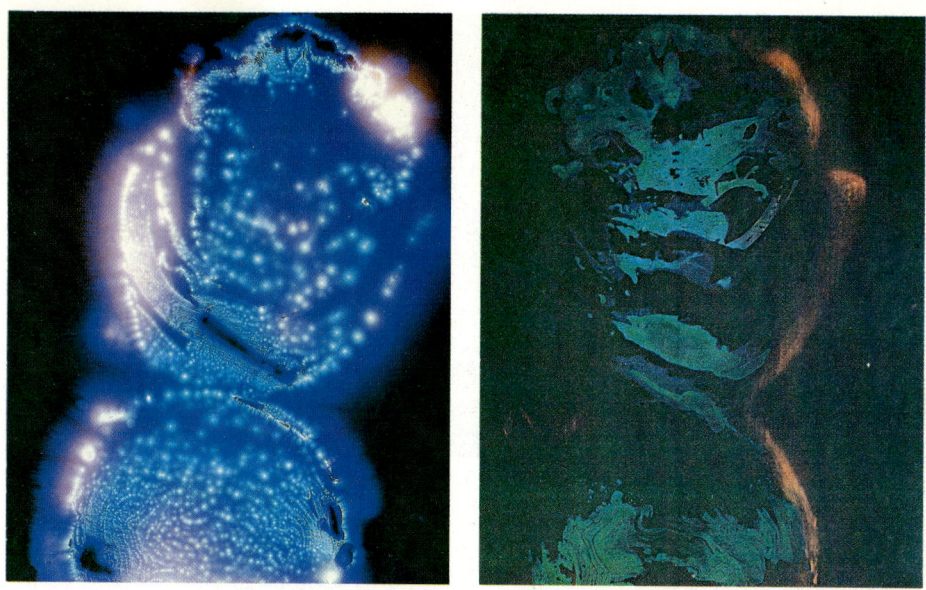

Fig. 7.6   The Kirlian field of the cabbage. Raw on the left and cooked on the right.

Fig. 7.7   The Kirlian field of oils. Olive oil on the left and refined lard on the right.

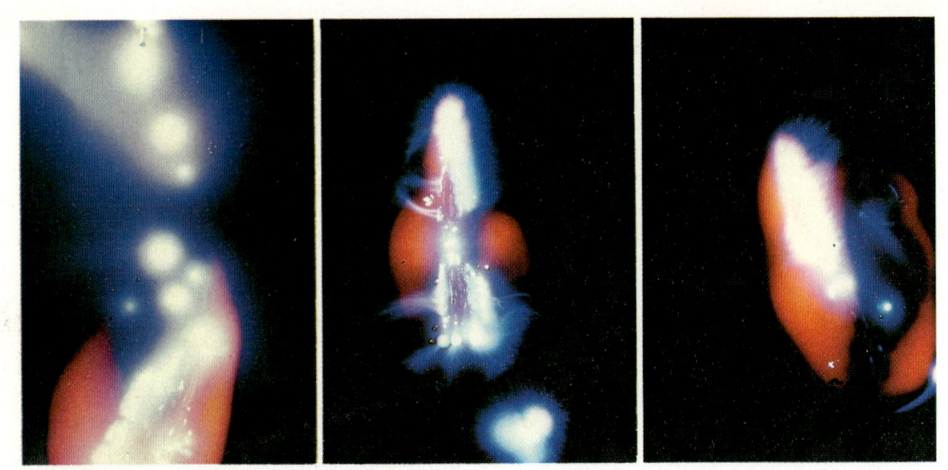

Fig. 7.8 The Kirlian field of onions. The first picture shows an onion kernel just removed from the bulb. The second, after five minutes, the energy field has significantly reduced. The third, after a further five minutes, shows how dissipated the field has become.

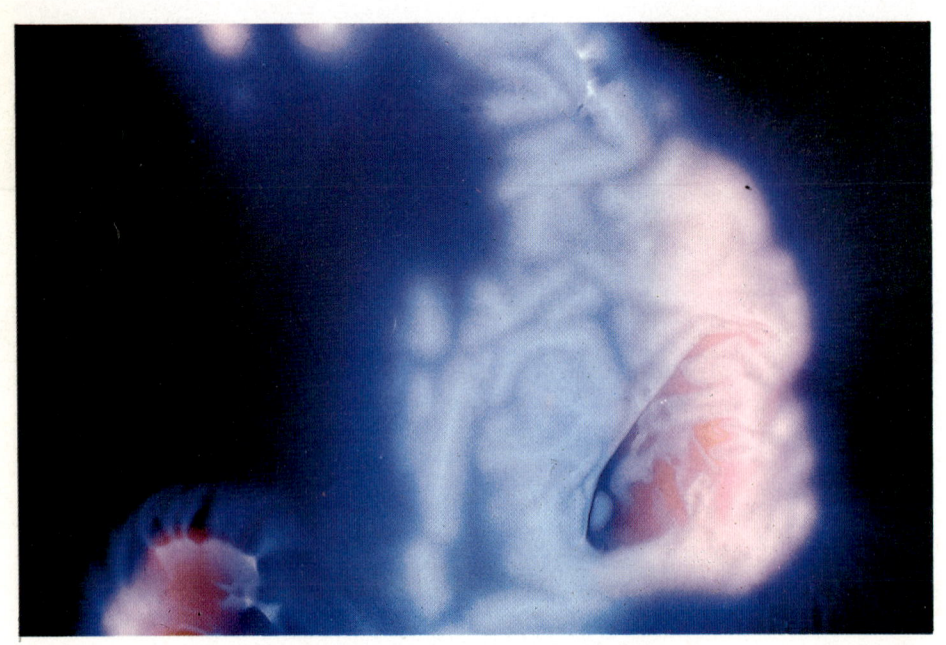

Fig 7.9 The spectacular Kirlian field of ginseng.

NUTRITION: PICTURES OF HEALTH

> In the pyramid of life, plants play an essential role. Man cannot ingest essential elements directly from the soil. They must be brought to him through the good graces of plants which likewise feed all animals, directly or indirectly. Plants can synthesise carbohydrates from the air, rainfall, and sunshine (i.e. light). ... Neither man nor animal can synthesise the necessary proteins from the elements. Animals can only assemble them from the amino acids, provided the necessary kinds and amounts of each can be collected or produced by plants with the aid of microbes. ... If the soil is not fertile, not teeming with microbes, the whole process grinds to a halt. It is a fact that plants grown on well balanced fertile soils have a natural immunity to insects and disease, just as a properly nourished body has an immunity to disease. Bugs and worms tend to gravitate towards plants which have grown on poor soil. One of the worst weakeners of plants turns out to be a chemical fertiliser, or NKP, which came into general use at the end of the Second World War.

What else could the huge factories previously devoted to making nitrites, the stuff of gunpowder, be turned to?

The main substances used to make up animal structure are proteins, carbohydrates, fats, mineral salts, vitamins, and so on. The animals themselves can in turn be eaten and their assembly can be broken down into its constituents called amino acids and then strung together again by the control of genetic codes to duplicate the ingesting organism. Thus we are actually eating processed sunlight at one or more stages removed.

Cornflakes are literally a sunshine breakfast, albeit a denatured one!

What we wish to establish here is a link, not in the biochemical sense, but one between the natural radiation still in the food we eat and the radiation which emanates from our own cells. We have already established in Chapter 5 evidence to show that all living things have a natural radiation associated with them which is either due to the electrochemical properties of living matter, or a force in parallel existence with it. This postulated force, simply a manifestation of electromagnetism, has been given many names by those who have tried to describe it: the auric field; bioplasma; chi; prana; and so on, all of which terms can, for the sake of convenience, be given a generic title of 'natural radiation'. And when we observed animals and plants at various times in their life cycle with the aid of Kirlian photography, certain changes were seen in this 'natural radiation', depending on the state of nutrition of the specimens.

In a controlled experiment in the United States using rats (yes, rats again!) exactly the same diet was administered to two groups, but in one group the food was processed. Their diet was eggs. The control group was fed on fresh eggs with mineral and vitamin supplements for an eight-week period, while the test group were fed for the same period on reconstituted powdered egg with exactly the same supplements.

The results were startling.

There was an increase in body weight and a maintenance of general condition in the group fed with fresh eggs, but the other group had lost weight and were in poor condition. The only difference between the two groups was that one group (the group that fared best) had eaten fresh food, while the other had eaten food where the natural DNA and cellular structure had been destroyed. In all other respects the two groups' diets were the same and, biochemically, the food contained exactly the same fat, protein, carbohydrates and mineral and vitamin content.

Could it be that, in addition to the ingested biochemicals, the fresh food had some sort of natural radiation essential to good nutrition which was contained within the cells but that whisking it up in a mixer destroyed it?

Mechanical mangling is not the only change which seems to affect the nutritive value of food. Chemical disturbance also reduces the nutritive effect: this disturbance can be enhanced by preservatives, artificial flavourings and colourants. Indeed, any chemical or mechanical disturbance of food such as cutting or mincing tends to affect the natural radiation present in foods. Therefore, it seems that if a salad is chopped and prepared and stood for some time before serving, a great deal of natural energy (or natural radiation) is lost. This effect can be clearly demonstrated using Kirlian photography.

It is becoming common knowledge that Vitamin C is lost at a steady rate by mechanical breakdown when fruits, vegetables and juices are cut and stored: fresh orange juice costs a lot more than pure orange juice which has been stored in containers, unfortunately!

The oranges in Fig. 7.1 give off a very spectacular corona discharge. Yet in fact, they have been stored for some time. So, if our hypothesis is correct, why do they appear so vibrant?

This question was put to Harry Oldfield at a lecture he was giving at Oxford. He had no answer, until a scientist, who had been involved in fruit importation, pointed out that oranges are picked from the tree in a green unripe state and are timed to be in the shops in a peak ripened condition. By contrast, fruit is sometimes deliberately irradiated with gamma rays (a wavelength range of around 10^{-2} nm and shorter even than X-rays, with a frequency of around 10^{-20} Hz). Avocado fruits irradiated in this way will never germinate, their natural radiation totally obliterated, possibly by a wave interference mechanism. This too can be demonstrated using Kirlian photography.

The practice of keeping food fresh by ionising irradiation is at last becoming the subject of some concern.

As we write, yet another article appears in Britain's most venerable newspaper, *The Times*, which puts the dilemma succinctly as follows:

> The choice is whether we continue to recognise which food most frequently causes illness and death and accept, annually, illness and death, or whether we apply a process which has been the subject of more toxicology and studies of wholesomeness than any other process used in the food industry.

Not a very convincing argument really.

At a recent conference a consultant to the London Food Commission said that there were strong reasons to demand a halt to the present rush to approve irradiation, and that research should be Government-funded rather than entrusted to those connected with the food industry. These reasons, including the dangers of ingesting high-energy radiation, and the fact that even if the food is microbe-free its toxic chemicals can still be present, and known adverse effects are well described by Webb and Lang in their new book *Food Irradiation, The Facts*.[298]

Has not this dilemma raised its head before somewhere? It sounds suspiciously as if the food industry's vested interests are once again being protected. Even the Government itself is not above suspicion: any political party which relies for its funds on political contributions from the large food conglomerates cannot afford to ignore their wishes.

Atqui custodiet ipsos custodes? as they say in the trade: who is going to guard the guardians?

Webb and Lang underline this possibility with the example, fortunately in America, of a company which was exposed by an Army investigation as having conducted fraudulent research on beef and pork irradiation for government and industry. Its three directors were imprisoned in 1983. But there are sinister happenings in Britain too: Britain's innocuous Health Education Council has just been disbanded after issuing a report unfavourable to certain large vested interests. And the strength of the tobacco lobby is notorious. Finally it must concern every ordinary thinking citizen that recently a BMA spokesman was castigated for confirming that AIDS is much more serious than even the official view. Surely politics has no part to play in medical diagnosis?

Using Kirlian photography we compared the natural radiation from fresh milk against that from formula milk, and found significant differences in the corona discharge. The picture in Fig. 7.2 shows the weak Kirlian field of powdered milk. (The red panel on the right is simply the control colour used.) There is also some evidence that breast-fed babies have less tendency to infection and neonatal complaints than bottle-fed babies. The medical reasons normally given for this are that the mother's antibodies are passed to the infant along with the milk. We believe, however, that more subtle energies, in the form of natural radiation, are also being passed on, and that these have nutritive qualities superior to bottled milk.

Using Kirlian techniques we modified the American processed-versus-fresh-food experiment, this time using young healthy human subjects instead of rats and shortening the test period to just one day. We selected one dozen average individuals on everyday diets. Most of them initially gave a Kirlian photograph much like that shown in Fig. 7.3. After a twenty-four-hour 'junk food' diet consisting of processed food including the usual chemicals, preservatives and colourants, Fig. 7.3 was a typical result. We then asked them to go on a twenty-four-hour wholefood diet, a balanced diet of natural foods to which no chemicals had been added. The result was a restoration of – and often an improvement to – the quality of the corona discharge.

Look now at Fig. 7.4. Here are the Kirlian handprints of a man who has been on a wholefood diet for forty years. He is in peak physical condition and states that even common colds are no problem since going on his health diet so many years ago. The photograph indicates a state of highly integrated and organised energy. One can only speculate that if our experiment with the dozen people on junk foods had been extended for as long as eight weeks the outcome would have been the same as with the poor rats in the US experiment.

We have already compared processed and breast milk, the first food of life under Kirlian analysis. We now describe an experiment with the first food of the day: breakfast!

In Fig. 7.5 we can see the comparison of a well-known breakfast cereal made of flaked corn with a wholefood cereal invented by Bircher called muesli. Both foodstuffs were photographed simultaneously on the same plate (and there was a red safelight, which accounts for the background). The food was isolated in each case with plastic transparent membrane. It is reasonable to propose that the cornflaked cereal has undergone much chemical and mechanical disturbance during its processing, whereas the muesli has not been produced by much more than simply mixing the ingredients, apart from a small amount of crushing of the larger kernels, so there has been very little mechanical and no chemical disturbance. The resulting pictures (which were repeated many times) illustrate the results in corona discharge of the two types. It would be possible to test all food in this way, and to assign them a Kirlian Factor, which would indicate the amount of natural radiation they contain.

We could go further than that. Webb and Lang assert that the official reason for not improving the legislation on irradiated foods is that there is no method for measuring whether food has been irradiated or not. Kirlian technology could, we believe, easily do so: the Kirlian discharge from irradiated food is much weaker than from unradiated food. This stands to reason if the nature of component cells have been fractured by ionising radiation. We would very much like to challenge anyone to supply us with irradiated and unradiated specimens to see if our equipment can distinguish them in a simple blind trial.

We next look at a typical vegetable prepared by many cooks each day, the humble cabbage. In Fig. 7.6 we show two different pictures of the corona discharge from the same cabbage. In one we have the fresh uncooked state: it is very active with lights twinkling like the stars at night. In the second picture we show the same vegetable after ten minutes of pressure cooking.

Whilst cooking certainly comes under the heading of mechanical disturbance, all methods of cooking can be grouped under this banner, since they all raise the temperature of the foods. Only the amplitude and depth of penetration of heat varies from one food cooking process to another. Bearing this in mind we were interested to identify which cooking process left the maximum natural radiation in the food after the cooking process was completed. The results of the survey we carried out were interesting: the least radiation from foods was after intense baking in an oven (we were careful to use the same foodstuffs in each process), and the best results came first from Chinese wok cooking, and second from (dim-sum) steaming, with microwave cooking third. We did not anticipate this, since we had thought microwave cooking would have been well down the scale. The high position of wok cooking did not surprise us, since in this process the wok is heated and oil added, vegetables and meats are shredded very thinly and the whole mixture is immediately stir-fried, while the vegetables are fresh. The resulting food is firm to the bite (*al dente!*) yet the inside is crisp because only the outside of the food has been subject to high temperature change. Within the food morsel there is an inverse square effect: a gradual decline in temperature has occurred as heat penetrated nearer to the centre. The speed of cooking was also a factor here we think: all the methods of cooking we tested showed a decline in corona discharge with time.

Here is our list of cooking processes in declining order of residual Kirlian corona discharge:

1. cooking with a wok;
2. steaming (dim-sum)
3. microwave cooking
4. pressure cooking and prolonged boiling
5. deep frying
6. oven baking

Barbeque cooking and grilling came between 5 and 6. There are many other types of cooking – we did not have time or means to test them all – but those were the main cooking methods in the West.

The polyunsaturated fats saga is now quite established in the history of twentieth-century nutrition: there has been a great focus on the investigation of saturated lipids in the context of heart and other coronary related diseases. An increased usage of polyunsaturated lipids has been the result, both in the UK and the US. One only has to watch TV commercials or read the labels in supermarkets to become aware of the impact on the consumer, who knows only too well now the difference between polyunsaturated margarine and butter.

However, this is not the issue here; we are looking only at the natural radiation difference between the two types of fat. Polyunsaturates are obtained mainly from plant sources, and saturates from animal sources.

In our series of experiments clear differences in radiation were seen (Fig. 7.7), the difference between dairy butter and cold pressed olive oil being particularly noticeable. A secondary radiation was also given off by olive oil: this was typical in Kirlian photography of that product, but we do not know why. In the next picture the olive oil is as before, but the small blue spot on an otherwise blank plate is all we could obtain as a Kirlian discharge from rendered lard or pork fat. We cannot avoid the thought that much of our lard and fat comes from Holland (have a look on your next packet) where food irradiation is less restricted than most other countries in the world.

As far as calorific energy is concerned (measured scientifically in K-joules) the saturated fats have much higher energy levels. One should clearly understand that Kirlian photography is not a measure of calorific energy potential, but that it is simply measuring a level of corona discharge, which may in turn reflect the natural (or, in the case of deliberately irradiated food, the artificial) level of radiation emanating from the food under examination.

Let us now, like Gurwitsch fifty years ago, have a look at the common or garden onion. Fig. 7.8 is a Kirlian picture of a living onion kernel, the centre of an onion bulb. We can see that the object is giving off many secondary or satellite effects, like a Roman candle! A clove of garlic also gives a similar picture. It would be interesting to see if the onion has an effect which can be measured on neighbouring onions, but we have not carried out this research yet. We have, however, observed circadian cyclical effects in the radiation levels of living plants.

Fig. 7.9 is Harry's favourite! One of the most beautiful Kirlian pictures he has ever taken. As you can see, here is a great deal of discharge coming from the specimen, and one might be forgiven for thinking it depicts a living plant. Surprisingly however, it is dead: a reconstituted piece of ginseng root. All we see is the radiation level still left over from the original living field. We had no living specimen of ginseng with which to make a picture, but would guess that it would be even more spectacular.

Finally, we would like to consider the problem of food preservation. If the food we eat has the highest natural radiation value just after death, and in the case of vegetables when still raw, then the best preserving method should aim to maintain food in a high state of natural radiation. We find that cooling to a temperature of 3° to 8°C slows down the decline curve of radiation loss dramatically. However, if the specimen is frozen, i.e. its temperature is reduced below 0° C, a sharp decline in radiation occurs at that point which flattens off in rate as temperature is further reduced.

On defrosting a radiation level of about 30 per cent is left in most foodstuffs. As shown, cooking defrosted foods will cause further declines in the radiation level, so the choice of cooking method is always important.

An interesting finding was that with freeze drying the residual radiation level after reconstitution was not 30 per cent but 75 per cent. Accelerated freeze drying methods are used in laboratories for the preservation and resurrection of micro-organism cultures. We speculate that cryogenic or accelerated freeze drying (AFD) methods may offer the best way of preserving the natural radiation in food, but have no experimental data to offer.

Our hypothesis to explain why ordinary freezing methods perform so badly *vis-à-vis* AFD and near freezing is that ordinary freezing, unlike cryogenics or AFD, produces ice crystals in the animal or plant tissue, which disrupts the microcellular structure in them – just as a domestic waterpipe bursts in freezing weather. This damages the ability of the cells to resonate its frequencies, and hence radiation levels fall in the same way as with mechanical or chemical disturbance.

Cooling food in a refrigerator, by contrast, does not actually freeze it, and does not damage cellular structure. With AFD furthermore, the water has been removed so that ice crystals do not form and disrupt the cellular structure. The worst falls in Kirlian corona discharge occurred with chemical preservation and gamma irradiation.

The list below shows preservation methods in descending order of Corona Discharge:

1. fresh-killed meat and raw food;
2. same cooled in refrigerator for four hours;
3. freeze drying;
4. freezing in ice compartment;
5. gamma irradiation;
6. chemical preservation;

We hope that this Kirlian approach to nutrition will prove stimulating. Though much research remains to be done, it should be apparent that Kirlian techniques offer an entirely new way of measuring nutritional values, and of supporting the hypothesis that all nutrition is ultimately a secondary ingestion of natural radiation.

8
The Birth of Electronic Medicine

'The work will be of great concernment, and what will give great light both to the Theory and Practice of Physick'

Sir Christopher Wren, 1656
(private letter to a friend).

We have already briefly discussed how Kirlian and electrographic techniques can expose tumorous cells, which show up as much brighter areas on a photographic plate, even in cases where X-rays reveal nothing.

These techniques point towards the possibility that cellular malignancy can be detected by monitoring electromagnetic radiation at lower than ionising levels; and further that viral infection might be acting by destroying the resonating apparatus of DNA. This hypothesis was explored in Chapter 5.

Is disease a sort of electronic warfare which takes place between the indigenous cells in an organism and invader cells from outside? Or even between the organic living cells and inorganic intrusions like chemicals? Empirical support for this view comes from calculations of the resonant frequency of a typical hydrogen bond within the DNA macro-molecule (see Chapter 5).

The results of our calculations of frequency suggest that the hydrogen bonds are resonating at ultraviolet frequencies, and ultraviolet radiations are known to modify DNA macromolecules. The mechanism could possibly work like this: there is a distance of about 3.4 Ångstroms (0.34 nm) between each pair of bases, and there are ten pairs of bases in one complete turn of the DNA's double helix. This means that the length of one 'wave' of the helix is about 3.4 nanometres, which is about one-hundredth of a typical wavelength of ultraviolet light. If a wave of that length is acting as a carrier, it is possible that the individual pairs of bases are modifying each carrier wave in a complex but unique sequence. It may even be that one strand of the helix to which the pairs are attached acts as the transmitter, and the other as a receiver. This might explain why when DNA is being formed it seems to be formed simultaneously from the −5 and the −3 end of the strand. We are not sure how any particular codon triplet modifies the wave-form. One guess would be that the distance between the hydrogen bonds varies slightly depending on the bases from which it originates. Certainly it was discovered very early by Rosalind Franklin[149] that the distances apart of the bonds varied according to whether the DNA was 'wet' or 'dry'. We would need to know a lot more about molecular chemistry to suggest a particular mechanism.

Further evidence for the impact of specific radiations on DNA comes from studying a certain 'slow' virus called scrapie, an agent which causes the disease of the same name in sheep. The symptoms commence with severe itching (from which it takes its name) followed by ataxia and paralysis. The incubation period can be up to two years, which is why it is called 'slow', and it can be transmitted by intra-cerebral innoculation. This agent, which in some ways resembles the AIDS virus, has the remarkable property that it is resistant both to boiling and to ultraviolet light. What is significant, however, from our viewpoint, is that it is very small (less than 30 nm by filtration). It appears to stimulate no immunological reaction of any type. Fortunately for us it does not infect human beings! But its action on sheep seems to be cerebral rather than by direct cellular invasion. That is why, in our opinion, it takes so long to show any symptoms: the local transceiving system of the cells is able to resist for a long time.

Actually there is a similar virus which causes an infection in human beings: it is called 'kuru', and once used to cause half the deaths in a small tribe in New Guinea, which was 'appparently due to a transmissible agent present in the brains of the dead'. It was formerly the custom of this tribe to show their respect for their deceased relatives by eating them almost raw. (Evidently not all raw food is wholesome!) The brain was regarded as a special delicacy, and was usually given to the children. The cannibalism has now largely ceased, at least officially, and the incidence of the disease appears to be declining. (We would find it significant if it turned out that a similar practice formed part of the voodoo cult in Haiti, where AIDS is a curiously prevalent problem.[48]) It is possible that the scrapie and kuru viroids are coding for only 70 or 80 amino acids. The point we make, however, is that there appears to be some connection between cerebral innoculation and a subsequent cellular malfunction.

Dr Kaposi first described the sarcoma which he discovered in the nineteenth century as 'a slowly progressive disease in which violaceous nodules appear first on the skin of the lower extremities'. This would fit well with our hypothesis that the radio control of cellular tissues emanates from the brain, and that in consequence any attenuation of its signal strength would have its first effect on the lower extremities. The same pattern, in fact, is observed with psoriasis, which is rare on the face and neck, but common on the extremities. Psoriasis also has a 'mirror image' pattern where marks on one side of the body are copied on the other: a clear sign that the effect is being centrally controlled, and not simply a local effect.

There appears to be a difference between the classical Kaposi's Sarcoma and the new form exhibited by AIDS patients, which also supports our hypothesis: in the 'new' form it is the head and face which first suffers lesions in many cases. Could this be because the retrovirus has early gained control of the 'radio station' so to speak which is the brain, and its signals are beginning to affect nearby cells in greater and greater numbers? The effect is similar to the plague of Athens already described, where the disease progressively worked its way through the body from the head. Clinicians have already observed that Kaposi's Sarcoma is incredibly sensitive to radiation, even down to a few hundred rads. The old limit for exposure to radiation of the extremities was 75 rem (a rem is the measure of biological damage done by radiation, and equivalent approximately to the rad. A new unit, the Sievert, has now replaced the rem, equivalent to 100 rem.)

Finally we note that those viruses most commonly associated with AIDS as opportunistic infections are nearly all much shorter or smaller than normal, at least as far as their capsids (their outer shells) are concerned. This is shown in Table 8.1. Pneumocystis Carinii Pneumonia, although one of the opportunistic infections most frequently associated with AIDS, is not a virus but a parasite, so does not appear in the table.

TABLE 8.1

Viral Infections Common in AIDS Patients	Size of Virus
Hepatitis B	27 to 42 nm
Polyoma Viruses	40 to 57 nm
Adenovirus	70 to 80 nm
CMV (this means 'the virus with the big case')	90 to 99 nm

Viral Infections not particularly associated with AIDS	
Pox Viruses	200 to 300 nm
Paramyxoviruses	100 to 300 nm
Arenavirus	50 to 300 nm
Rhabdovirus	80 to 180 nm
Arbovirus	20 to 130 nm
Rhinovirus	80 to 160 nm
Myxoviruses	80 to 120 nm

Why should capsid size have anything to do with the wavelength we claim is emanating from the brain? The following quotation[13] from a famous nineteenth-century Swedish physicist, Svante Arrhenius, explains why:

> Owing to the refraction of light, this will, according to Schwartschild, further necessitate that the circumference of the spherule should be greater than 0.3 times the wavelength of the incident rays. When the sphere becomes smaller, gravitation will predominate once more. But spherules whose sizes are intermediate between these two limits will be repelled. It results therefore that molecules, which have far smaller dimensions than those mentioned, will not be repelled by the radiation pressure, and that therefore Maxwell's Law does not hold for gases. *When the circumference of the spherule becomes exactly equal to the wavelength of the radiation, the radiation pressure will act at its maximum* ... .

Arrhenius goes on to say that many living cells have diameters in the range 0.00016 mm to 0.0015 mm (16 nm to 150 nm), so we can translate these into circumferences of 50 nm to 470 nm which is the broad wavelength range of ultraviolet radiation. Obviously much further research is needed before firm conclusions can be drawn, but there appears to be a direct relationship between organic cells and radiation.

The effect of ultraviolet light on DNA has not gone unnoticed by microbiologists: A. H. Rose, Professor of Microbiology at Bath, wrote in the 1976 edition of *Chemical Microbiology*[249] (an excellent introduction to the subject): 'Ultraviolet radiation resembles ionising radiation in that its action can be either lethal or mutagenic, depending on the organism, the wavelength of the radiation, and the dose administered.'

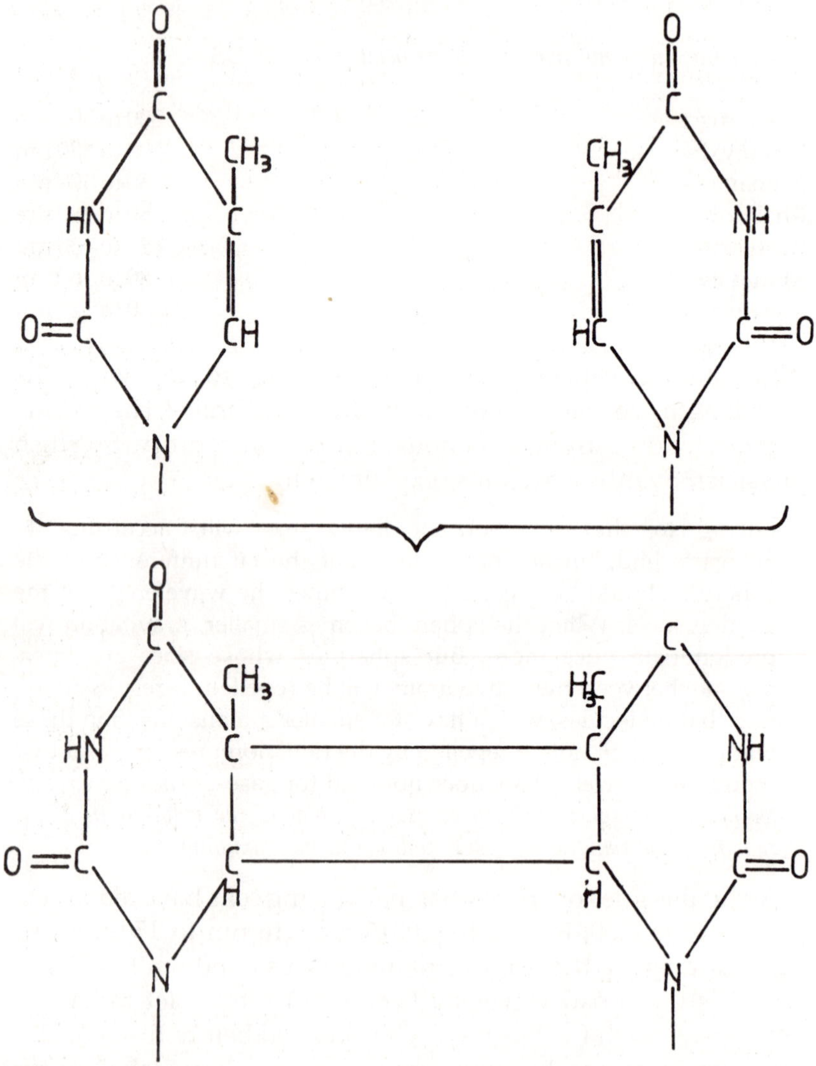

Fig 8.1 Dimerisation. In the lower picture ultraviolet irradiation has caused the carbon bonds to forge between C – 5 and C – 6 atoms to give a cyclobutane ring between the two thymine residues. (Source: A. H. Rose)

He goes on to point out that vegetative microbes are extraordinarily varied in their response to ultraviolet radiation. The dose of ultraviolet radiation needed to inactivate a harmless bacillus common in our intestine (*E. coli*), for instance, is 7,000 times less than the amount needed to inactivate the highly resistant *M. radiodurans* bacterium.

The lethal effect of ultraviolet radiation is greatest at a wavelength of just below 280 nm, which is the wavelength of maximum absorption by pyrine and pyrimidine bases in DNA and RNA. Ultraviolet radiation causes a number of different effects on DNA when examined *in vitro* (in the test tube), effects such as chain breakage, intra-strand cross linking, and formation of DNA protein cross linkages. The inactivating effect of the radiation on microbes, explains Rose, is attributable to formation of covalent linkages between pairs of pyrimidine residues in DNA. This is known as pyrimidine dimerisation (Fig. 8.1).

'There is wavelength dependence in this process, longer wavelengths (around 280 nm) being more effective than 240 nm,' says Rose.

It is possible that the effects described above are examples of external radiations controlling the linking and schism of DNA macromolecules from outside the cell. The same author continues:

> The effects of ultraviolet radiation on microorganisms are not entirely irreversible. With many microbes the effects can to some extent be reversed by exposing irradiated organisms to visible radiation (*this is radiation at lower frequencies* [our italics]), a phenomenon known as photoreactivation. ...Repair of DNA after ultraviolet irradiation can also take place in the dark, a process known as dark repair. This dark repair can also take place following damage to DNA from other causes such as ionising radiation and mutagenic compounds.

Sheila Callender in her 1985 book on blood disorders[49] throws further light on the possibility that external radiation can activate intracellular DNA changes:

> Recently a virus has been identified in a type of lymphoblastic leukaemia (the human T-cell leukaemia virus, or HTLV). Such viruses may enter cells and become integrated into the genetic material leading to uncontrolled growth, or possibly they remain latent for many years and are only activated by a trigger factor *such as radiation* ... Although clusters of leukaemia cases do occur, there is little as yet to

suggest that these are associated with an infectious agent, or that they could not have occurred by chance.

There could indeed be an electromagnetic radiation effect at work with leukaemia clusters, just as we proposed was at the root of influenza 'epidemics': Lakhovsky noted that the upward radiation from some soils seemed to be responsible for cancers in the inhabitants living directly above them.

It would be natural to suppose that specific small differences in ultraviolet radiation could energise or alter the resonant hydrogen bonding between different DNA bases without actually damaging them: the genetic coding table suggests 64 'half tones' (about the same number as on a cello) each of which represents a different codon triplet. Each of these might respond to a different specific ultraviolet wavelength.

The shorter the wavelength the higher the frequency, and the higher the energy of radiation. Whereas our eyes can perceive only the visible electromagnetic frequencies, our cells within us (and the viruses in our bodies) can clearly respond to ultraviolet and higher frequencies.

The differences are shown in Table 8.2.

	Infra-Red	Visible	Ultraviolet
Typical wavelengths (nm)	1000	750 to 450	250
Frequencies (10^{14} Hz)	2.99	4.00 to 7.12	14.96
Energy (KJmol−1)	119.6	159.5 to 284.7	478.4

Without going into technicalities, it is easy to see that ultraviolet radiation is about twice as energetic as visible light.

Dr Frances Balkwill studies interferon at the Imperial Cancer Research Laboratories in London and her lucid articles for *New Scientist* magazine[19] explain the problems of research into this new 'natural' drug. Interferon is the great white hope in the search for a cure for cancer, the leukaemias, and possibly even AIDS. Yet no one really knows how interferon works. Our morphogenetic radiation hypothesis seems to be one which fits the diverse and somewhat bizarre profile of this drug, which is only slowly being manufactured by natural cloning.

Take, for example, the curious fact that interferon can cause considerable changes in the electrical activity in the brain, activity which is related, it seems, to the amount of interferon in the bloodstream. This is odd because there is a blood-brain barrier, and little or no interferon is ever found in the fluid that bathes the brain. If the interferon is broadcasting its genetic frequency rather than simply delivering it physically, then the explanation becomes clearer. Furthermore, there are many varieties of interferon, not only of alpha, beta, and gamma, but at least twelve sub-types of alpha-interferon. If these sub-types are different because they each have a slightly different complex wave-form or resonant frequency – and 20 per cent of their amino acids are different – it would again begin to make sense to researchers. As the level of interferons in the body increases, the phenomenon of 'loss of executive function' also begins to occur: patients with high interferon levels can develop brain-related disorders like states of confusion, inability to concentrate, and even suffer hallucination and coma. These symptoms are just as similar to the effects of high-frequency electromagnetic fields as they are to chemical toxicity.

Interferons are known to slow down cell growth, but can simultaneously make eyelashes grow so quickly that they need trimming twice a week! (Remember how, in Tesla's laboratory one object would start resonating as another stopped.) Furthermore, just like a musical chord, combinations of types of interferons can work better than one type alone. Finally, interferons seem to give encouraging results when used in conjunction with radio waves, possibly the most telling clue of all.

Researchers have been much too chemically oriented in their thinking about biology: as the great Tesla said, the moment scientists stop thinking in purely physical terms, science will make greater strides in one decade than in the previous century. Pharmaceutical companies are truly facing great problems in grappling with modern retroviral infections, principally because they cannot develop one solution to the myriad varieties of the virus in the individual and unique bodies of sufferers.

One theoretical approach to cancer therapy begins to recognise the radiative importance of the organic cell, suggesting that attaching monoclonal antibodies to radioactivity creates a sort of 'magic bullet' to kill specific antigens attached to cancer cells.

The same concept may well already be operating with interferon, whose specific radiative frequency (more likely to be in the ultraviolet frequency range than in ionising frequency ranges) will build up its radiative signal strength as more interferons permeate the body: a chorus is louder than one choirboy. Interferons would, therefore, act directly on the cells by 'normalising' any defective cells, rather than having a nullifying resonant effect on the invading virus: and they do not need to be physically adjacent to do so. Warts, long regarded as being a cutaneous radiation effect, are sensitive to interferons.

Indeed it cannot have escaped everyone's notice that many diseases which could have a radiation etiology – e.g. cytomegalovirus, hepatitis, herpes, shingles, keratitis, meningitis, cancer tumours, and oncogenes – are all treated to some extent by interferons. 'Interferons', suggests Dr Balkwill, 'are the first of a whole series of agents that will become available this decade, collectively called "biological response modifiers". These substances are produced naturally by our bodies as part of our defence against infectious agents, and maybe even cancer cells themselves ... and the beneficial effects we see with interferons may well be enhanced by other naturally occurring immune regulatory substances that are currently being tested in the laboratory.'

How interesting! If that concept were to be coupled with a radio-communications device, then we would have reinvented the homoeotron!

Controlled mid-frequency radiation techniques represent an almost totally unresearched area, which could well work in association with the so-called 'natural' drugs.

Bearing in mind that DNA turns perpendicularly to a magnetic field – and anyway the DNA helix is not really a helix but a collection of atoms which lie on imagined helices, its electromagnetic sympathy should already be implicit in its structure and behaviour. Linus Pauling thought that right- and left-handed chains of atoms could actually exist. In fact, however, only left-handed amino acids occur in living things; and an electric current will only create a left-handed magnetic field.[95] Could this be further support for the view that DNA is radiating a frequency, and its helix reflects the direction of the emanating field?

The microtubules, microfilaments and intermediate filaments which seem to pull chromosomes apart when cells divide (mitosis) were discovered only after the invention of immunofluorescent microscopy made it possible to study intracellular molecules; they are only between 6 and 25 nm in length, which is the same as the very short end of the ultraviolet wave-length. It is these which may be damaged by ultraviolet action, and indeed the 'cytoskeleton', as the fine net is called, is smashed rapidly by a mysterious mechanism during cell division, and then equally rapidly reassembled after the division is complete. Could we be witnessing the actual dematerialisation and subsequent regeneration of material form by means of electromagnetic radiation? Certainly no change in cell metabolism has so far been detected as the net collapses, so the mechanism may well be activated by non-physical controls, perhaps from neighbouring cells, or more distantly by the brain itself. There is something infinitely more majestic about a brain which controls its body by telecommunication than one which fires comparatively slow electrochemical signals down nerve fibres. (Nervous impulses only travel at 40 metres a second, which is painfully slow compared with the speed of light and other electromagnetic waves.)

Significantly an increasing number of chemists are examining the nature of interactions between molecules (extramolecular chemistry), and how molecules 'recognise' each other.[57] It turns out that receptor molecules have specific electronic characteristics that complement their 'guest' molecules, so that the guest can be received in comfort. The electrostatic forces which accomplish the bonding of host to guest molecule can be disturbed by external perturbation of their electron clouds: differing pairs of molecules will act as very efficient electronic relays: the herbicides Diquat and Paraquat are like this, shorting out the metallic pathways of weeds at a cellular level.

It seems we just can't keep electronics out of molecular biology!

We are getting the picture of a tumorous cell which has not only become 'deaf' to the normal radiated wave-form which controls its growth, but which can actively influence adjacent cells to change their wave-form to a similarly malignant structure by modifying the sequence of their DNA bases.

Disease is defined in many ways. Before concluding this part of the chapter, we would like to suggest to the reader a classification of disease which breaks away from the conventional one which classifies by symptoms. Instead let us classify by aetiology, as follows:

(1) Environmental
Dietary deficiency, airborne chemical contamination (coaldust, asbestos, car exhaust fumes). A subdivision of this category would be allergies, all types of inhaled pollens – and surface allergies such as fur, plant and animal products, clothing and other materials which manifest their effect by skin eruption.

(2) Structural
The breakdown of body maintenance systems – circulatory, respiratory, digestive, nervous. Any of these may have an inherited origin, and thus may already be incorporated (potentially) in the structure of an organism. Accidental somatic injury or deliberate wounding would form a special sub-set here.

(3) Psychosomatic
The development of disease as a consequence of psychological trauma: anorexia nervosa, bulimia, certain asthmatic conditions, any stress-related somatic disorders such as rashes or stomach ulcers, and psychiatric conditions which have not manifested a physical counterpart, like neurosis, psychosis, drug-related syndromes and hysteria.

(4) Hereditary
Certain diseases of the blood, mongolism, phenylketonuria, multiple sclerosis, haemophilia and other disorders caused by deficiencies in the genetic structure of chromosomes. These can also sometimes be acquired.

It is often difficult to put a particular syndrome wholly into one category: there is also an emerging class of socio-economic diseases, such as hypothermia amongst the elderly poor, suicide amongst the socially disgraced, ill health following grief or early retirement, all of which have psychological and structural components. We ourselves observed, and the finding was confirmed by other researchers, that if you ask a cancer sufferer the question whether within the last year or eighteen months he or she has undergone any physical or emotional trauma or shock, in a great majority of cases, the answer is in the affirmative. Failure of a business or a marriage, or the loss of a loved one can bring organic disease in their train, heart disease being a common residual. One could run through a catalogue of famous people who have passed away as a result of organic disease brought on by documented trauma. Who knows what turbulence in the breast of Rosalind Franklin during the 1950s caused her to slip away betimes, thus robbed of a certain Nobel Prize. Russell Davis, in his textbook *An Introduction to Psychopathology*[252] links trauma to mental illness and thus starts the chain which we link in turn to physical disease, saying:

> Retrospective investigations of patients suffering from schizophrenia, who come under observation in their late teens or twenties, suggest that the origins of their disorders lie in their relationships, as children, to their parents. Moreover the origins lie not so much in the gross disturbances in parent–child relationships which result from break up of the home ... as in the intimate factors in the relationships, which if they can be assessed at all by retrospective inquiries, can be assessed only unreliably.

Elsewhere he points out a correlation between the seriousness of the mental condition and early age, the earlier being the more traumatic: 'The approach is similar to one that has proved fruitful in the study of disorders of foetal development due to noxious physical agents. It has been shown that the organs most affected, e.g. irradiation by X-rays, are those developing and differentiating at the time at which the noxious agent acts.'

We conclude from this view that mental trauma has a physical effect on the young, by acting on the cells which are in the process of maturation at the time the trauma took place. Other relatively common causes of physical post-natal defects are accidental injury to the brain and infections causing brain damage,[254] including irradiation and maternal rubella. It may prove to be that many mental illnesses can be better understood when looked at from the viewpoint of our central hypothesis.

So much by way of introduction.

The contribution of Kirlian photography to disease lies principally (but not wholly) in its ability to diagnose abnormality early, often before the physical symptoms appear, and its use as a research tool in the investigation of morphogenetic fields. We have already referred to Dumitrescu's results in the early detection of tumour growth as compared with X-ray diagnosis. Following the concept that the body acts as a transmitter and receiver, there are a number of useful diagnostic results which can be obtained from Kirlian analysis.

Before going on to discuss individual diseases, there is one other phenomenon which merits description in our discussion of the way brain and cell interact. We would like to introduce to readers the interesting and replicable technique of applied kinesiology (AK). This unorthodox technique aims not only to test the general energy level of the subject, but more specifically it can test for allergies.

AK tests are of two main types:

The Finger Loop test. The method of operation is very simple, the thumb and the index finger of the strongest hand is formed into a ring and held rigid while the experimenter loops his little finger through that of the subject. In this position, he holds the wrist of the subject firmly and tries to pull his little finger (in a crooked position) through the joined gap of the subject's joined gap between the index finger and thumb. Moderate pressure should reveal the state of the subject's overall muscle tone. The test condition is now applied: this can be as varied as simply asking the subject to think of a particular trauma, or to place his other hand on various parts of his own body. Any weakness in energy levels or dysfunctioning organs will show up when the experimenter finds that a fall in muscle tone by the subject has enabled him or her to to pull a finger through the closed finger-thumb gap of the patient. If there is no change in the subject's muscle tone then the body's energy field is unimpaired. A modified version of this AK test can also be used to test a surrogate who is too weak, small, or unconscious. For example, a mother can test her baby's muscle tone or search for allergy by substituting her own body for that of the child. By a process which seems to be a radiative one the information flows from one to the other.

2. *The Deltoid muscle test.* In the Deltoid test the subject and the experimenter both stand. The experimenter then asks the subject to hold his/her strongest arm out in a horizontal position. He then places an index finger near the wrist and asks the subject to resist any pressure from the finger in a downward direction. It should be very easy for the normal subject (except perhaps those suffering with MS or MD) to resist the experimenter's moderate pressure from one finger. The subject then rests while food or other material to which the subject is sus-

pected of being allergic is introduced. After about twenty seconds of the subject's contact with the suspect item the test is repeated. If the subject's arm is then easy to move down just with very moderate finger pressure, and muscle tone has weakened, then the item is the allergy. This test can be made more objective by using bathroom scales: by setting these at arm height the scale of pressure can be read off during each test.

These tests are the crude equivalent of what electroscanning and Kirlian photography does on a more precise basis. When a 'negative' field is introduced into a patient – negative not in the electrical but in the metaphysical sense in that it may be an invading organism or a psychological trauma – there is a bio-electric change which causes a temporary loss of tenacity and tone in any group of muscles in the body convenient for testing. The subject's hand can be used as an energy transducer, being placed over a zone suspected of being malignant (again the use of malignancy is not confined to physical disorder).

It is becoming generally accepted by psychologists that resistance to disease is impaired by depression and related 'low spirits'. In a more sophisticated way the Kirlian 'camera' can measure the negativity by which both acute and chronic psychological events distort the body's bio-electric field (this is nothing to do with the so-called biorhythms), and perhaps even more subtle energy lattices within the soma. Only later in time may such distortions produce a somatic disease event.

Before discussing individual diseases we would like next to review some of the other pieces of equipment which use conceptually similar techniques.

Kenyon[153] suggests that bio-electronic regulatory control techniques (BER) clearly indicate that looking for an energetic change in the body is 'a real possibility', whereas looking for physical change in the body, no matter how small, is unlikely to produce a major change in diagnosis.

Kenyon believes that the technology available in BER needs to be developed to much higher levels of sensitivity before it can register the subtle electrical changes indicated before, and when, a tumour exists in the body. In the same work he provides a useful summary of two BER techniques, the segmental electrogram (SEG) and the Vegatest. Whereas the EMI whole body scanner and nuclear magnetic resonance (NMR) machines only investigate structure, BER techniques can diagnose the advent of a tumorous condition by changes in the energetic electrical conditions which precede disease.

The SEG equipment records skin impedance over eight body quadrants, after the introduction of a 13 Hz frequency at low (2 v) voltage. The response, in terms of change of impedance with time, is recorded for each pair of segments in the four quadrants on a moving paper graph. In this way abnormality can only be detected in the area of one quadrant.

Where abnormality is present, the relevant segment record appears either too exaggerated or too flat.

The sign of a healthy patient is an even result from all segments. Whilst it is fairly non-differential, there is evidence that the SEG can identify diseased tissue when conventional techniques like X-rays show no irregularity. The SEG does not, however, localise which organ is diseased.

The Vegatest similarly relies on changes in the resistance to the flow of electricity over acupuncture points on the ends of fingers or toes, but introduces different substances into the testing circuit. The technique was invented only in the 1950s by a German doctor, Dr Voll. The instrument includes a honeycomb of small container holes into which a potentially curative medicament is placed and connected in series with the patient via a probe at one end and a metal cylinder which he grasps at the other. A small direct current (0.87 volts) is applied. The probe is applied to the acupuncture point relevant to the illness. Thus the Vegatest is not so much a diagnostic instrument as a means of testing for the appropriate homoeopathic cure. It is especially useful for identifying allergies to which a patient might be sensitive. Its use was for a long time confined to Germany, but it is now spreading amongst homoeopathic practitioners throughout the world. Voll's technique showed that nearly always more than one remedy was needed in order to normalise the readings from a patient, and this is further discussed by Kenyon.

No investigation into the emerging field of electronic medicine could fail to mention MORA therapy. The word MORA comes from the initials of its two inventors, Doctors Morell and Rasch from Germany. The first units were introduced in 1975, and during the early eighties they were refined into the current range.[89]

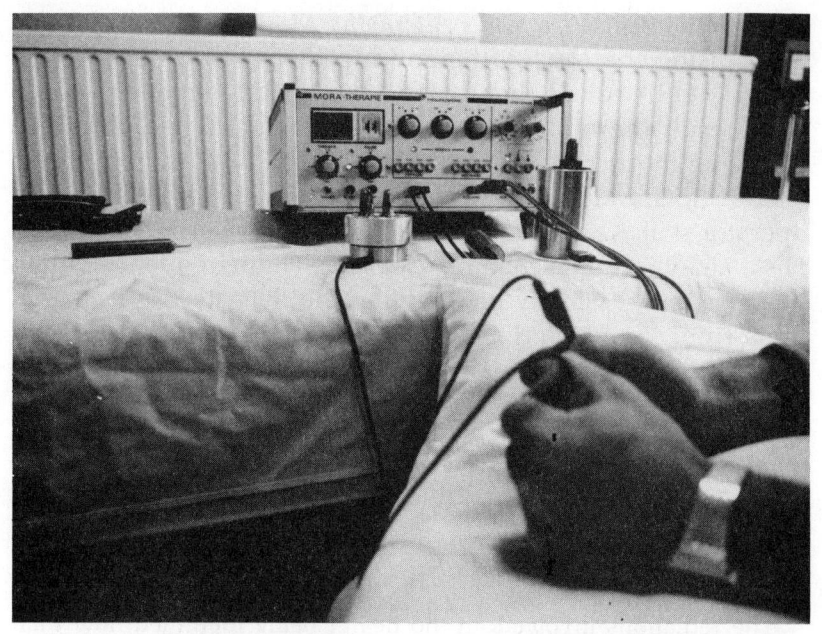

Fig 8.2 The MORA equipment in use. (Julian Kenyon)

The key to the MORA machines is the understanding that all organic functions are caused and controlled by electromagnetic field forces. The hypothesis is similar to our own (Fig. 8.2).

The MORA machine uses the patient's own electromagnetic oscillations to give the therapy. This is done by feeding the healthy and unhealthy frequencies from the imput of the MORA unit to the patient via a hand, foot or other electrode. A process of filtration and wave inversion then occurs and the output is fed back to the patient as a relatively harmonic or healthy waveform. Like the Vegatest, the MORA machine can be used for testing homoeopathic medicines. Newer variants of the same principle apply coloured light of high frequency converted to low-beat (pulsed) frequency oscillations. A similar device known as INDUMED magnetic field therapy, developed by Dr W. Ludwig of Tübingen[183] in the early 1970s, which imputs a very low field strength, again pulsed to induce harmonics, can be used in conjunction with the MORA equipment.

During a recent conference in Germany on the MORA therapy the adult daughter of a medical consultant fell down the stairs, suffering contusions and cuts, relates an article in the July 1984 issue of the *British Journal of Alternative Medicine*. Treatment was given using the MORA therapy together with a new variant called MORA colour therapy and Indumed Magnetic therapy. As a result the mouth had almost completely healed by the following morning.

Both SEG and Vegatest, points out Kenyon, rely much on operator skill. Kenyon is equally critical of Kirlian photography. His main objection is that the use of such high frequencies must destroy any possibility of receiving the delicate wave emanations from tissues and cells. (The answer to that objection is that cellular resonance is not emanating from one cell, but from the whole organism.)

Even more critical of such machinery is Lyall Watson. (It is unusual for him to throw the baby out with the diagnostic bathwater.) In his latest book, *Beyond Supernature*, when discussing Abrams, De La Warr and radionic equipment in general, he says:

> The radiations involved are no nearer being identified now than they were in 1924, and suspicion grows, even amongst practitioners, that they don't exist. The healers themselves are almost certainly more important to any success they may achieve than the increasingly elaborate devices they choose to focus on. ...
>
> I am surprised that no practitioner of radionics has yet had the courage to take the final step in the sequence begun by Abrams and Drown. They removed first the patient, and then the abdomen of a living detector. Now even the rubber imitation diaphragm has gone. All that is left is the machinery, which stands as the only remaining barrier between them and their logical admission that what they do as humans is to divine disease in others of their kind, and treat it, if they can, by psychic means.

Yet for all his scepticism Watson also concedes: 'We ride these [earth] waves like veteran surfers, dealing instinctively with their fluctuations, anticipating changes in frequency which lie beyond the limited scope of our usual sense organs. We learn to read between the lines. We resonate in natural sympathy with our planet.'

Either the lines are there or they are not. The substitution by Abrams and Drown of sophisticated electronic instruments for previously crude manual or physical methods of detection can never be construed as a retrograde step: it is a step towards scientific method and away from purely 'psychic' explanations.

In any case, we must emphasise that the early practitioners of radionics follow somewhat different principles from those which we have ourselves developed.

Though Lyall Watson comes face to face with morphogenetic fields when describing that famous experiment with red and yellow sponges, it is uncharacteristic of him not to look any further. The experiment, which demands explanation, was one of the most simple ever carried out in this area: a red encrusted sponge called *Microcliona prolifera* was sieved together with a yellow sponge called *Cliona celata*. After being thoroughly mixed they were left for a day, and by the end of that time had reassembled themselves into their original forms. What, one asks was the nature of the communication system which reunited them? We believe that the phenomenon was caused by intercommunication of a radiative kind between the sponges' microorganisms, and is an example of how the whole process began in living things.

To return to Kenyon. His basic criticism of BER systems is that they are too crude. He dismisses Kirlian photography on account of its being too powerful to detect such subtle energies as intracellular resonance. The Vegatest and SEG, though operating on low voltage, rely too much on their operators' skills. Nevertheless, Kenyon remains optimistic that techniques will be refined and that such instruments will be part of the armoury of the twenty-first-century doctor, a creature who will be a generalist supported by specialists.

Kenyon, as a qualified doctor himself with a very open mind, occupies a half-way position regarding electronics-based medicine. He believes it can assist in diagnosis, but has not made that step over the yawning chasm which accepts its use in actually treating patients. His book *Twenty-first Century Medicine*[153] is, as a result, a mixture of electronic diagnostic methods and conventional complex homoeopathic treatments. We believe that by the twenty-first century medicine will, in fact, have stepped across that chasm, assisted by a better understanding of the homoeopathic principles first unearthed by Paracelsus.

Julian Kenyon, like Leslie Kenton, makes some important points about the effect of 'good' nutrition on health. He brings out and amplifies the important concept of dysbiosis: the sometimes deadly, sometimes helpful action of intestinal flora (bacteria), the intestine being an organ in which most of the body's bacteria lie, from which they occasionally sally forth up the gut, to wreak havoc with other organs. Colonic cleansing is coming into vogue in the Health Exhibitions: none too soon, for the colonic flora offer an unrivalled natural pathway for viral infection, whether via the anus, the vagina, or the penis. It is via these open doors that most AIDS retro-viruses arrive, and it is significant in this stress-laden age that stress is well known to affect the gastro-intestinal membrane. This in turn can cause changes in the intestinal flora, so that they become incapable of fighting off invading foreign viruses or bacteria.

We pause here briefly to offer a sub-hypothesis to explain the mechanism of how stress might cause illness.

Stress starts, we think, in the brain, where it builds up synaptic loops in the long-term memory areas. This may consequently weaken the brain's ability to broadcast its cellular regulatory signals at the proper strength (decreased muscle tone is a symptom of stress). Thus the correct resonant frequencies which call on DNA to carry out mitosis are impaired, and may even go off tune, as a result of which, as the stress becomes chronic, mitosis diminishes and viral frequencies gain a foothold in the cellular broadcasting apparatus.

It is a recurring fact that cancer patients with 'willpower and determination' are those most able to overcome the illness. Similar successes are recorded with many other diseases, and even AIDS patients who fight back mentally are the last to succumb. (See refs. 42, 85, 93, 220, 261, and 300.) 'They can because they know they can', to quote an old Latin poet.

Part of the determination may be the unconscious barricades put around the stress currents in their brain, or it may be that there is a way of de-emphasising stress, so that their cellular control broadcasts are continued at unimpaired signal strength. A neat concept, but, unfortunately, one which we do not have space to develop here. (We would welcome a study of the effects of stress on young homosexuals in a partially hostile society, in relation to the spread of AIDS; AIDS patients report persistent tiredness, confusion and other disorientations of brain function long before the more serious opportunistic infections arrive.) Suffice it to say that the build-up of stress 'loops' in the brain could have an adverse effect, being an electrophysical phenomenon, and thus support our hypothesis of cellular control by radiations from the brain.

It is a hypothesis which unifies under one principle, causative factors as far apart, in the case of cancer, as cigarette smoking, radiation, excess lipids, insufficient raw foods and general exposure to radiative carcinogens.

Despite contrary expectations, the hypothesis of morphogenetic radiation is essentially a Newtonian/Cartesian hypothesis. It makes the postulate that man is still only a machine; the novel feature is the concept of man as a much more advanced machine than science has so far given him credit for. When Descartes said 'My thought compares a sick man and an ill-made clock, with my idea of a healthy man and a well-made clock', he was right; all we are suggesting in this book is that the clock is regulated, as it were, by quartz crystal, not clockwork, and affected by piezo-electric pulses or frequency changes, not rust, which can put it out of time. Not for nothing are the meditative states becoming so popular in a Western world full of noise, electromagnetic bustle and social stress. The brain and its body are controlled, we propose, by mechanisms too delicate to be unaffected by such influences. We need space to hear our clocks ticking and to read the information they give us. To borrow gratefully again from Kenyon:

> The emerging science of biophysics is consistently finding that very small energy changes in magnetic fields are of major biological importance. Recently it has been found that minute electrical potentials co-ordinate the balance of electrical activity in the brain. By comparison a nerve action potential is enormous. Slowly, therefore, evidence is being gathered which leads us to believe that monitoring subtle changes is going to be a useful exercise.

A glance at the various kinds of brain 'waves', the first of which, alpha rhythms, was discovered by Hans Berger in 1928,[30] will tend to support the idea that they are controlling the body by non-neural methods. There seems to be a basic pulse at about ten cycles per second, which as it dies away introduces harmonics of a very complex nature. The pattern changes if the subject closes his eyes: the amplitude increases noticeably. And if the subject is irritated a crescendo of waves is emitted: could these be giving instructions to the adenosine triphosphate (ATP) to get some energy into the relevant muscles by a route far faster than the parasympathetic nervous system?

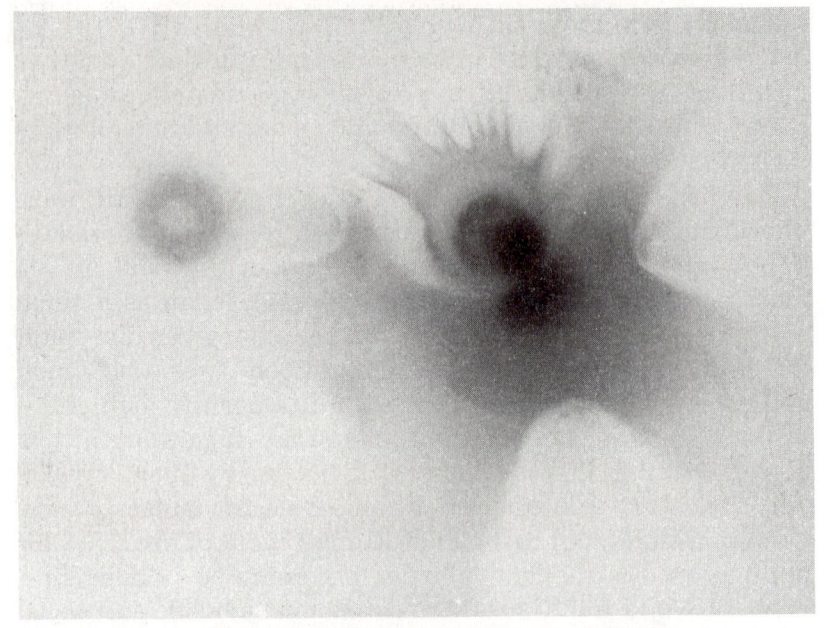

Fig 8.3 Person with active cancer in their body.

A variant of Kirlian photography throws light on this possibility. There is in medical circles an application of the technique called the Skin Hydration Test, introduced by Mr Leonard Konikiewicz,[164] the director of the Medical Photography Department of the hospital at Harrisburg, Pennsylvania. In this application the normal cyclic pattern of the skin around a fingertip can be speeded up and changed in a normal subject. However, if the person tested has active cancer anywhere in the body, this test will show a different result (Fig. 8.3). In the normal control we have a wipe-out of the electrical energy, but in the cancer subject there is a chaotic pattern of very active energy. The same effect is observed in a series of tests where we prepared test tubes, some with normal cells and some with cancer cells. In nearly every case, as the pictures (Fig. 8.4) show, a steady glow from normal cells but a chaotic eruption, both inside and outside of the test tube, with cancer cells. Other pictures (Fig. 8.5) confirm the result: comparing a preparation of adrenal cancer tissue with normal adrenal tissue shows that the cancer tissue was very energetic indeed, sending flares over a centimetre away from its container. The possibility exists that the chaotic energy radiating from cancer cells is a malfunction

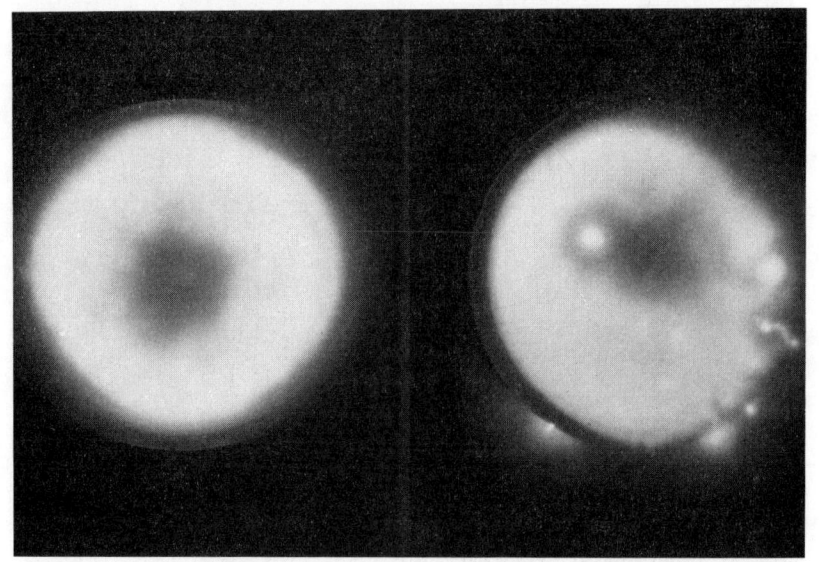

Fig 8.4 Normal cell.   *Fig 8.5 Cancer cells.*

of frequency: W. Grey Walter[288] recalls a conversation with F. L. Golla, Professor at the Maudsley in 1929, in which Golla surmised that there would be variations of brain rhythms in disease. This was soon verified, giving rise to the ability to locate tumours in the brain. It would be interesting to know whether such tumours are accompanied by any slowdown in cell growth in the rest of the body.

In a book such as this we can do little more than point towards avenues of research which might refute or support our hypothesis. Should it prove well-founded then much of the credit must go to the Kirlian equipment which helped evolve the idea.

We would like to conclude this chapter by discussing five specific diseases and relating them to our hypothesis. These are cancer, arthritis, psoriasis, multiple sclerosis, and AIDS.

Cancer

There are distinct differences in the photograph of a cancer sufferer's fingers from those of an arthritic (Fig. 8.6). In the latter is displayed a severe attenuation of energy flow: the energy, measured by the strength of the corona discharge, seems to withdraw into the joints, or to build up in rheumatic patches. A cancer patient's fingers by contrast display a chaotic,

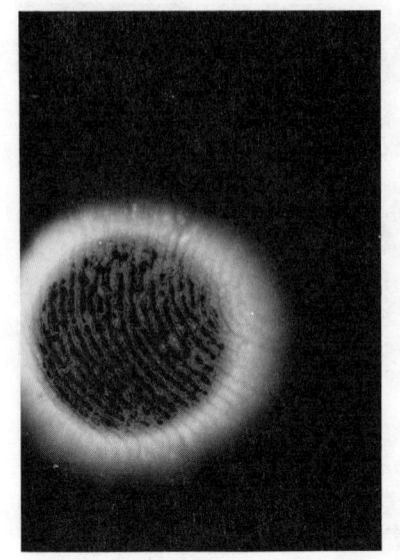

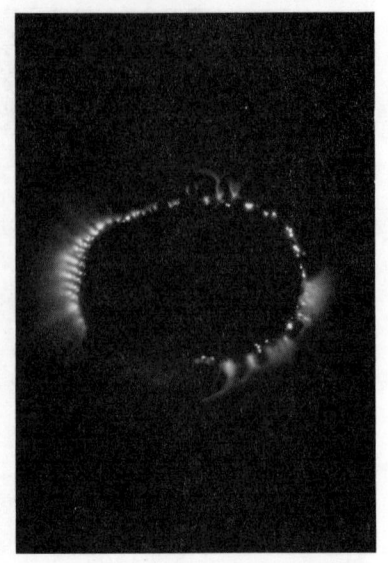

Fig 8.6 Comparison of a cancer sufferers fingers (left) with those of an arthritis sufferer (right).

volcanic eruption of energy, with highly distorted signals as measured on the electroscanner as well as in the Kirlian photograph. Interestingly, both the scanner and the Kirlian 'camera' suggest some functional failure in the thymus in both cases. Before proceeding to discuss each type in detail we would like to stress that both instruments should be used only in conjunction with other means of confirmation, and not by themselves alone, even when the practitioner has become skilled, to avoid mis-diagnoses.

The odd thing about cancer, despite all the research and the success which has been achieved in treating it, is that experts still do not know what is its cause. (See Table 8.3.)

TABLE 8.3
Proposed Causes of Cancer Identified to Date
1. Cigarette smoking
2. Free oxidising radicals
3. Fats and cooked meats
4. Psychological trauma
5. Ionising radiation
6. Sunbathing
7. Skin irritants

Treatments of Cancer having Some Claim to Success
1. Surgery
2. Raw vegetables
3. Will-power
4. Complex Homoeopathy
5. Chemotherapy
6. Radiation treatment
7. Freedom from stress

The postulate that Kirlian photography can detect the presence of tumorous cells in advance of their physical manifestation is a useful beginning to both aetiology and diagnosis. The Kirlian effect was confirmed by Dumitrescu's electronographic methods, and we feel that both are compatible with our radiated morphogenetic radiation hypothesis.

In a sensitive chapter on cancer treatment in his book *Twenty-first Century Medicine*, Dr Julian Kenyon suggests that the US National Cancer Institute's objective of halving the number of cases by the end of this century 'seems to be based on little more than faith in the brilliance and innovation of cancer researchers. The hopes for attacking micrometastases (small secondary tumours) demand a great deal of optimism'.[153]

Looking briefly once again at the seven potential curative treatments listed above, we can see how they each have some beneficial effects, but that none makes full use of the concept we have expressed: surgery would work, according to our proposals, by physically cutting out the malignantly radiating cells. Recurrence would, however, be likely, not just in adjacent areas, but in quite different loci, and this is what in practice is found. Surgery should in our view not be attempted if it involves massive excision, since it will have no major beneficial effect on the prime source of the radiation, which is, in our view, the brain.

Raw vegetable treatments will certainly introduce energy to the remaining normal cells and enable them to improve their combative signal strength. Since they are only peripheral signals, however, unless the brain's signals can also be modified, this treatment by itself will only result in minor improvements, and relapse is likely if the diet stops.

Will-power is a more direct attempt to control malignancy by isolating previously extant stress loops and reimposing at a subconscious level the correcting controls on the aberrant cells.

Of all treatments this is likely to be the most potent of those reviewed. Will-power improvement techniques such as deep hypnotherapy should be explored for their contribution to this treatment.

Complex homoeopathy is a positive step in the right direction in that it consists effectively of transmitting corrective resonant frequencies to the malignant cells. But it is still only a half-way house: the transmitted wave-forms are derived from natural substances, and may not be as accurate a reflection of the malignancy as might be achieved from a purely electronically designed wave.

Chemotherapy is also making a radiative contribution to the disease, but its action is far too violent, and likely to do more harm than good. It will probably destroy the normal tissues alongside the abnormal, and introduce damaging side effects.

Radiation treatment in the ionising range is also a purely destructive method, and does not attempt to normalise the malignant tissues, simply to eradicate them. Like surgery it should not be used where the result is to lose large volumes of tissues, particularly specialised types of cell where the restitution of function may not be possible.

Finally, freedom from stress is obviously going to improve the brain's chances of reimposing corrective control over its cells. It must however be accompanied by some psycho-mechanism which eliminates any existing stress loops, by 'taking the patient's mind off things', for example, and by restoring energy levels to the normal cells so that they too can help re-establish the correct morphogenetic signals.

As might also be expected the causes of cancer are also compatible with our hypothesis. The action of cigarette smoke is directly on the brain's signalling capability. Free oxidising radicals are likely to have a more peripheral effect on the cells' hydrogen bonds and may therefore act by damaging the reception mechanisms of DNA. The low level of natural radiation present in fats and cooked meats will certainly have no beneficial effect on cellular signal strength, and may even damage it. Psychological traumata by contrast are a direct interference with and weakening of the brain's signal strength. Sunbathing is an external radiation effect and its action would normally be confined to epidermal tissues. Once established, however, our hypothesis would predict that the abnormal pellicular cells would start affecting subcutaneous tissues and become progressively malignant. Certain skin irritants might have the same effect, and we would not rule out the possibility that some kinds of ingested items would also act internally in the same way. That is why it is so important to control the irradiation of foods and the level of inhaled irritants like coaldust and asbestos, in case these damage the normal morphology of the ingesting organism.

What we are briefly suggesting here is an entirely new approach to the treatment of cancer. We leave it to medical practitioners to explore the concepts we have propounded, using their experience with individual cases. In our view, as we have said, the best treatment method is to copy the organism's normal wave-form precisely and re-broadcast it to affected areas electromagnetically.

We have mentioned Lakhovsky's theory of cellular radiation already, and also his Multiwave Oscillator. What we have not described are the documented applications of these. During the twenties and thirties, doctors in Paris, New York and other hospitals made extensive use of his equipment to treat both cancer and arthritis. Here are some of the documented case histories in brief:

Cancer Treatments

Case One (report made to the Congress of Radiologists held in Florence in May 1928)
C.T., aged 25. Diagnosis: relapsing sarcoma of the hand. Two years ago the patient was operated on for a sarcoma of the hand. After six months she had a relapse for which she underwent another operation. For a few months she remained well, but in November 1927 she had a relapse. A Lakhovsky's oscillating circuit in the form of a bracelet was applied which she wore without ever taking it off. Fifteen days after it had been put on, the patient declared that the pain had almost disappeared. After about a month the tumour had become less hard, and after two months it had disappeared.

This case, reported by Dr Attilj, director of the Radiological Service at the San Spirito Hospital in Sassia, Rome, is one of four similar cases with which he started an experimental programme to test Lakhovsky's theory.

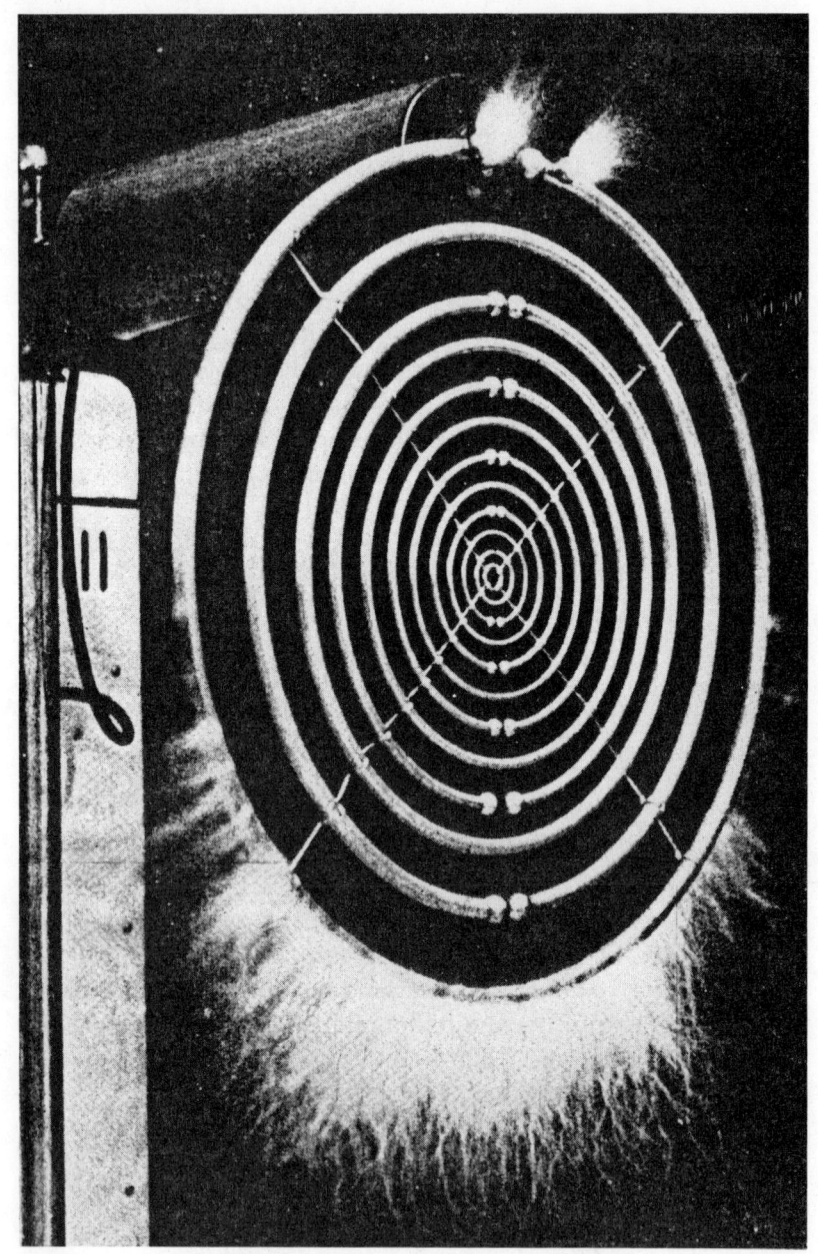

Fig 8.7 Lakhovsky's multiwave oscillator.

THE BIRTH OF ELECTRONIC MEDICINE

Fig 8.8 Tesla's high-frequency machine, the forerunner of the multiwave oscillator pioneered by Lakhovsky.

Case Two: (reported by Dr Cincin of Sevran, Seine et Oise, 6 March 1929)
One of my patients was operated on in 1925 for a sarcoma of the ovary. In January 1928 the patient complained of oedema, abdominal pains and general fatigue. Since May 1928 she has been wearing a Lakhovsky's oscillating circuit constantly. At the present time she feels very well. The surgeon who operated on her does not know what to make of it. Since the application of Lakhovsky's oscillating circuits (collar and belt) the patient is better than she has ever been.

These reports were some of many where Lakhovsky's theory was put into practice using a portable circuit. In 1931 he brought out the multiwave oscillator (Fig. 8.7) and some of the results obtained with it in cancer cases are reported below. (It is remarkably similar to Tesla's equipment in appearance (Fig. 8.8).)

Case Three: Madame C., aged 68.
Diagnosis: rodent ulcer situated in inner angle of the left eye, diameter about half an inch. Duration three years. The diagnosis was confirmed by biopsy (microscopic examination).

This patient was treated twenty-three years previously with X-rays for a facial lesion. An improvement resulted, but sub-

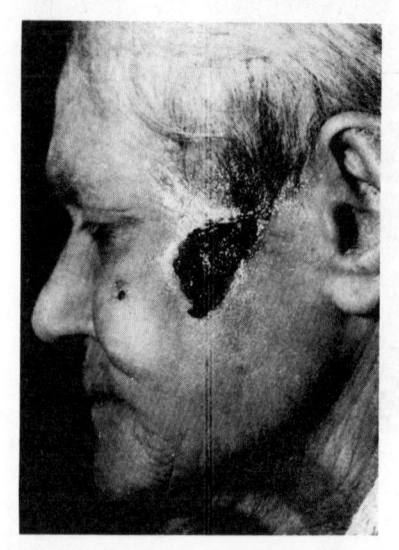

Fig 8.9 The cancerous ulcer before treatment.

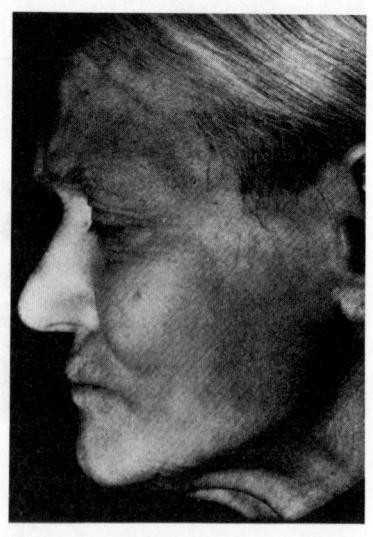

Fig 8.10 After treatment the cancerous ulcer has disappeared.

sequently a suspicious crust developed in the site. Treatment with Lakhovsky's multiwave oscillator began on 8 September 1931 at the Hospital St Louis, Paris. After the third session, lasting fifteen minutes each, there was an improvement in the general state of the patient and a diminution in the size of the lesion. On 19 November 1931 the cancerous ulcer had completely disappeared (Figs. 8.9 and 8.10).

Case Four: Madame S, aged 82.
Diagnosis: Epithelioma of upper part of left cheek (2½ x 1¼ inches). As the general condition of the skin was gradually becoming worse she was sent to the Calvaire Clinic. Treatment with the MWO began on 26 April 1932, and lasted fifteen minutes. After only two applications an improvement was observed. With further treatment the improvement was maintained and on 12 May 1932 a final treatment of twenty minutes duration was given. The enlarged submaxillary glands and oedema noticed at the time of the examination before treatment began were no longer present.

Arthritis

The mechanisms and symptoms of arthritis are quite different from those of cancer. Arthritis means acute or chronic inflammation of the joints, and there are several distinct types, all classified by their symptoms, of which one example is gout, where uric acid is lodged in the feet and ankles, and rheumatoid arthritis where fluids encompass the affected joints.

Kirlian photographs reveal abnormally low corona discharges with arthritic subjects. Why? Is it because the affected parts are immersed in what amounts to electrolyte, and so their ability to transmit or receive radiated morphogenetic signals has been damaged or impaired? And if so, what can be done to dry out the fluid and restore normal communications? Leslie Kenton reports that a raw food diet is most effective against arthritis. But bones and keratinous tissues (like hair or fingernails) generally must have a family of frequencies different from soft tissues if our hypothesis holds, and penetration by the ultraviolet range is likely to be less invasive in the case of hard tissue. What are the correct frequencies? Stiner found that adding pasteurised milk to the diet of guinea pigs induced arthritis, and Lars Erik Essen of Sweden, an expert in arthritis, prescribed three-day fasts, followed by a cleansing diet high in raw vegetables. Carl Otto Aly also prescribed a 'high-raw' diet, this time also low in protein. Finally another substance which is said to have a beneficial effect on the ailment is superoxide dismutase, which discourages the formation of free radicals. The substance occurs naturally in organic cells, appearing to protect DNA against the wrong radiation, possibly by preventing the hydrogen bond from being weakened by oxygen molecules. Raw foods are very rich in this superoxide dismutase, so its ingestion may be one of the ways to protect the radiative health of cells.

Nevertheless, the central problem with arthritis, as with tumorous cells, is to make the joint's cells hear; this time through a sea of fluid. Interestingly, the electrical pulse techniques which have been so useful in knitting bones together faster than normal, or joining bones which cannot normally be healed, is of special use in cases of arthritis. The small electric current is possibly helping to increase the signal strength from adjacent reference cells, so that it can penetrate better the hard tissues and electrolyte which has accumulated at the joint. There is the further possibility that B-lymphocytes, which are generated from bone marrow, are also less actively manufactured when the signal strength falls.

Szent-Yeorgyi, one of the most eminent biologists of our time, suggested in 1960[272] the use of small electromagnetic currents to assist in mending bones or to regenerate nervous tissue, and Robert Becker's pioneering work with electromagnetic therapy applied to bones confirms its efficiency. These successes point towards a radiative aetiology for arthritis, or rather the lack of ability to receive radiations of the correct frequency. The cells are not themselves diseased or, as it were, hard of hearing; they are wearing balaclava helmets, so to speak, and only by shouting louder (introducing electrical carrier waves) can we make them hear.

When Lakhovsky arrived in New York in 1941 his multiple wave oscillator was used experimentally in a large New York hospital by the head of the physiotherapy department who authorised him to publish the results. Only those relating to arthritis have been extracted, though other cases where major improvement or complete cure are claimed include exophthalmic goitre, enlarged prostate (Presidents please note), gastroduodenal ulcer, encephalitis, alcoholic paraplegia and chronic inflammations. In cardiac asthma, however, results were negative.

TABLE 8.4

Patient	Illness	Number of Treatments	Summarised Results
X	Arthritis (both knees)	14	Good improvement.
F.T.	periarthritis of the shoulder	6	Condition good.
M.M.	Osteo-arthritis	7	Marked improvement after two treatments, stiffness diminished.
M.K.	General chronic arthritis	11	Slight improvement.
M.O.	Arthritis of ankle	3	Results good.
C.V.	Arthritis (both knees)	11	Marked improvement.
S.I.	General arthritis	10	Marked improvement.
B.M.	Arthritis and circulatory disturbances	6	Improving.
M.L.	Arthritis of ankle and knee	7	Improvement, no recurrence.
M.B.	Arthritis of shoulder	7	Marked improvement.

And so on ... The translator, Mark Clement, notes:[55]

> Remarkable results in cases of enlarged prostate which confirm those already reported by continental physicians, hold out new hope of treating this distressing condition, for which orthodox medicine has no treatment except surgical operation with all its attendant dangers and complications.

Today the Food and Drug Administration of the United States officially bans the multiwave oscillator. Why? It seems sad to us that modern medicine is floundering about in its attempts to cure cancer and arthritis when electronic methods are available right now.

Multiple Sclerosis

There have been many medical advances in the course of this century: the great scourges of tuberculosis, poliomyelitis, syphilis, and smallpox have largely been eradicated by the discovery and refinement of vaccines and antibiotics; in the field of surgery organ transplants, microsurgery, and the application of NMR and laser techniques have been paralleled by equal but less popularised developments in instrumentation and anaesthetics, leading to incredible improvements in operative techniques. One group of afflictions, however, remains a total mystery, despite decades of patient assimilation of data research effort and theoretical consideration. This group embraces such ailments as arthritis and cancer, but adds multiple sclerosis, previously called disseminated sclerosis because it seemed to pervade, mysteriously, all parts of the body, and psoriasis with its attendant internal forms, called psoriatic arthritis.

Of all of these, multiple sclerosis (often abbreviated to MS) is the most distressing in many ways, in that it rarely attacks until the subject is fully grown. Personal attachments of family and friends are therefore already strong before the first symptoms appear. More than that, it seems to select those people who are hardworking, intelligent, sociable and productive members of their society. These it strikes in their prime years, often in their twenties and thirties, quietly, and so insidiously, and with such trivial symptoms which then disappear, giving rise to hopes of complete remission. But slowly over the succeeding years its symptoms progress through years of worsening relapses. Its mechanism has so far proved unfathomable, and even the testing of possible treatments is most difficult to evaluate because of the peculiar remissions which tear at the heart of human relationships, lifting then dashing hopes.

In one of the best books for laymen on multiple sclerosis[190] Bryan Matthews analyses in detail the many strange facts which must be taken into account in any comprehensive theory of causation of the disease. At the risk of oversimplification we list these below, recognising that the very early symptoms are so slight and fleeting that they may not even now have been noticed by patient or physician.

1. MS is exceedingly rare in childhood: its frequency slowly begins to increase around the age of 17, and reaches a peak in the early thirties.

2. There is a striking pattern of geographical distribution: in tropical countries it is rare, whereas in Northwest Europe, the Northern States of the United States and in Canada, and in their corresponding latitudes in the Southern Hemisphere, prevalence is high: in Great Britain prevalence is 50 per 100,000 with at least 20,000 registered cases.
3. There is lower incidence in the black population, suggesting a hereditary factor. Yet MS does not behave like other hereditary diseases.
4. There is evidence of 'clusters', where incidence is high in some small locality, its sufferers being unrelated by blood or marriage.
5. It is relatively more common in the higher socio-economic groups.

Anatomically there is no doubt that MS is a progressive demyelisation of the lipid sheathing round the central nervous system, and some features of the disease can be related directly to this structural disability. But overall the specific symptoms of MS (as opposed to the demographic symptoms listed above) are quite bizarre:

1. The onset is marked by a fleeting moment or two of double vision, or a feeling of 'pins and needles', or an inflammation of the optic nerves.
2. There is a remarkable pattern of remissions when the patient returns, for a while at least, to normal.
3. A common mode of onset is a sensation of numbness in the feet, ascending in the course of a few days to the waist. (This will now come as no surprise to our readers.)
4. Giddiness is an accompanying symptom. This could arise from hardened plaques forming in the cerebellum, since the cerebellum is traditionally associated with balance, and the plaques or hardened neural plates are how the sclerosis gets its name.
5. Apart from these symptoms patients generally do not feel unwell at all, except that even in older sufferers the first symptoms are a progressive weakness in one or both legs, with accompanying incontinence and (in men) loss of sexual drive. These latter symptoms have an astonishing degree of variability: sometimes there is a persistent localised pain, often in the arm or in the trunk. More commonly a trigeminal neuralgia is set off by touching the face and occurring many times in a day, with an accompanying tic douloureux, a sharp but brief pain and associated muscular spasm. Loss of the myelin sheath could here be leading to nerve impulses spreading to other axons and causing massive discharge. In our view it is important to distinguish between the electrical and the electronic effects.

6. A pronounced effect of temperature is common: a very hot bath can cause unpleasant sensations, and blurring of vision. Yet only in the terminal stages, say twenty years after onset, is there any impairment of mental function, since before this the patient retains normal memory and reasoning power. As the disease progresses the hands become more shaky and ataxic, with a symptom known as 'intention tremor' because the hands start shaking whenever a voluntary action is contemplated. At the end a euphoria sets in as memory and concentration fail. Opportunistic diseases gain a foothold often bringing mortality in their train. Sometimes other diseases, similar to MS, can confuse the diagnosis: sarcoidosis, polyarthritis, and Behcets disease are examples, mostly producing their effects by insufficient oxygen carried by the blood; syphilis of the nervous system has similar effects. Certain hereditary diseases can also be confused with MS, as can spinal cord damage resulting from a deficiency of vitamin B12.

Though diagnosis is therefore sometimes difficult, one surer way of distinguishing MS is by recording onto an EEG the brain's response to a single stimulus. An MS patient's response cannot be distinguished, being 'swamped by background noise arising from the contraction of muscles, spontaneous electrical activity in the central nervous system, and other unwanted interference'.[190] This phenomenon can be detected even after a remission and in the absence of relevant symptoms.

Turning to causative factors, the section in Matthews' book on this problem does nothing if not underline the conclusion that nothing seems to explain the cause to date. Diet, poison, viral infection, and heredity have all been examined as the potential cause without real success, except that there does seem to be an inborn defect in the immune reaction which permits the persistence in the nervous system of a virus which in turn may stimulate autoimmunity to the patient's own myelin. In this regard there are similarities to AIDS.

Matthews concludes his book with a useful section on treatments, and quite properly identifies the vulnerability of the patient's family to fraudulent or genuinely misguided treatments. Furthermore he mentions other attempted treatments like arsenic, tubercle bacillus injection, and the so-called Russian vaccine, all of which have been tried and discarded in the past. Current ideas under investigation include steroids like ACTH, immunosuppression, transfer factors, anti-viral treatments, gluten-free diets, the witholding of saturated fats, rest/exercise programmes, dorsal column stimulation, and even alternative medicines like herbs, rays, manipulation, and acupuncture. These are as much a measure of the wide scope of research as a mere catalogue of possibilities, and show just how perplexed is medical science about the disease. Matthews' attitude, born of bewilderment, is, thank goodness, an open one. Any new technique should not be dismissed out of hand, he says, concluding: 'The essential clue that will permit the trail of causation to be followed back to the point at which effective treatment can be applied is to be found in a systematic research, although a shaft of genius illuminating the scene from a quite unexpected source is also possible.'

Our experience with electrocrystal therapy in the treatment of multiple sclerosis has been limited to only a dozen patients. We are therefore even more mindful of Matthews' cautionary admonition that even if a cure were found this would not become apparent for years, since natural and temporary remission might be raising undue optimism, only to be followed by a relapse with even more serious consequences for the members of those families whose hopes are thereby dashed. It is with this prefatory caveat that we offer the tentative subhypothesis based on a morphogenetic radiation approach.

The first and most obvious sign that we are dealing with a brain/body control aberration comes from the onsetting symptom of numbness from the patient's feet, progressing upwards to the waist, a symptom which has manifested in others of the diseases we have considered. This, together with periodic remission, smacks very much of an attenuating radio broadcasting signal, becoming fainter at one time, and strengthening at another, dependent on the 'radio weather' or density of the signal-noise ratio. Knowing that there is progressive demyelinisation in course, which will clearly cause leakage and loss of power to the brain's radio transmissions so that the organic cells of the patient have to rely on their local power supplies from the mitochondria to supply the normalising radiative morphogenetic field signals. Some support for this view comes from taking a closer look at the retinal and optic nerve inflammation (optic and retro-bulbar neuritis) which is a feature of MS. One eye will typically give a delayed EEG occipital response whilst in the other there will be no response at all. Since the electrical charge is, so to speak, 'shorting out' via the demyelinised areas, any attempt either artificially or by the body itself to replenish the lost energy will simply have deleterious effects such as trigeminal neuralgia and similar pains associated with the leak. Eating raw fruits and vegetables will certainly supply more radiative energy to the body's cells to help them take over the brain's radiative function, and this may manifest as partial remission, but the cells are fighting a losing battle, and the result of such a diet by itself may not be curative. If the radiating component of the brain turned out to be the corpus callosum, for example, then the transmitting capability of the brain might have become impaired on one side; hence the occipital response delay.

The cells' transmission levels are likely to vary with local mitochondrial energy levels, and this will show up in Kirlian pictures. The common syndrome of the MS patient who attempts to run a race but after a few minutes becomes exhausted and weak, particularly in the lower legs, may be as a result of a quite different mechanism: it is possible that ATP has been wrongly programmed to strip myelin from the spinal cord sheath instead of from other lipids, or that the myelin itself is being wrongly encoded and has become like ordinary lipids.

Whatever mechanism is at work, some means of remyelinisation must be found before remission can become permanent. The observed temporary remissions could be as a result of higher signal-to-noise ratios operating for a while. Matthews has already given examples of the low signal-to-noise ratio observed in EEG studies of patients' responses to visual stimuli.

If our suggestions, albeit tentative, are correct then how can the patient even begin to remyelinate his central nervous system?

One solution might be to obtain a sample of the patient's myelin and from it derive its wave-form, which can then be amplified and rebroadcast to help regeneration of the myelin morphs. Alternatively one might attempt to uncover the cerebrovirus responsible for the incorrect broadcast signal and introduce a signal which would neutralise it. Remyelinisation would then at least be free to grow, though this might be a slow process without a strong orthomolecular signal. At this stage, since we can only guess at the mechanism involved, we can do little more than point the way to the development of treatment techniques. It is not known whether remyelinisation occurs naturally in the CNS. It does occur in the peripheral nervous system, with consequent recovery from paralysis, so there must be some hope that myelin morphs can be created once the complex point mutation has been corrected.

We are not yet in any position to make positive claims for our hypothesis in the case of MS. We have, however, seen good and apparently permanent remissions following electrocrystal therapy. The MS clusters reported from time to time (just like the clusters of leukaemia reported earlier by Sheila Callender), the temperature-related effects on MS incidence, and the fact of 'intention tremor' can all be explained by a radiated morphogenetic field in operation: the clusters might be evidence of extra-organism transmissions, or a radiative effect from the soil, a suggestion made by Lakhovsky himself. The temperature effects could be more related to the 'shorting out' of the energy levels in the central nervous system, just as a battery might lose charge after a sudden cold snap. And intention tremor studies might show whether they develop even in the absence of neural action potentials to the relevant hand. Similar tremors in other diseases like Parkinson's or Huntingdon's Chorea seem to be related to a deficiency of L-dopa, which is normally generated in the mid-brain area, another hint that the brain's transmission system has gone awry. Unless a clear correlation between intention and tremor can be proved then some other mechanism must be at work, and this mechanism could well be a radiating morphogenetic field which has been impaired by the absence of some part of its generating component.

Psoriasis

We have already touched on the disease of psoriasis in Chapter 5. The connection between that disease and arthritis is clear in cases of psoriatic arthritis, where psoriasis, normally a skin disease, attacks the internal joints.

As with the other diseases we have discussed, there is a stress-related component in nearly all cases, and as usual it is the extremities which are most affected. Temporary remission is easily achieved by means of ultraviolet light in the 300 wavelength range, but this treatment will only hold off the symptoms for about eight weeks. Jane Waters of the Alternative

Centre assures us that complete remission has occurred, but there is no clear reason why it happens.

The Alternative Centre, which confines itself to the study of eczema and psoriasis, is beginning a small research programme designed to analyse the records of the thousands of cases they have treated, in order to see if a single factor can be isolated. It is sad to record that the Centre is the only one of its kind in Britain, and is funded entirely by private patients. Indeed there was originally much opposition to its creation on the grounds that its directors had no licence to practise medicine. Fortunately for their thousands of grateful clients these objections, which emanated from the major pharmaceutical companies, were overcome, and the centre has gone from strength to strength.

We would predict that a major cause of psoriasis is a mis-broadcasting of the brain's instructions to epidermal cells, and in this case do not think that adjacent intracutaneous cells would normally have the capability or signal strength to penetrate these tissues, which are designed to protect the organism from radiative influences in the first place. Otherwise the ultraviolet treatment would be a permanent cure. But some restoring agent is restructuring the lesions, and according to our hypothesis this can only be the brain.

AIDS

Lakhovsky did not come across the acquired immune deficiency syndrome, which was first recorded in the United States only in 1981. By mid 1985 there were just over 11,000 cases in the world that met the strict clinical criteria of AIDS, of which 9,000 were in America. By the beginning of 1986 the world total for the disease had doubled and new cases were being reported at the rate of 2,500 per month. In *AIDS, the Deadly Epidemic*, Hancock and Carim pull no punches when they point out[119] that ultimately it appears that every AIDS patient will die, if not from an opportunistic disease like pneumocystis carinii, then from the direct invasion by the retrovirus responsible into the cerebral cortex, causing dementia. This was observed only in 1985, and national governments have not yet had the courage to mention it fully in their various campaigns. What is surprising to us is that the experts should believe that the virus only arrives in the brain so late in the day. According to our hypothesis it arrives there first.

THE BIRTH OF ELECTRONIC MEDICINE

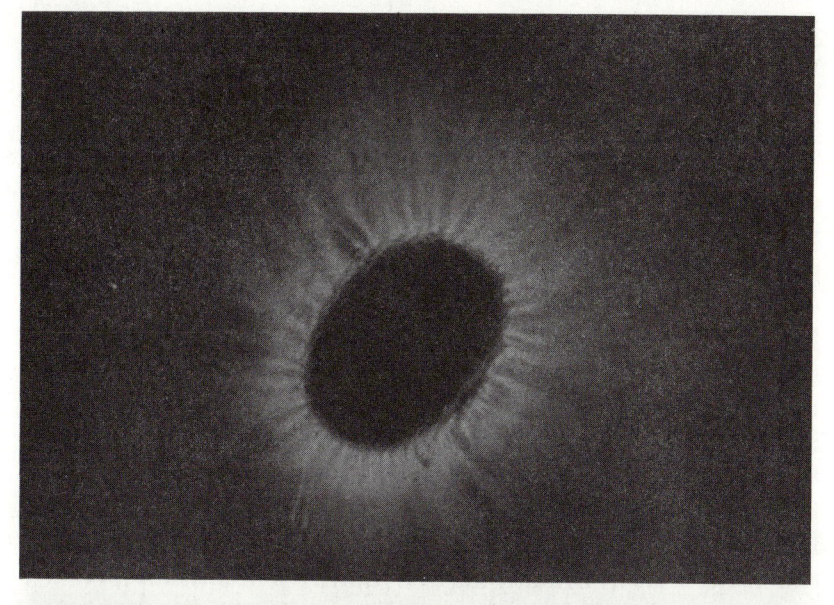

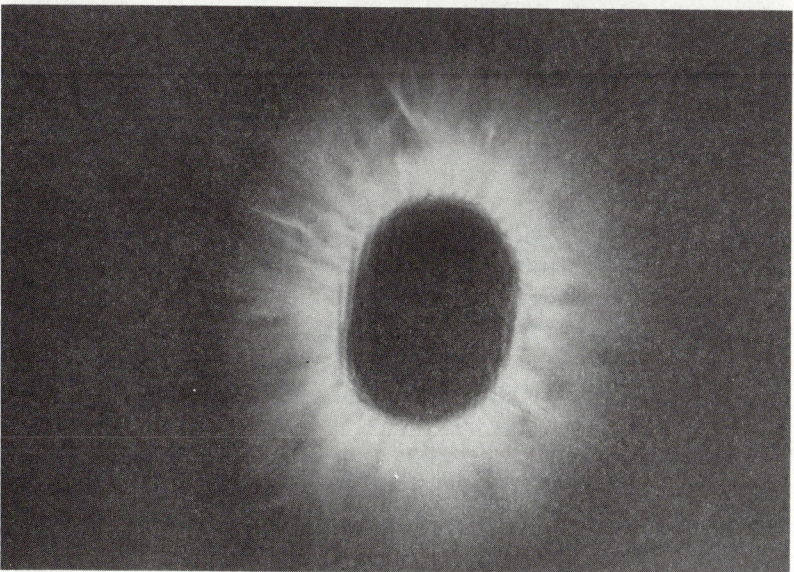

Fig 8.11 The Kirlian print of an AIDS sufferer before and after treatment with electrocrystal therapy.

Unless an effective means of combating AIDS is found, and quickly, some millions of people already carrying the AIDS virus will eventually die. According to our hypothesis every person who is soma-positive will eventually find that the radiative build-up of the aberrant signal emanating from his brain will damage his body cells and eat out his cerebral cortex with dementia as the result. We are facing the modern equivalent of the plague of Athens, in slow motion.

Yet St Mary's Hospital Medical School at Paddington in London was able to confirm that no research into the effects of Lakhovsky-type multiwave oscillating equipment, nor even any general studies utilising specific frequency ultraviolet radiation on malignant cellular tissues had been attempted. No one had heard of him there. The one thing which was confirmed was that no treatment had yet been discovered which proved effective. The real problem is that the AIDS virus attacks the cerebral cortex immediately, and thus any antiviral agent has to break through into the brain via the blood-brain barrier. Yet such treatments as these (Suramin, Ribavirin, HPA-23 – which Rock Hudson tried to no avail, and even Burroughs Wellcome's AZT, called Retrovir in Britain) may be 'quite useless when it comes to preventing or halting the spread of AIDS-related encephalitis'.[119]

Without wishing to prejudge the issue, but in order to initiate this section with an open mind, we quote one case from Lakhovsky's casebook relating to encephalitis:

> A case of encephalitis, contracted at the age of 3, left the patient, now aged over 50 with a hemiplegia (a stroke) which greatly impeded his movements. After about three months' treatment with the multiwave oscillator a great deal of mobility in the inferior limb and a little less in the upper limb was restored. It is really astonishing that a curative effect could be obtained in such a case in which pathological changes had been established for several decades.

Our hypothesis would predict that despite Hippocrates' pessimistic statement that hemiplegia is incurable,[130] if the transmission from the damaged side of the brain can be normalised electronically then partial or full recovery is possible.

But where does AIDS come from, if it is a radiated dysfunction? We believe that an AIDS retrovirus of the lentiform type could be easily developed in an environment where semen – a cellular organism structured specially for mitosis, and generating very strong frequencies – is anaerobically placed among intestinal bacilli or flora which are programmed to destroy all invading resonances except those near to normal human frequencies. The anaerobic condition is vital to prevent the oxygen molecules impairing the recombination of DNA. As Hancock and Carim put it: 'Semen is anathema to leucocytes.'

Accordingly residual cellular resonances near but not exactly the same as normal may be left unaffected, and retroviral cells could develop.

'One view (of viruses) which has been widely held is that they have arisen by a process of retrograde evolution from bacteria' say Stewart and Beswick in their classic textbook on virology.[267]

In which case it may be fruitless to look for a geographic source of AIDS. It may be that Stanley Miller's experiments with the ultraviolet irradiation of simple organic chemicals can be made to throw light on the issue.

To summarise we quote (perhaps somewhat out of context) from Colquhoun, Stoddart and Williams in *New Scientist*:[50]

> What of the future? With the knowledge we are acquiring of extramolecular chemistry, it should one day be possible to make molecules that replicate themselves (so imitating DNA synthesis) and transmit information between molecules.
>
> Materials science will be revolutionised by the former, while a possible 'sixth generation' computer (one operating with molecules, not chips of semiconductor material, the ultimate in miniaturisation) will consign present machines to the stone age.
>
> By the turn of this century, therefore, classical covalent chemistry may simply be a vehicle for exploring the nature of the non-covalent bond, and extending the horizons of chemistry beyond the molecule and out into new and exciting areas of science and technology.

A close investigation into the principles behind the electroscanner and electrocrystal therapy should, we feel, form part of that exploration. With time electroscanning will develop and improve, particularly when allied to computer enhancing techniques.

Investigations could be carried out with the kind of apparatus which was designed by Mitra, Sen, and Crothers of Yale,[196] where a polarised laser pulse at 308 nm was fired at herring sperm DNA and the extent of covalent attachment of psoralen to the adjacent pyrimidine bases assayed by scintillation. Sure enough, it worked. The ultraviolet pulse bound the DNA. Harry's machine generates pulsed frequency of much lower wavelengths, but it is possible that between the pulses the harmonics – which are much higher – are having their effect on interior cellular tissue.

To summarise, given all the weight of experimental evidence that radiation affects organic cells and that these organic cells are controlled by the brain, we find it surprising that medical research establishments have not already developed this method of diagnosis and treatment. It is not beyond their expertise. With acute problems like AIDS now adding to the chronic problems of arthritis, cancer, and other diseases, the time for a re-evaluation is long overdue.

Conclusions:
'A Thinge Worth Ye Tryalle'

In the mid 1600s Dean Wren was conducting experiments with the venom of a dying snake. He found that by injecting small quantities of it into persons afflicted with the poison, they were saved. He noted this curious finding in the margin of his book,[309] thus antedating the discovery of innoculation by 150 years. 'A Thinge Worthe Ye Tryalle', he wrote in his notebook ... Sadly, no one did try it out; and immense numbers of people died of the Great Plague a few short decades later, ignorant of a mechanism of nature which could have prevented it.

We are driven inescapably by the large tracts of evidence we have reviewed towards the conclusion that a two-way electromagnetic communication system exists between the brain of all organisms which possess them, and their individual cells, in that the brain acts as a central controlling transmitter with a receiving capacity, and that individual cells have a local transceiving capability.

This local mechanism is within the chromosomes: the amplitude and wavelength of a DNA macromolecule is specified uniquely for each organism by the sequence of hydrogen bonds bridging its paired purine and pyrimidine bases, and by the hydrogen bonds holding the helix in place. Since each DNA macromolecule holds a copy of the genetic and transmissive code for the whole organism it can communicate with any other cell, using the principle of electronic resonance, and the energy from this probably comes from the mitochondria of the same cell where transmission is involved. No energy is required to receive signals via resonance; the energy comes from the source of the transmission.

The central mechanism is in the cerebrum and the limbic system of the brain: whilst the cerebellum and the fundamental lower brain functions control the central and peripheral nervous systems, the central mechanism not only acts as a di-pole receiver and transmitter for its own organism, a view patently supported by its anatomical disposition, with two hemispheres each surrounded by a plate (the cerebral cortex), connected by filaments (the corpus callosum), whose traffic is monitored and directed by a number of specific instruments (the limbic system, thalamus, hypothalamus, and pineal gland, etc.); but this system can also be affected by exterior electromagnetic fields, some of which may even convey intelligence to the structure. We ourselves have not researched the possibility that the brain also transmits intelligence extracorporally (see refs. 8, 184, 193, 223, 224, 240, etc.), but it would not be unduly surprising.

As a consequence of this two-way telecommunications system, mutations or invasive damage to individual cells are likely to induce a cerebral effect, and, vice versa, any abnormalities of brain function such as tumours, stress patterns, electromagnetic, mechanical, or chemical damage, will weaken the brain's controlling radiative wave-forms, leading to cellular dysfunction.

The so-called 'phantom leaf effect' we have observed in Kirlian photography is a manifestation of locally induced waveforms emanating from adjacent organic cells, which are still being energised by their mitochondria: these radiations die away after cell death as the automatic delivery of energy from the mitochondria is depleted, and could therefore act as an indicator of nutritive strength, the onset of viral infection, or of intracellular mechanical or chemical damage. Whilst experience of the photographic counterparts of these various types of damage may be possible, and these diagnostic techniques are indeed practised by some researchers, the analysis of such wave-forms is now possible via more sophisticated techniques such as our instruments and those of MORA therapy and others.

These radiated morphogenetic wave-forms appear from experimental evidence to be in the ultraviolet range. Accordingly it is possible, we believe, having analysed an individual organism's unique and complex wave-form, to reamplify and rebroadcast that specific wave-form to abnormal areas, which can also be detected, with a consequently normalising effect. Using pulsed high-frequency and resonant principles such waveforms can be induced to act on interior tissues via the harmonics they generate, and not as simply a surface or pellicular phenomenon as seen in sarcomata.

There are a multitude of examples supporting our view, embracing not only the organic fields and including viruses, bacteria, small organic lifeforms, plants, insects, animals, primates and man, but there is even evidence that inorganic forms have a similar radiative capacity which announces their characteristics at a distance electromagnetically.

The hypothesis we are suggesting we have called the Morphogenetic Radiation Field Hypothesis.

A very small selection of examples of its mechanism at work would include the fact of cerebral Mass Action, whereby cortical abilities are transferable to other parts of the cortex following lesion; the natural progression and remission of certain stress-related diseases like psoriasis, asthma and eczema; the local disposition of cellular dysfunctions like Kaposi's sarcoma and the whole spectrum of neoplastic abnormalities (cancers); arthritis; point mutational diseases like phenylketonuria and multiple sclerosis; and rebroadcasting anomalies like the range of immune deficiencies including AIDS beginning to invade human populations.

Some neoplastic diseases seem to arise on occasion as a result of mucous coatings around cells which impair or prevent the relevant intercellular signals from being transmitted or received.

Proximity to high-voltage power lines, electromagnetic ionising radiation, and the ability of people fitted with plastic replacement corneal implants to perceive ultraviolet radiations emanating from organic tissues are a few examples of cases where the brain is affected by exterior electromagnetic radiation. In such cases mental confusion, depression, loss of cerebral function, and cellular dysfunction have been observed. Patients injected with Interferons also suffer disruption of higher cerebral function, which supports the view that the system is a two-way communications system between brain and cell.

The AIDS virus can, by means of our hypothesis, be explained as a cerebroviral cellular dysfunction, where the virus has captured the mechanism with which the brain transmits information to the cells, having altered slightly the wave-form specific to each individual organism so as to cause dysfunction to the T4 cells. This in turn leads to opportunistic disease.

Where do we go from here?

The world pharmaceutical industry is, like conventional medicine, suffering a crisis of confidence. The old systems whereby the family doctor acted as bedside comforter to his patient are steadily being replaced by waiting rooms crowded with people more likely to have a mental than a physical complaint, to be tranquillised or energised by drugs whose action may ultimately be more pernicious than curative. Whereas the pressures of demand and the structures of public health services are being seriously overstrained and underfunded, the pharmaceutical conglomerates by contrast move from strength to international strength, and, swollen by profit, spend millions on research into developing new product lines with which they can subsequently hold health authorities to oligopolistic ransom, and keep their corporate structures intact.

Sooner or later the whole system will have to change.

The wholesale dispensation of tranquillisers, antibiotics, and narcotics to people, chemical fertilisers to plants and cereal crops, and pesticides to insects, is breeding strains resistant to all three classes of participant in this planet's natural riches. The colorado beetle has learned to survive. The harassed and valium-ingesting housewife or executive has become a drug addict. The soil overladen with NKP has become self-destructive. Even the rain is becoming acid.

No wonder there is a groundswell of revolution among the aware public, in favour of gentler, non-invasive alternative medicines, organically grown vegetables, and raw or wholefood diets. It is unfortunately the revolution of desperation, and in consequence often turns down blind alleys, or is prone to clutching at the straws of charlatanism and quackery.

The book you have been reading invites an equally scientific, but much less invasive solution to the problems of nutrition and the treatment of disease. It personalises the treatment of the individual, accepting that each human being is unique, and may not always respond to a blanket pharmacological approach. It recognises the need to look at the whole organism, whether plant, man, insect or beast, and what is more to relate them to their whole environment. It shuns the symptomatic approach to disease. Treating one localised symptom may be fine where one is simply aiming to purvey a consumable product and capitalise on its continued consumption, but it does little to satisfy the sufferer's ultimate aim of curing him or herself.

The mechanisms we have uncovered have always been there: the laws of physics do not change, and those of biology only slowly. But it is a new alternative; and from it will derive the electronic medicines of the twenty-first century. Modern man

CONCLUSIONS: 'A THINGE WORTH YE TRYALLE'

has ignored these possibilities for long enough. Any further delay now will expose large sections of our world's population to the risk of horrendous diseases which may never be contained by conventional pharmaceutical ideologies, which are quickly losing their potency.

We have found a Thinge Worthe Ye Tryalle.

APPENDIX
How To Make Kirlian Pictures

Warning

The authors and publisher would like to stress that these instructions are written for the researcher who has a working knowledge of electronic safety, and while the equipment is perfectly safe when set up and used correctly, no responsibility can be accepted for any negligence or misuse on the part of the practitioner.

The Kirlian machine used to make pictures, is not a camera in the ordinary sense. There is no lens and no shutter. The only common denominator between the two is that they both use photographic film or plates, onto which a record is made (Fig. A.1).

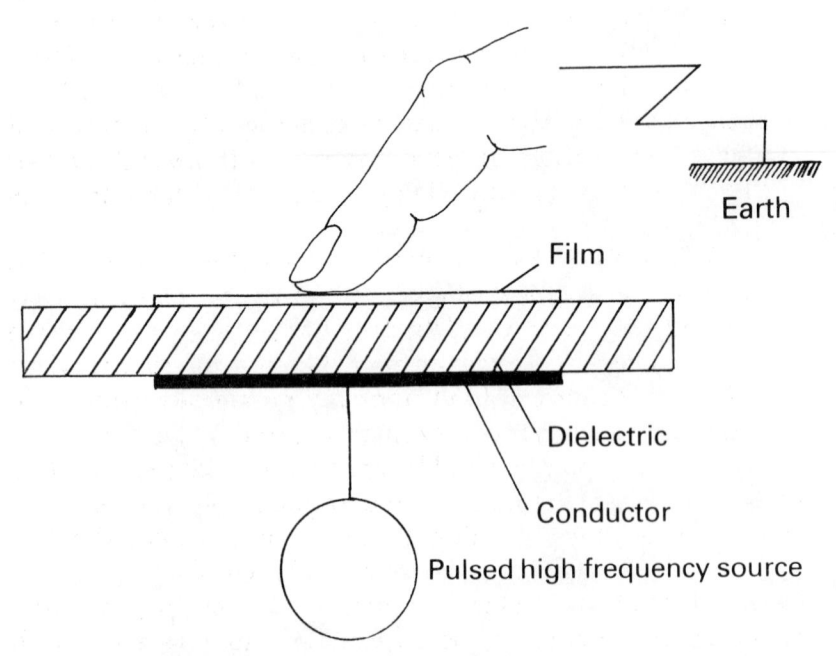

Fig A.1 A schematic diagram of the Kirlian apparatus.

APPENDIX: HOW TO MAKE KIRLIAN PICTURES

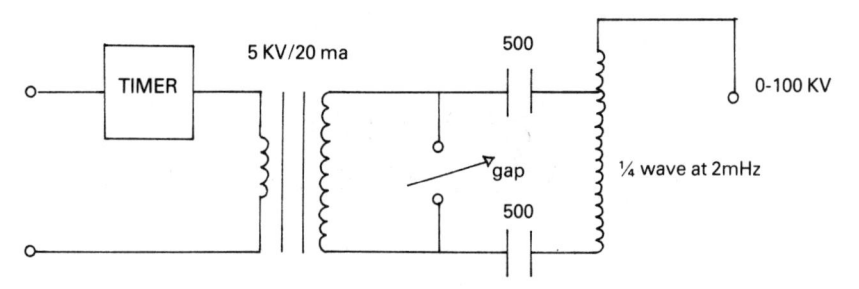

Fig A.2 A high-frequency high voltage oscillator for Kirlian photography.

The Kirlian camera as such is more accurately described as an electrical generator. It generates high voltage and high-frequency electrical pulses (Fig. A.2). These pulses are fed from a secondary coil to an electrode, normally located at the top of the apparatus. The means by which high electric voltage is generated is very simple. If a wire is coiled say ten turns round a bobbin and attached to the terminals of a small battery, electrons will flow down the wire. If a second wire is now coiled round the first wire, say a thousand turns, this 'secondary' winding will also have electrons flowing down it by a phenomenon known as inductance. Since the ratio between the two wire lengths is 100 to 1 the electrons in the secondary will travel much faster than those in the primary, with a resulting large increase in voltage, though a corresponding drop in current. If this secondary current's direction alternately flows and reverses at a high rate then the current will alternate at a high frequency (Fig. A.3).

An electrode is simply the place at the end of a wire used to produce some electrical effect. On top of this electrode is a non-conductive plate of dielectric. Dielectric is a substance which insulates an electric current, like the plastic round an electric wire. Electrons don't normally pass easily through it. (By contrast electrolyte is a substance, often a liquid, through which electrons pass easily, like the acid in a car battery.) This serves to protect the object being studied and the generator from direct electrical shorting. It also serves to spread the flare pattern more evenly. The object to be photographed (with the exception of people and live animals) is then earthed by a wire to the earth terminal on the apparatus or to a separate earth site. A potential difference is now set up between the high

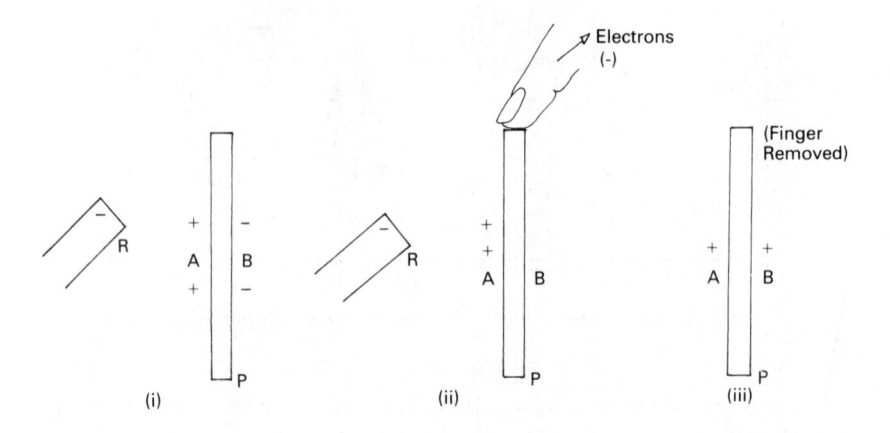

Induced Charges (Electrostatic)

Fig A.3 i. The principle of electrostatic induction.

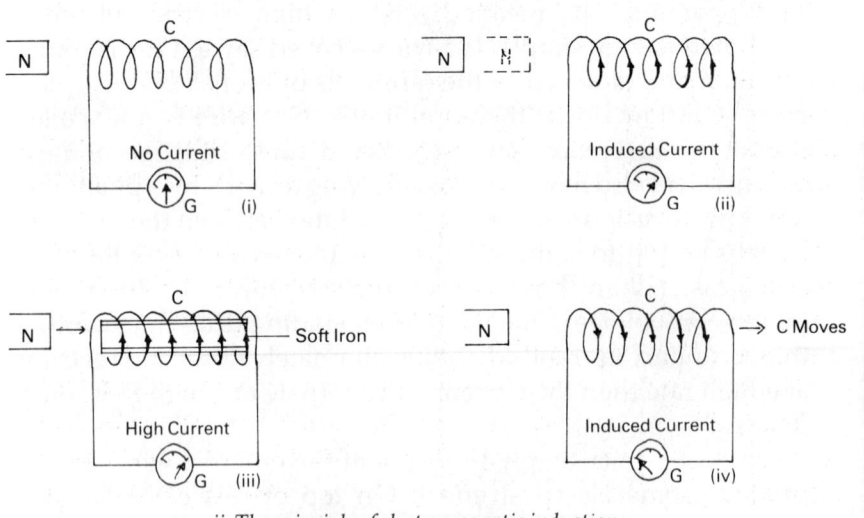

ii. The principle of electromagnetic induction.

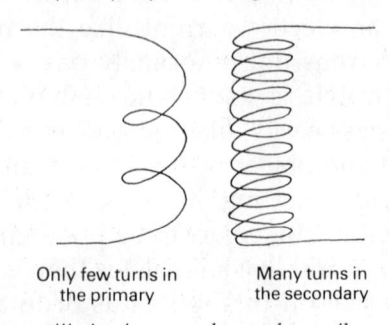

iii. A primary and secondary coil.

APPENDIX: HOW TO MAKE KIRLIAN PICTURES

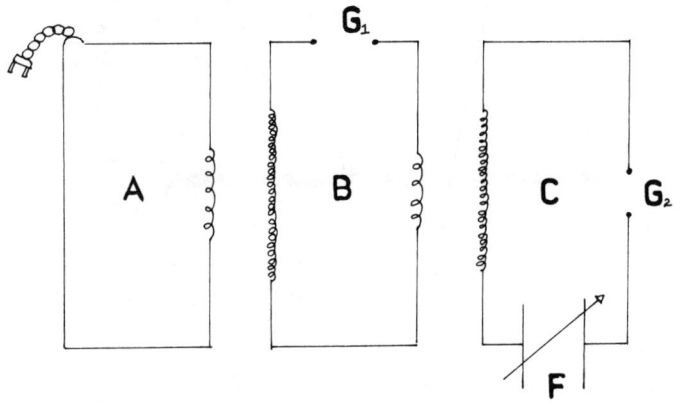

iv. The principle of the Tesla coil. The rheostat (F) controls the resistance through the tertiary winding. G_1 and G_2 are spark gaps.

voltage, high frequency of the generator and the object. If the apparatus is now switched on, the high-voltage pulses are sent along into the dielectric by induction and into the object. The current then flows to earth through the earth connector. When all this takes place, a corona discharge is emitted from the object which is luminous and this is recorded onto a film or plate under the object. A corona discharge is simply another word for a luminous spark-sheet generated by electrons moving across a large gap between high voltage and low voltage. The exposure varies with the subject being photographed; this will be discussed in more detail later.

The film is then developed in a normal manner and the result is analysed. This system has, of course, been oversimplified. It serves only as a brief description of what is a complicated procedure in practice. We say complicated because if repeatable and consistent results are required then there are certain working parameters to follow.

Let us first examine other methods in which Kirlian photography can be recorded. In the method just described, the object itself is the negative electrode. (An electrode is positive when it loses electrons. When an electrode or object gains electrons, it is said to be negatively charged.) In some systems of Kirlian photography, the object can be the positive electrode, in other words, the polarity is reversed. In even more complicated systems, the specimen is placed between the positive and negative electrodes with an air gap in between (Fig. A.4). The field then

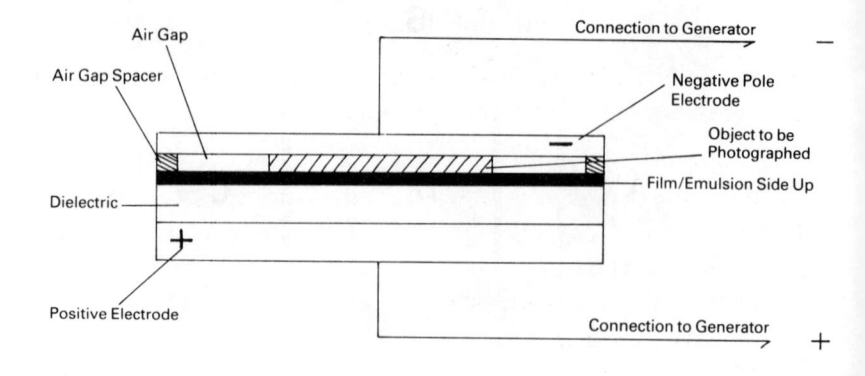

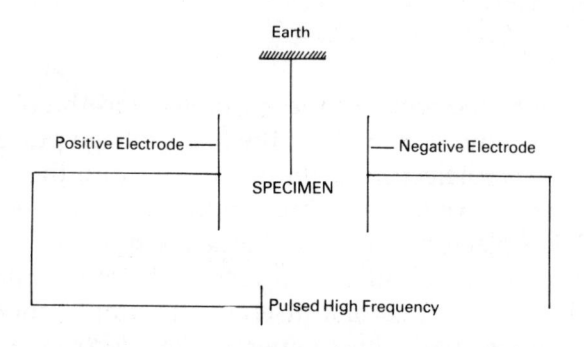

Fig A.4 The set-up making use of Kirlian apparatus with an air gap.

travels from the object: the object gives off light and the film records its pattern.

Parallel with Kirlian photography are the variety of electrographic methods described by Dumitrescu in 1976 and translated from the original Romanian with the assistance of Dr Julian Kenyon. Dumitrescu also developed micro-electronography, which involves exposing a biological preparation as a monocellular layer to an electromagnetic field generated by a single impulse, or by series of impulses at an experimentally predetermined amplitude.

Dumitrescu believed that of all the methods he had experimented with electronography offered most possibilities for immediate use. This technique uses a relatively compact medium for the passage of the electromagnetic field, at a single impulse, in one direction only. It measures the electron emission from the subject, and their different positions and energies.

APPENDIX: HOW TO MAKE KIRLIAN PICTURES

Working Parameters

Whatever particular method is used in taking these pictures, the variable factors are the same:

1. stability of equipment;
2. object/specimen topological features and mass;
3. temperature control;
4. humidity control;
5. barometric pressure control;
6. film characteristics;
7. exposure time;
8. plate pressure of specimen;
9. angle of incidence in fingertip studies;
10. frequency and pulse repetition rates.

These ten very important factors must be taken into account if serious applications are intended. We will now explain and expand upon each factor in turn.

STABILITY OF EQUIPMENT

Many early investigators of Kirlian photography were sometimes put off by inconsistent results. Most of these inconsistencies could be traced to involuntary variations in the electrical parameters of the equipment. These included fluctuations in voltage, variations in pulse rate, pulse length and variations in the input frequency through fluctuations in the mains voltage supply. If these problems are not taken into account with Kirlian equipment then results, no matter how relevant and spectacular, are unlikely to be repeatable. These problems have to be considered at the design stage of equipment!

Frequent problems concern electrode variations, dielectric imperfections, and associated imperfections in the field distribution across the plate. Scratches and imperfections in the dielectric can cause tracking errors in the high-voltage field. Earth leads and high-voltage delivery leads should be of consistent impedance and physical length to avoid capacitance problems and current flow variations. If this is not done then variations in fields on photographs are probably due to these factors and not to any change in the object! Some early researchers were perplexed by early equipment which gave changes when the specimen was moved to different positions on the plate. This was due to imperfections in the dielectric of the plate.

OBJECT/SPECIMEN TOPOLOGICAL FEATURES AND MASS

When taking a Kirlian image of any object the topology and mass of the specimen must be considered. The electrode plate and its dielectric cover is two-dimensional and the photographic image when recorded will be in two dimensions also. It then follows logically that the specimen and/or object should have ideally at least one surface in fairly complete contact with the plate. If this condition is not observed then uneven specimens (for example of large mass and size) will give an image only where the points of physical contact with the electrode occur. Another factor in the recorded image is the conductivity of the specimen and ionisable material in its make up. This is where a high impedance meter would be very useful for the serious researcher. Specimens with a high impedance and therefore low conductivity will require longer exposures and the opposite will be true of low impedance or specimens of high conductivity. Shape problems and conductivity variations can be solved by placing the specimen in a vessel of adequate size and transparency, i.e. glass, perspex, etc. These types of containers will act as a dielectric and, as long as the object inside is earthed, enough potential difference will occur to provide corona discharge. This depends, however, on the thickness of the container, especially the part in contact with the plate, which should be flat and of even thickness. The specimen of uneven topology or poor conductivity can be covered with an electrolyte to overcome these problems. Be sure, however, to take a control picture of an empty container in which there are the same combined volumes of electrolyte and specimen. For safety purposes, only saline solutions are used as an electrolytic medium. (Even strong acid solutions do not add any significant increase to the intensity of the final recorded image.) It is also advisable when making pictures of this sort, for example in flat-bottomed test tubes, to earth two tubes or more for simultaneous records. This is particularly the case where control shots are needed. Make sure that the tubes have a common earth return, on a split cable function system. However, if separate earth return leads are used, make sure that they are of identical length, make and

APPENDIX: HOW TO MAKE KIRLIAN PICTURES

impedance. They must have also identical insulation.

TEMPERATURE CONTROL

There are only two main factors to consider when taking temperature measurements. These are temperature recording of the surrounding air and the temperature of the object itself. When trying to repeat certain interesting effects, this has to be taken into account. Mercury thermometers are the most accurate for air temperature. However, for flat objects such as leaves, etc., we have found that the new liquid crystal colour change strips are very good indeed. (You can buy them in your local pet shop where they are made for the tropical fish aquarium.) They can also remain attached to the object throughout the experiment for constant reference. When trying to replicate recorded events, the researcher must try to reproduce all the parameters of the experiment under control conditions (e.g. was the central heating on in the room, etc.) which can be achieved without too much trouble. The researcher cannot prevent changed solar or lunar influences or differences in atmospheric electricity, but by dating and recording them he can build up experience of their importance.

HUMIDITY CONTROL

Humidity meters should always be used as a reference, whenever serious Kirlian records are made. As with temperature, these variable parameters are important. When conducting a series of experiments on the same subject, try to keep the conditions the same. With humidity this is easy to accomplish with a chemical or electronic dehumidifier (commercially available). An alternative is the use of silica gel, spread in trays near the equipment and stored with specimens to be photographed. The mechanical machines used in offices to keep electronic equipment, such as computers, etc. in good working order are, of course, quite expensive.

However, if you wish to observe Kirlian images under higher humidity conditions than normal, then water troughs hung over radiators in the workshop or laboratory create a good constant flow of water vapour. For greater accuracy, there is yet another electronic alternative, the office humidifier, used where air has become too dry.

BAROMETRIC PRESSURE CONTROL

Of all the variables in Kirlian photography, barometric pressure is the most difficult to control. It is, however, very lucky for the Kirlian researcher that this is also a variable which seems to affect results on a small scale. Only about a 10 per cent increase in corona discharge is seen during low pressure conditions, rain storms, etc. However, in this case, there are also increases in humidity to watch out for! It is a very simple procedure to record the pressure readings on any day when a particular experiment is executed. If in some subjects humidity or barometric pressure is an important factor then other researchers will be able to wait for the correct pressure levels to obtain the same results. On days of higher barometric pressure similar results are obtained if the pulse repetition rate is increased slightly and vice versa. There have been experiments done in the United States and the USSR on atmospheric sealed chambers where the entire apparatus can be placed inside. It can then be observed under high and low pressure conditions and even the gases can be changed inside the chamber. Whilst there have been reports of dramatic changes when the proportion of gases has been changed, pressure variations seem only to produce the least change (within the range of normal atmospheric pressure).

FILM CHARACTERISTICS

As mentioned earlier, nearly any commercially available film or even film print paper will produce Kirlian type images. There are many considerations to be made when choosing the type of film to be used in any given experiment. It should be noted that a good proportion of the corona discharge from the object or specimen is in the invisible violet and ultraviolet part of the spectrum. It is, therefore, advisable to have film which is sensitive to this part of the electromagnetic spectrum (10–300nm). Another choice depends on the analytical objectives of the experiment. In most experiments the main information is contained in the flare patterns of the discharge and the intensity of light coming from the discharge. If this is all that is required then we advise any researcher to look no further than black and white photographic materials. They are quick to develop

APPENDIX: HOW TO MAKE KIRLIAN PICTURES

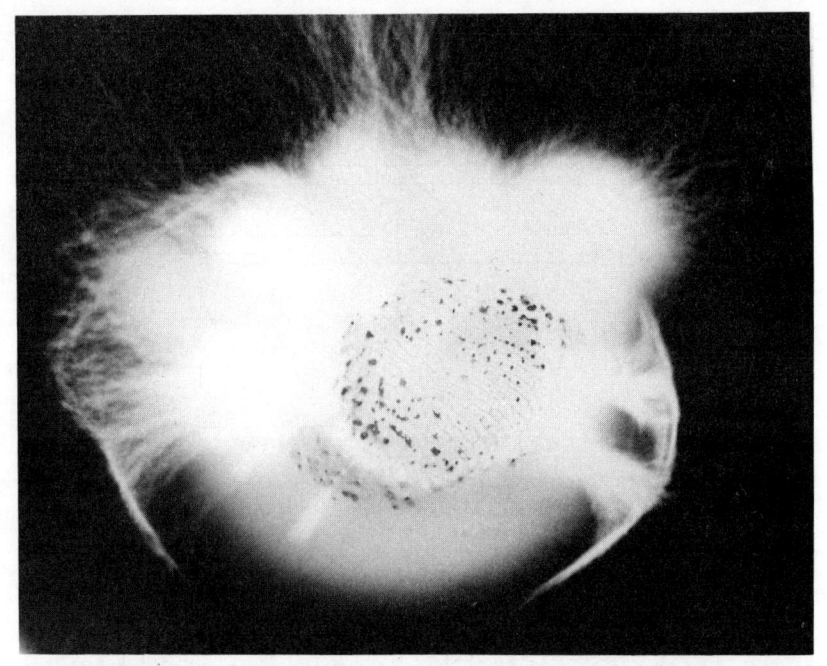

Fig A.5 Finger-tip showing the amount of energy given off in a split second of time.

in trays or daylight tank. They also have the advantage of sometimes being able to be used with a red safelight. This would include all black and white print papers. There are also proper sheet films, blue line lithofilms, and most of these can be used in a very dim red light. This is because they are very insensitive to this part of the spectrum. This means ease of operation in the dark room, no problems with breaking specimen bottles, etc.

The film sensitivity to light is measured with a Din or ASA number: the higher the number, the more sensitive the film: therefore less exposure time is needed with high ASA or Din numbers.

The print papers are a different matter. Please remember here that these will give you a black image on white background, so the light image comes out black on a white background (Fig. A.5). This gives a good contrast for pattern analysis. The sensitivity of the print papers is lower than film, and compensation has to be made with exposure times which will be dealt with more fully in the next section. However, there is a guide to the light sensitivity of the paper, which starts at zero (the most sensitive) and goes up to six being the least sensitive and with

```
                                    Transparent ─────┐        ┌───── To Earth
                                    Electrode
```

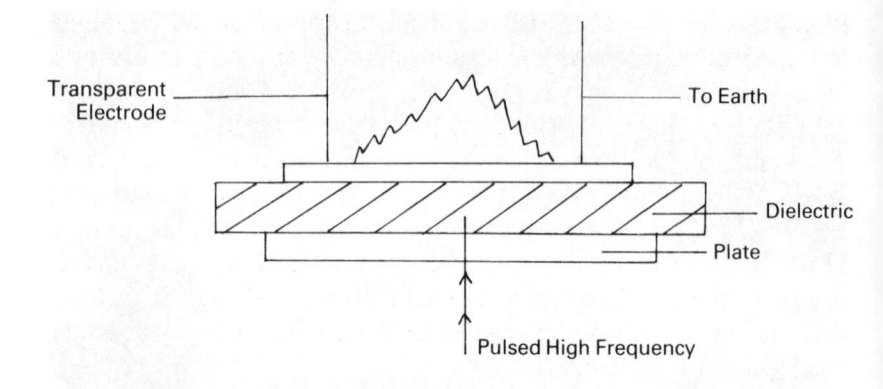

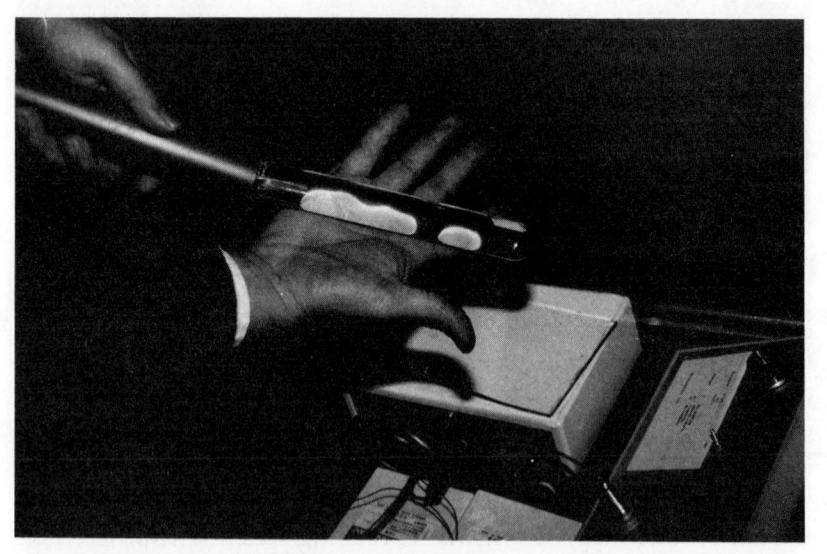

Fig A.6 Kirlian apparatus set-up for use with a transparent electrode.

higher contrast. These scales are used by most manufacturers of papers. When developing the films or papers always use the finest grain developer. This is slightly more expensive but the fine images are worth it.

What about colour photography with Kirlian techniques? If colour changes are required then more accurate results can be obtained by transparent electrode techniques. Here a thin glass plate electrode is used, which is filled with clear salt water or weak sulphuric acid. The pulsed high frequency is fed into this and an ordinary camera is placed near one side of the electrode: underneath on a shelf arrangement or perpendicular on a tripod

APPENDIX: HOW TO MAKE KIRLIAN PICTURES

(Fig. A.6). The object is then placed on top of or held against the electrode and earthed. In completely darkened conditions light will be seen coming from the specimen and the camera set on long exposure can record this. A close-up lens or converter is also needed for this work. Quartz lenses transparent to UV light might also be preferred, to capture more of the image. You may have noticed that this method does not involve contact of the film in the high-voltage high-frequency field. The reason we recommend this method over contact methods in colour work is because any colour recorded on the film is true transmitted light colour information.

The problem with contact analysis is that one cannot always be sure if the colour seen is true colour or an artefact of electron and photon emission impinging on a layer in the colour emulsion. In colour films or colour papers, the sensitive emulsions are in layers: one layer of red, one of blue and one layer of yellow. If electron excitation of the colour emulsion occurs, photons can be produced in one or more layers. This means that colour could be seen when developed which did not come from the object. However, the pattern of the energy would still be valid. Another disadvantage with colour is the need for total darkness, which entails a lot of problems in the darkroom with equipment, etc. If colour film is to be used we would recommend Kodak Ectochrome 64, which gave negligible artefacts of this nature.

EXPOSURE TIME

In Kirlian photography this can vary with the conductivity of the object, amplitude of the field and the frequency of pulses of the field in any given second of time, the sensitivity of the film or paper already discussed, and the dielectric thickness. All these variables can be compensated for by varying the field strength or pulse repetition rate of the Kirlian apparatus. The actual physical set-up for this can be controlled by an ordinary dark room timer used in photography enlargers which is wired in series with the power supply of the camera. On our apparatus there were variable pulses from one cycle per second to 250 thousand pulses per second; we have found that for nearly all purposes this is adequate. When the frequency is set, the duration can be set on the timer from 1/10th second to exposures of over 5 minutes if needed.

With transparent electrode techniques it is possible to tune in with the naked eye the most visible corona discharge that the object can produce. This method dispenses with all trial and error settings of frequency. If a transparent electrode is not available an ordinary mirror the size of the electrode can be placed on top, and the corona is much more visible coming from the object in blackout conditions.

PLATE PRESSURE OF SPECIMEN

This is easily solved by placing the apparatus on the spring balance, if the weight and pressure is critical in a picture (e.g. a human hand). In a case like this if pressure ratings are not taken results could differ from exposure to exposure. If making clinical tests, where many pictures have to be taken, then pressure should be the same in every case, especially where A/B comparisons are needed. Even a difference of an ounce of pressure has been seen in our research to make a difference which could be explained by no other working parameter.

ANGLE OF INCIDENCE IN FINGERTIP STUDIES

There is no doubt in our minds that a fingertip pattern can give very interesting information about the condition of a human

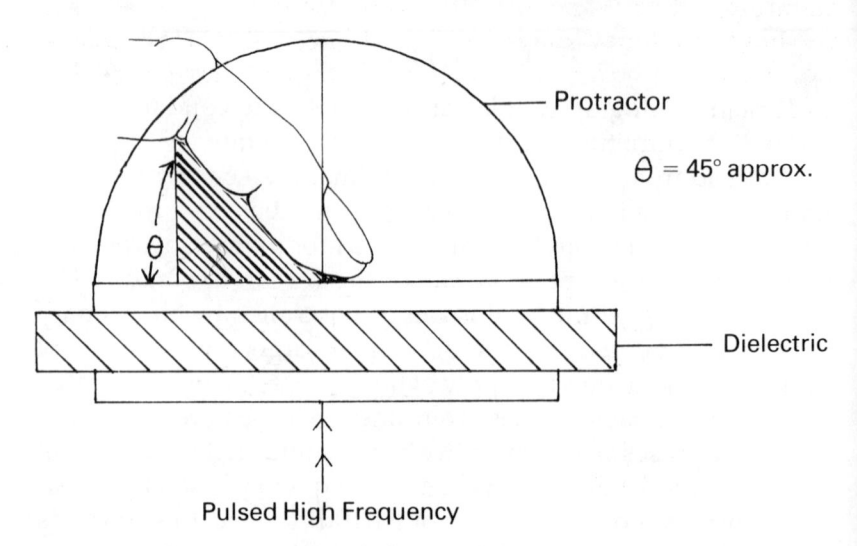

Fig A.7 Controlling the finger angle for a Kirlian photograph.

APPENDIX: HOW TO MAKE KIRLIAN PICTURES

subject. This can be clearly seen for example in the skin hydration test (Fig. A.7). It is very fortunate that the angle of the finger on the plate is not very critical in this particular test, because the energy field in a cancer patient is the same leaking disorganised field whatever the angle.

However, in studies of multiple sclerosis, viral infections, etc., the angles that fingertips subtend can make a great deal of difference to the picture. It is essential therefore that the finger angle is taken in the same position for the initial and subsequent comparison studies. We have found that an angle of 45 degrees will give the most accurate results. Use a wood or metalwork protractor where consistent accurate results are needed (Fig. A.7).

FREQUENCY AND PULSE REPETITION RATES

There has been to the non-technical researcher a great confusion between these two terms. Some have even said that there is no difference between the two! I am afraid that this is very wrong and there is a great deal of difference between the two.

Let us examine closely what happens in a Kirlian camera or generator. Stable oscillating circuitry feeds a frequency, in this case a signal of electrical energy in the form of a wave. The wave in this kind of electrical circuit is usually a 'square' waveform because most modern signal circuitry (microchips, etc.) are designed to work with this wave shape (Fig. A.8). This wave, which is rising and falling just like visible waves in the sea, is fed into an amplifier of some sort. The function of this

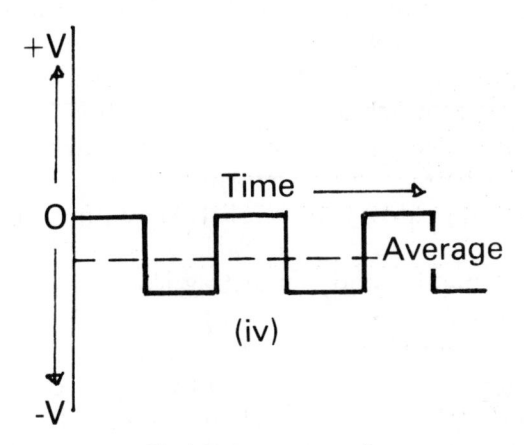

Fig A.8 A square wave form.

amplifier is to add amplitude (wave height) or electrical volume to the signal. When the correct threshold has been gained, it is sent into an induction coil apparatus – this coil is made up of continuous coils of wire. In the primary side of the coil there are say, a few hundred turns of wire. In the secondary part of the coil there are many thousands of turns which can in some coils add up to two or three miles of copper wire. The purpose of this apparatus is to turn a low primary voltage to a high voltage. The waves sent into the primary side of the coil, which is really switching on and off at great speed, make an oscillation. When this first wave enters the primary, nothing happens in the secondary; however, when this cycle stops, a secondary impulse is set up in this side of the coil, which due to its many thousands of turns of wire sets up a secondary field effect. This then increases to many thousands of volts. However, as the voltage increases the current drops to very low values. This process described is similar to the ignition coil apparatus in a car, but that is a crude mechanical make and break system, whereas in a good-quality Kirlian camera we have a stable transistor switching system controlled by microchip circuits.

The high voltage is produced in pulses from the secondary coil. As a result of the pulses of energy there are many frequency harmonics. This can be shown up by the fact that car radios need suppressors. It very often is the case that no matter where your car radio is tuned in, AM or FM setting, an interference of pulses will be heard (without screening). The pulses are energy bursts from the coil, and the number of pulses per second is the pulse repetition rate. This is completely different from the resonant frequencies generated in each pulse from the coil. The resonant frequencies of the coil do not affect the Kirlian picture results as much as the pulse repetition rates.

If a suitable darkroom is not available one can be made underneath the stairs (once in Mexico Harry had to work in a light-proof broom cupboard!) The basic list of equipment is as follows:

1. Kirlian Generator and connecting leads.
2. Three medium-sized developing trays.
3. Running water facilities and/or water trough/basin.
4. Film/film print papers, black and white or colour.
5. Thin glass plate 3–5 mm approximately, 8" x 5" (for the barrier between film and specimen). Clear polythene can

APPENDIX: HOW TO MAKE KIRLIAN PICTURES

be used, but only if it has a smooth surface. (Crinkles can cause distortion of results).
6. Thermometer (mercury).
7. A humidity meter (greenhouse type can be used).
8. Red safe light (black and white photography only). This cannot be used with black and white panchromatic or with colour film.
9. Suitable developing chemicals. i.e. developer, stop bath and fixative solution.
10. A pressure balance (with zero feature).
11. Barometer.

With this basic equipment you are ready to begin. Please note, however, that the parameter measuring equipment (thermometer, humidity meter, barometer) is not essential for making preliminary pictures. However, if you get interesting results, it becomes important to refine the conditions of their production if you wish to replicate them. These instruments are also indispensable for advanced research.

How he proceeds from here depends on the experimenter. Are objects or people to be investigated? Are the objects of organic origin or inorganic? Let us deal with each section in turn, with an example of the best procedures in each case.

If we start with inanimate objects of either organic or inorganic origin, we always begin by cleaning the electrode with a damp (lint-free) cloth of cotton, dampened with distilled or deionised water. The electrode is then wiped down with a dry cloth and allowed to dry (a hair dryer can come in useful in the darkroom for this, or for drying prints quickly). The film/print paper is placed emulsion side up on the electrode, and a thin sheet of glass 3-5mm is placed on the film. (This is only used as a precaution in critical experiments where moisture from a specimen might produce a distortion.) If the specimen, however, is dry (e.g. a crystal) or is in a watertight container, then this procedure is unnecessary. The specimen is then placed on the film and/or glass plate and the object is earthed to a suitable point on the generator (a separate earth is an advantage on a unit or can be earthed via a mains terminal earth socket). The pulse repetition rate is set and the time exposure meter is also set at this moment. (Pulse and exposure time varies by specimen type, conductivity, etc.) The generator/camera is switched on via the exposure device for the desired time. In completely dark conditions a light will be seen coming from the edges and surrounds of the specimen. The exposure completed, the film is removed from the plate by the edges (no finger prints please) and developed according to the film type. For black and white photography this is via developer, stop solution and fixative. After these three baths the film strip/plate/paper is washed and hung on a clip to dry in a dust-free environment. If panchromatic film is used then no safe light can be used and all procedures have to be completed by touch alone. A luminous timer in the darkroom is essential for this type of film processing. If 35 mm colour film is used then this can be sent off for normal processing to a suitable laboratory. Careful notes, however, should be taken between exposures on the order of pictures and where controls have been used. A dispensing and take-up cassette arrangement can be used in a set-up where 35 mm film is going to be used a great deal. Film can be also used in daylight conditions in which case the film is first placed in light-proof plastic sandwiches or polythene envelopes. The procedure of taking the picture is the same, however, minus the glass plate. There is some loss of quality and sharpness with this method which can to a certain extent be made up by longer exposure times. The envelopes or sandwiches should be labelled and careful notes of specimen type kept. Another method of daylight photography can be accomplished by an electrostatic resin method. This is where a light coating of special electrostatic sensitive resin, as used in photocopiers, covers a sheet of paper. The specimen itself can also be evenly coated with the dust if care is taken, with excellent results! The object is energised in the usual way via the generator and the pulse repetition rate altered until a sharp pattern is seen around the object/specimen. The object is lifted off the sheet and an infra-red lamp is brought a few inches away from the pattern left on the sheet. After the lamp has shone for a few seconds on the image the latter will change its chemical structure and stick fast to the sheet as an image! This method is very good where darkroom facilities are impossible and where only pattern analysis is needed (Fig. A.9).

In organic and low-conductivity specimens greater detail can be obtained by longer exposures or by using a thinner, or in some cases, no dielectric layer! If this is done, take care that no direct earth shorts occur as this could damage the electrode by

APPENDIX: HOW TO MAKE KIRLIAN PICTURES

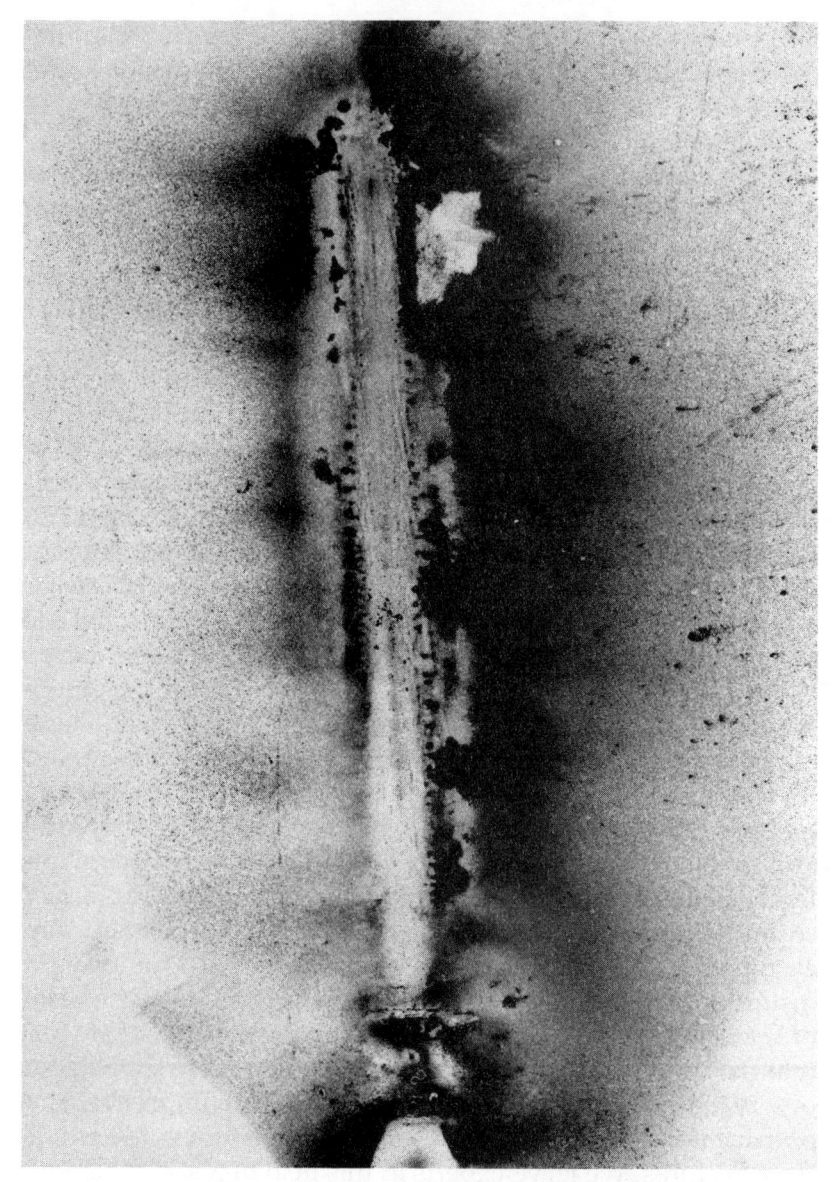

Fig. A.9 Photograph produced using the electrostatic resin method.

high-frequency burning. This can be avoided by using the reverse side of a mirror a few millimetres thinner than the electrode plate. This is placed non-reflective side up on the plate top. The film is placed directly onto this and, if the specimen contains moisture or electrolytes, it should not be used without the protection of a dielectric insulator. Exposures in low conductivity specimens can sometimes last several minutes or more! Always take several trial pictures of a specimen at various exposures, before deciding on a set procedure.

Let us now turn our attention to human subjects. I am afraid that of all objects and specimens available for Kirlian research, the human subject can be the most difficult to study. People with cardiac pacemakers, for example, should be photographed only under medical supervision. Do not earth a human subject or live animal through the equipment! This could produce a current density discharge to earth, which could shock the subject! Electrical energy always finds the shortest and least resistive channel to earth. All human subjects are naturally earthed unless they are standing on a completely insulated surface. It should also be noted that their footwear must be taken into account. If A/B comparisons are going to be made on different occasions, the same footwear should be used, or footwear should be removed. The need for this is due to the effect of the field flowing to earth via the feet discharging at different intensities with different types of shoes. Also do not have the equipment on metal surfaces or near metal filing cabinets, etc. These can also cause field variations. All bracelets and watches should be removed for the same reason. Fingertips should be used in preference to whole hand pictures. These are easier to control and are not prone to as many distortions. There are many differences in surface area between individual hands. This is not so much the case in fingerpad areas. The hand can also trap air under the surface in the palm sector which can cause slight distortion. There are, however, acupuncture points in the palm of the hand which can give interesting information, but we feel that flat transparent electrode techniques are more suitable for observation. We do not wish to comment here on mental and or psychic analysis techniques which sometimes use whole hand pictures. We leave experts in this field of research to offer their findings and describe their conditions.

APPENDIX: HOW TO MAKE KIRLIAN PICTURES

SAFETY PRACTICES

There is always the possibility of danger with any high-voltage electrical apparatus. Always use extreme caution when making measurements. Most Kirlian devices, however, produce high voltage at very low currents. It is also the characteristic of the Kirlian field that it travels as a surface effect over the skin and does not enter vital organs, etc.

- When making measurements do not stand on wet or damp floors. Do not work near or on any earthed metal object. Contact between a grounded metal object and the apparatus or any object or person connected to the apparatus may cause a shock hazard! This would not be a lethal shock, but could be unpleasant because of the current concentration on metal surfaces.
- Always use only well-insulated test leads. Do not allow your fingers to touch the bare metal part of any earth test leads when the circuit is in operation.
- Never use leads with frayed or broken-down insulation, high voltages can break through at these defects.
- Disconnect all test earth leads as soon as exposures have been made for safety reasons.
- Always turn off the generator when connecting or disconnecting leads to specimens.
- Do not expose your Kirlian camera to excessive moisture; avoid high humidity for long sessions. Excessive dust and dirt also should be avoided, from the point of view of contamination of exposures.
- Avoid excessive vibration or mechanical shock, since the generator could be damaged or its performance accuracy affected thereby.
- When exposures are being made on the apparatus, do not touch the specimen or subject, otherwise there may be a short to earth through you. This could not only cause an unpleasant sensation but also invalidate the exposure. Many early researchers tried to show the increase in corona from individual fingertips by people joining together by holding hands in a chain. There was an increase in the photographed subject. Not because energies were added together, but because of capacitance effects!

BIBLIOGRAPHY

1. Ali ABBAS, Perfect Book of the Art of Medicine (10th century).
2. Dr Albert ABRAMS, New Concepts in Diagnosis and Treatment, Philipolis Press, San Francisco (1922); also - Iconography: Electronic Reactions of Abrams, Philipolis Press, San Francisco (1923).
3. Viktor ADAMENKO, Living Detectors (on the expts. of K. Bakster - sic -) (in Russian), Tekhnika Molodezhi no. 8, pp. 60-2 (1970).
4. W. R. ADEY, Magnetic Field Effects on Biological Systems. Brain Res. Inst.
5. W. C. AGAR, F. H. DRUMMOND and O. W. TIEGS et al., Fourth (final) Report on a test of McDougall's on the training of Rats, Jnl. Exptl. Biol. 307-2l, Melbourne (1954).
6. Charles I. ALLEN, The Sexual Relations of Plants, New York (1986).
7. Carlos M. ALLENDE, Notes on Jessup's 'The Case for UFO's', Saucerian Press, P.O. Box 2228, Clarksburg, W. Virginia 26302.
8. M. D. ALTSCHULE, (ed.), Frontiers of Pineal Physiology, MIT Press, Cambridge Mass. (1975).
9. H. G. ANDRADE, A teoria corpuscular do espirito, Private Publication, Sao Paulo (1958).
10. ARAGO, Annales de Chimie et de Physique, Tome 32 (1826), pp. 213-23.
11. D. ARCHER, Intestinal Infection and Malnutrition Initiate AIDS, Nutrition, Research Vol 5, 1.9-19 (1985).
12. ARISTOTELES, Philosophus, De Generatione Animalium, ed. I. Bekker, Berlin, 1831-70.
13. Svante ARRHENIUS, Worlds in the Making, Harper & Row, NY and London (1908).
14. Edwin BABBITT, The Principles of Light and Colour, USA (1878).
15. Dr Edward BACH, Heal Thyself, C. W. Daniel Co., Saffron Walden (1931).
16. Cleveland BACKSTER, Evidence of a Primary Perception in Plant Life, Intl. Jnl. of Parapsychology, Vol. 10, No. 4, pp. 329-48. Winter 1968.
17. A.E. BAINES, The Origin and Problem of Life (Published 1920s).
18. K. P. BALITSKY, K. P. KAPSHUK, and V. F. TSAPENKO, Some electrophysiological peculiarities of the nervous system in malignant growth. Annals of the NY Acad. Sci., 1969, 164, 520-5.
19. Frances BALKWILL, Interferons: from common colds to cancer. New Scientist, 14 March 1985, pp. 26-8.
20. John BANVILLE. Kepler, Granada, St Albans (2nd edn, 1983).
21. Julian BARNARD, Patterns of Life Force, Bach Educational Programme, Hereford (1987).
22. Madeleine BARNOTHY, (ed.), Biological Effects of Magnetic Fields, Plenum Press, New York (1964).
23. M. J. BAUM, Physical Behaviour, 1970. 5. 325-9.
24. B. BECK, The Russian Lakhovsky Rejuvenation Machine, Borderland Sciences Research Foundation.

BIBLIOGRAPHY

25. Michael M. BECKER and James C. WANG, Use of Light for Footprinting DNA in vivo. Nature, Vol. 309, 21 June 1984, pp. 682-7.
26. Robert O. BECKER, and Andrew A. MARINO, Electromagnetism and Life, State University of N.Y. Press (1982).
27. John S. BELL, Article, Physics, Vol, 1, p. 195 (1964).
28. J. A. BENNETT, The Mathematical Science of Sir Christopher Wren, Cambridge University Press, Cambridge (1982).
29. Itzhak BENTOV, Stalking the Wild Pendulum, E. P. Dutton, New York (1977).
30. Hans BERGER, Uber das Elektrenkephalogram des Menschen (1929).
31. Charles BERLITZ and William MOORE, The Philadelphia Experiment, Panther (Granada), St Albans (1980).
32. M. l'Abbé BERTHOLON, De l' Electricité des Végétaux, Alyon (1783).
33. Dr A. BIERACH, Bioelektrizitat, Wilhelm Heyne Verlag, Munich (1984).
34. R. BIRCHER, A Turning Point in Nutritional Science, Lee Foundation for Nutr. Res., Milwaukee, Wis., No. 80.
35. M. BIRCHER-BENNER, The Prevention of Incurable Disease, James Clarke, London (1981).
36. Dr Francis BITTER, Magnets, the Education of a Physicist, Cambridge, Mass. (1956).
37. Ra BONEWITZ, Cosmic Crystals, Turnstone Press, Wellingborough (1983).
38. Sir Jagadis C. BOSE, The Nervous Mechanism of Plants, Longmans, London (1926).
39. André BOVIS, Pamphlets on Dowsing, Privately printed in Nice (1971).
40. Prof. Israel BREKMAN and I. V. DARDYMOV, New Substances of Plant Origin which increase Non-Specific Resistance, Annual Review of Pharmacology, Vol. 9 (1969).
41. Stewart M. BROOKS, The World of Viruses, A. S. Barnes and Co., Sth Brunswick and NY, Thos. Yoseloff, London (1970).
42. B. BROWN, New Mind, New Body, Harper & Row, NY (1975).
43. G. I. BROWN, Introduction to Physical Chemistry. Longman, Harlow (3rd edn, 1983).
44. Thos. BROWNE, Pseudodoxia Epidemica, In Bennett (1974), pp. 30-76.
45. Hans BRUEGEMANN, Diagnosis and Therapy Methods in the Ultrafine Bioenergy Sector, Haug Verlag, Munich (in German).
46. Harold Saxton BURR, Blueprint for Immortality: The Electric Patterns of Life and An Electrodynamic Theory of Life (1935). Neville Spearman, London (1952).
47. W. E. BUTLER, How to Read the Aura, Aquarian Press, London (1971).
48. Kevin CAHILL (ed.), The AIDS Epidemic, Hutchinson, London (2nd edn, 1984).
49. Sheila T. CALLENDER, Blood Disorders, The Facts, Oxford University Press (1985).
50. Fritjof CAPRA, The Tao of Physics, Fontana (Collins), London (2nd edn, 1976).
51. D. P. CARDINALI, et al, Proc. Natl. Acad. Sci., USA. Vol. 69. 2003-5 (1972).
52. Edgar CAYCE, Handbook for Health Through Drugless Therapy, Macmillan (Jove), 1975.

53. Margaret CHENEY, Tesla: Man out of Time, Prentice Hall, Englewood Cliffs, London (1981).
54. Ronald W. CLARK, Albert Einstein, World Publishing, NY (1971).
55. Mark CLEMENT, The Waves that Heal, Health Science Press, Sussex (1949).
56. Hugh F. COCHRANE, Gateway to Oblivion, W. H. Allen, London (1980).
57. Howard COLQUHOUN, Fraser STODDART et al., Chemistry Beyond the Molecule, New Scientist, 1 May 1986, pp. 44-8.
58. C. A. COULSON and A. JEFFREY, Waves: A Mathematical Approach to the Common Types of Wave Motion. Longman, London (2nd ed, 1977).
59. Prof. Guido CREMONESE, I raggi della vita fotografati (1930).
60. Francis CRICK, Life Itself, its Origins and Nature, MacDonald, London (1982).
61. George Washington CRILE, The Phenomena of Life: A Radio-Electrical Interpretation, MacMillan, New York (1926).
62. George Washington CRILE, The Bi-Polar Theory of Living Processes, MacMillan, New York (1926).
63. Dr Manfred CURRY, Bioklimatik, Amer. Bioclimatic Res. Inst. Reiderau, W. Germany (1946).
64. Charles DARWIN, The Formation of Vegetable Mould through the Action of Earthworms (1881).
65. Paul DAVIES, Superforce: The Search for a Grand Unified Theory, Unwin Paperbacks (Heinemann), London (1984).
66. Mikol DAVIS & Earle LANE, Rainbows of Life, Harper/Colophon Books, San Francisco (1978).
67. George DE LA WARR, Article, Do Plants Feel Emotion?, Electrotechnology (April 1969).
68. George DE LA WARR and Douglas BAKER, Biomagnetism, De la Warr Labs. Oxford (1967).
69. Paul DEVEREUX, Earthlights, Book Club Associates, London (1982).
70. Richard DIXEY, The Effect of Pulsed Electromagnetic Fields on Cells in Culture, Ph. D. Thesis, St Bartholomew's Medical College (1985) Summary: Nature, Vol. 296.5854, pp. 253-6, 18 March 1982.
71. Dr John DOUGLASS, Is 'How Vitamin C Works' Medicine's Best Discovery?, Nutrition Today (March/April 1980).
72. S. DRABKINA, Tobiscope, Sputnik No. 5 (1965).
73. H. DREICH, Science and Philosophy of the Organism, A. & C. Black, London (1908).
74. Ruth Beymer DROWN, Theory and Technique of the Drown H. V. R. and Radiovision Instruments, Artists' Press, Los Angeles (1939).
75. Aleksandr P. DUBROV, The Geomagnetic Field and Life, Plenum Press (1978).
76. Ion DUMITRESCU and D. CONSTANTIN Modern Scientific Acupuncture, ed. Junimea, Iasi (1977).
77. Ion DUMITRESCU and Julian KENYON, Electrographic Imaging in Medicine and Biology (trans. L. A. Galia) Neville Spearman, Suffolk (2nd edn, 1983).
78. Sir John C. ECCLES, The Neurophysiological Basis of Mind. Oxford University Press (1953).

BIBLIOGRAPHY

79. Sir John C. ECCLES, Brain and Conscious Experience, Springer Verlag, Berlin (1966).
80. L. E. EEMAN, The Curative Properties of Human Radiations, Fredk. Muller, London (1947).
81. Arnold EHRET, Mucusless Diet Healing System, Ehret Literature Publishing Co., Cody, Wyoming (1953).
82. Stephen T. EMLEN, The Stellar Orientation System of a Migratory Bird, Sci.Amer. Aug. 1975: 102-11.
83. H. ENGELHARDT, H. GAUB, et al., Viscoelastic properties of erythrocyte membranes in high frequency electric fields, Nature, Vol. 307, 26 Jan. 1984, pp. 378-80.
84. Hans EPPINGER, Transmineralisation und Vegetorische Cost, Ergebnisse der Inneren Medizin und Kinderheilkunde, Vol. 51 (1936).
85. Dr Elida A. EVANS, A Psychological Study of Cancer, Dodd Mead & Co., NY (1926).
86. Dr William T. FERNIE, M.D., The Occult and Curative Powers of Precious Stones, Blauvelt NY, Rudolf Steiner Publications (1973).
87. A. FIFE, Moon and Plant, Society for Cancer Research (1958).
88. Ernst FLOREY, General and Comparative Animal Physiology, W. B. Saunders Company, Philadelphia (1966).
89. Geoffrey FOULKES and Anthony SCOTT MORLEY, MORA Therapy: a revolution in electromagnetic medicine?, Jnl.Alt.Med. July 1984, p. 10.
90. Raoul Heinrich FRANCE. The Love Life of Plants and Germs of Mind in Plants, A. and C. Boni, New York (1923). Originally published in Stuttgart (1905).
91. Dr E. H. FREI, Medical Applications of Magnetism, Bulletin of the Atomic Scientists, Oct. 1972.
92. M. FRY The development of equipment for investigating the biological effects of pulsed magnetic fields, M.Sc. Thesis, St Bartholomew's Medical College (1986).
93. GALEN, De Tumoribus, c. 2nd century AD.
94. Mark L. GALLERT, New Light on Therapeutic Energies, James Clark, London (1966).
95. John GALLOWAY, 'Helix through the looking glass', New Scientist, 27 Jan. 1983, pp. 242-5.
96. Luigi GALVANI, De viribus Electricitatis in Moto Musculare Commentarius, trans. E. Licht, Cambridge, Mass. (1953).
97. Martin GARDNER, Fads and Fallacies in the Name of Science, Dover, NY (1957).
98. Luigi GENNARO, Fulvio GUZZON, Pierluigi MARSIGLI, Kirlian Photography, East West Publications (UK) (1980).
99. Max GERSON, A Cancer Therapy: Results of 50 Cases, Totality Books, Del Mar, Calif. (1977).
100. Iran U. GHYSSAERT, The Therapeutic Use of Gem Remedies, Mont de Plan, Ch-1605,Chexbres, Switz.
101. Sandra GIBBONS, Living With Psoriasis, Alternative Centre (1986).
102. Dr Ronald GLASSER, The Body is the Hero, Random House, NY (1976)
103. Joscelyn GODWIN, Athanasius Kircher, A Renaissance Man, Thames &

Hudson, London (1979).
104. Johann Wolfgang von GOETHE, Theory of Colours, Frank Cass (1967).
105. June GOODFIELD, Playing God, Hutchinson & Co., London (1977).
106. Simon GOODMAN, The bones of a cell, New Scientist, 4 Oct. 1984, pp. 44-7.
107. Celia GREEN, The Human Evasion, Institute of Psychophysical Research, Oxford (3rd edn, 1983).
108. John GREEN and David MILLER, AIDS, The Story of a Disease, Grafton Books, London (1986).
109. George GREY, Radiation and Plant Research (1934).
110. John GRIBBIN, In Search of Schrösdinger's Cat, Corgi Books (Wildwood House), Transworld Publishers, London (2nd edn, 1985).
111. John GRIBBIN, In Search of the Double Helix - Quantum Physics and Life, Corgi Books (Transworld) (1985).
112. Dr George GUILBAULT, Article, Sunday Times, 1 Feb. 1987, p. 76.
113. P. GULYAEV Cerebral Electromagnetic Fields (transl.), Intl. Jnl. of Parapsychology, NY, Vol. 7, No. 4, (1965).
114. A.G. GURVICH, The Theory of a Biological Field, Sovyetskaya Nauka, Moscow (1944).
115. A. and L. GURWITSCH, L'Analyse Mitogénétique Spectrale, Hermann, Paris (1934).
116. Samuel HAHNEMANN, Organon on the Art of Healing, Published 1810.
117. Daniel S. HALACY, Jnr., Radiation, Magnetism and Living Things, Holiday House, New York (1966).
118. Manly P. HALL, The Mystical and Medical Philosophy of Paracelsus, Philosophical Research Society, Los Angeles (1964).
119. Graham HANCOCK and Enver CARIM, AIDS, The Deadly Epidemic, Victor Gollancz, London (1986).
120. D.J. HARAWAY, Crystals, Fabrics and Fields, Yale University Press, New Haven (1976).
121. Sir Aleister HARDY, The Living Stream, Collins, London (1965).
122. K. HARRISON, A Guidebook to Biochemistry, Cambridge University Press (1960).
123. Z. V. HARVALIK, A Biological Magnetometer-Gradiometer, Virginia Jnl. of Science, Vol. 21, No.2. (1970) pp. 59-60.
124. J.B. HASTED, Speculations about the Relation between Psychic Phenomena and Physics, Psycho-energetic Systems 3. 243-57 (1978).
125. J.B. HASTED, The Metal Benders, Routledge & Kegan Paul, London (1981).
126. Alfred HAY, Alternating Currents, Harper & Brothers, London (1923).
127. HERACLITUS of Ephesus, De Natura, c. 513 BC, ed. H. Diels Vorsokr. i. p. 67, Mythographi Graeci iii (2) Leipzig (T.) (1902).
128. M. B. HESSE, Forces and Fields, Nelson, London (1961).
129. T. Galen HIERONYMUS, The Truth about Radionics and some of the Criticism made about it by its Enemies, Intl. Radionics Assocn., Springfield, Mo. (May 1947).
130. HIPPOCRATES MEDICUS Opera, Esp. On wounds of the head, and On the Skin, ed. E. Littre, 10 vols. Paris (1839-61), & H. Kuehlewein, Leipzig (1894).

131. Francis HITCHING, Pendulum, The PSI Connection, Fontana (Williams Collins), Glasgow (1977).
132. A. HOLDEN and P. SINGER, Crystals and Crystal Growing, Heinemann, London (1961).
133. R. E. HOPE-SIMPSON, Person-to-person transmission of influenza, Jnl. Hyg. Camb. 83.11 (1979).
134. R. E. HOPE-SIMPSON, Correlation of 20th century pandemics with sunspot activity, Nature, 275 (1978), 86.
135. Fred HOYLE and Chandra WICKRAMASINGHE, Space Travellers, the Bringers of Life, University College Cardiff Press (1981).
136. Richard HUDSON, Kirlian Photography, B.A. Social Science Degree, Polytechnic of Central London (May 1984).
137. Kenneth HUNT, Experiments in Kirlian Electrophotography. Unpublished (c. 1976).
138. IAMBLICHUS, Philosophus, Life of Pythagoras (De Vita Pythagorica), John M. Watkins (1965).
139. Brian INGLIS, Wilhelm Reich, A biography.
140. Brian INGLIS, Fringe Medicine, Faber, London (1964).
141. Vladimir INYUSHIN, On the Bioenergetic Aspects of the Influence of Light Energy on the Organisms of Animals. Some Questions of Applied Biology, Alma Ata (1967).
142. Vladimir M. INYUSHIN and N. N. FEDOROVA, On the Question of the Biological Plasma of Green Plants (in Russian), Alma Ata, USSR (1969).
143. K. JACH Researches on Telepathy Phenomena in Connection with Hypothesis of Electromagnetic Waves. Unpublished: Refce. The President, Polish Copernicus Soc. of Naturalists, Warsaw.
144. Hans JENNY, Cymatics, Basilius Press, Basel (1967).
145. Morris JESSUP, The Case for the UFO (Annotated) Varo Mfg. Co., Garland, Texas (1955).
146. Kendall JOHNSON, Photographing the Non-Material World, Aquarian Press, Wellingborough (1975). Hawthorn Books Inc.,New York (1975).
147. Pascual JORDAN, New Trends in Physics, Saint Paul de Vence (1954).
148. Matthew JOSEPHSON, Edison, McGraw Hill Book Co., N.Y. (1959).
149. Horace Freeland JUDSON, The Eighth Day of Creation, Jonathan Cape, London (1979).
150. Dr Henning KARSTROM, Protectio Vitae. Also Rätt Kost, (Feb. 1972), Skandinavska Bokforlaget, Garle (1982).
151. M. KATO et al., Proc. Jap. Acad. (967). 43. 220-3.
152. Leslie and Susannah KENTON, Raw Energy, Century, London (1984).
153. Dr Julian N. KENYON, Twentyfirst Century Medicine, Thorsons, Wellingborough (1986).
154. Johannes KEPLER, De Fundamentis Astrologiae, Prague (1602).
155. L. E. KEYES, Toning: the Creative Power of the Voice, De Vorss Co. , Santa Monica, Calif. (1973).
156. Dr Walter J. KILNER, The Human Aura, University Books , NY (1965).
157. William KINGSLAND, The Great Pyramid in Fact and Theory.
158. Athanasius KIRCHER, Ars Magnetica, Wortsburg (1631).
159. Semyon D. KIRLIAN and Valentina H. KIRLIAN, The Significance of Elec-

tricity in the Gaseous Nourishment Mechanism of Plants, Alma Ata, USSR (1968).
160. Semyon D. KIRLIAN and Valentina H. KIRLIAN, Photography and Visual Observations by Means of High Frequency Currents, trans. Foreign Techn. Divn.,U.S. Air Force Systems Command (1963).
161. Semyon D. KIRLIAN and Valentina H. KIRLIAN, Investigation of Biological Objects in High Frequency Electrical Fields - Bio energetic Questions - and Some Answers, Alma Ata USSR (1968).
162. Werner KOLLATH, Der Vollwert der Nahrung und seine Bedeutung für Wachstum und Zeller satz, Experimentelle Grundlagen, Stuttgart (1950).
163. K. KOLLERSTROM & M. DRUMMOND, Article. The Astrol. Jnl. (UK) 1977, 19. 100-5.
164. Leonard KONIKIEWICZ, Introduction to Electrography. Leonard's Associates, Harrisburg (1979).
165. Stanley KRIPPNER and Daniel RUBIN, The Kirlian Aura, Photographing the Galaxies of Life, Anchor Books (Doubleday) NY (1974).
166. Stanley KRIPPNER and Daniel RUBIN, The Energies of Consciousness. Interface Books (Gordon & Breach) NY (1975).
167. Stanley KRIPPNER and Daniel RUBIN, Galaxies of Life, Interface Books (Gordon & Breach) NY (1973).
168 Stanley KRIPPNER and Daniel RUBIN, The Human Aura in Acupuncture and Kirlian Photography.
169. Dr Masanore KURATSUNE, Experiment of low nutrition with raw vegetables, Kyushu Memoirs of Medical Science Vol. 2, Nos. 1-2 (June 1951).
170. Georges LAKHOVSKY, The Secret of Life, MacMillan Scientific Publishing, London (1939).
171. Georges LAKHOVSKY, L'Origine de la Vie, Editions Neillson, Paris (1925).
172. Georges LAKHOVSKY, The Waves that Heal (trans. Mark Clement), Health Science Press, Sussex (1949).
173. Earle LANE, Electrophotography. And/Or Press, San Francisco, CA (1975).
174. K. R. LASHLEY, In Search of the Engram, Symp. of Soc. for Exptl. Biol. 4, pp. 454-82 (1950).
175. K. R. LASHLEY, The Neuro-Physiology of Lashley. Selected Papers, McGraw-Hill (1960).
176. Drs LEMEX and GIBBS, Brainwaves do correlate with phases of the moon. Jnl. Heredity. Via Analog Vol. XIX No.1, p. 72.
177. Dr Lawrence LESHAN, You Can Fight for Your Life, M. Evans & Co. NY (1977).
178. Selim LEMSTROM, Electricity in Agriculture and Horticulture, Electrician Publishing Co., London (1904).
179. Mario LENZI, A report of a few Recent Experiments on the Biological Effects of Magnetic Fields, Radiology 35, pp. 307-14 (1940).
180. A.B. LERNER et al., Melatonin production controlled by light of long wavelength, J. Biol. Chem (1960) 235. 1992-7.
181. Sir Oliver LODGE, My Philosophy, Ernest Benn (1933).
182. LOPER, AHR, and GLENDENNING, Basic Electricity and Electronics, Chapter 19. p. 461, Litton (1979).
183. Dr W. LUDWIG, The Development of the Schumman Wave Generator,

BIBLIOGRAPHY

Tubingen University W. Germany (1976).
184. E. J. LUND, Bioelectric Fields and Growth, University of Texas Press, Austin (1947).
185. Dr J.E.R. McDONAGH, The Universe Through Medicine, James Clark & Co., London (1966).
186. Frank McGILLION, The Opening Eye, Coventure, London (1980).
187. S. MANCZARSKI, Questions of Telepathy in Radiotechnical Studies, Telecommunication Review Nos. 10,11/12 (1964) and Nos. 1/2,3 (1947).
188. Professor F. MARGRASSI, Article on Influenza Epidemic in Sardinia, Minerva Med, Torino, 40 (1949), 565.
189. Thomas C. MARTIN The Inventions, Researches and Writings of Nikola Tesla, The Electrical Engineer, New York (1894).
190. Bryan MATTHEWS, Multiple Sclerosis, The Facts, Oxford Medical Publications, OUP (1978).
191. James Clerk MAXWELL, A Treatise on Electricity and Magnetism (2 vols.) Clarendon Press, Oxford (1892).
192. F. M. MEISSNER, W. HEPTING et al., Laser Stimulation within the Scope of Combined Therapy in the Pain Centre, Stuttgart, Schmerz 2 (1983).
193. Franz Anton MESMER, Le Magnétisme Animal (Reprint) Payot, Paris (1814: 1971).
194. John MICHELL, The View over Atlantis, Ballantine Books, NY (1969).
195. Earl MINDELL, The Vitamin Bible, Arlington Books, London 1982 (1979).
196. Sekhar MITRA, D. SEN, and D. CROTHERS, Orientation of nucleosomes and linker DNA in calf thymus chromatin determined by photochemical dichroism. Nature, Vol. 308, 15 Mar. 1984. pp. 247-52.
197. Clifford T. MORGAN and Eliot STELLAR, Physiological Psychology, McGraw-Hill Book Co.,New York (2nd edn 1950).
198. C. MORGAN et al., Intracellular crystals associated with viral development. Transact. Acad. Amer. Physicians. 71; 281 (1958).
199. Thelma MOSS, The Body Electric, Paladin Books (Granada) (1981).
200. Thelma MOSS, The Probability of the Impossible, J.P. Tarcher, Los Angeles (1974).
201. Thelma MOSS and K. JOHNSON, Radiation Field Photography, Physics Magazine, July 1972.
202. Indumati L. MULAY, Article: Cancerous Cells die in Magnetic Field of 4000 gauss, Nature, 10 June 1961.
203. Dr Jean MUNRO Article (in press) on treatment of allergies with specific frequencies, Clin. Ecol. March 1987.
204. Guy MURCHIE, Music of the Spheres, Rider/Hutchinson USA (1951).
205. Dr Larry E. MURR, Physiological Stimulation of Plants Using Delayed and Regulated Electric Field Environments, Intl. Jnl.of Biometeorology, Vol.10, no. 2, pp. 147-53.
206. Hans NEIPER, Lecture given at Royal Society of Medicine, London (May 1980).
207. M. NELKON and H. I. HUMPHREYS, Electrical Principles, Heinemann Educational Books, London (4th edn, 1981).
208. Kristine NOLFI, My Experience with Living Foods, Humlegaarden, Humlebaek, Denmark (undated).

209. M. L'Abbé Jean Antoine NOLLET, Recherches sur les causes particulières des phénomènes électriques, Paris (1754).
210. Dr Bjorn NORDENSTROM, An Electrifying Possibility, Discover, April 1986, pp. 24-37.
211. Dr Bjorn NORDENSTROM, Biologically Closed Electric Circuits. Clinical, Experimental, and Theoretical Evidence for An Additional Circulatory System (1983).
212. P. L. NUNEZ, Electric Fields of the Brain, Oxford University Press (1981).
213. Harry OLDFIELD, Article, Medical News Weekly, 17 Dec. 1981, Vol. 13. p. 48.
214. John G. O'NEILL, Prodigal Genius, The Life of Nikola Tesla, Panther (Granada) 1980, Neville Spearman Ltd (1968).
215. Sheila OSTRANDER and Lynn SCHROEDER, PSI: Psychic Discoveries behind the Iron Curtain. Abacus (Sphere Books), London (2nd edn, 1973).
216. PARACELSUS, Sämtliche Werke von Theophrast von Hohenheim gen. Paracelsus, (20 vols.) R. Oldenbourg, Munich (1922-1965).
217. Linus PAULING, The Nature of the Chemical Bond. Cornell University Press. Ithaca (3rd edn, 1960).
218. L. P. PAVLOVA, Some EEG Indices in Exptl. Research into Bio-telcommunication. In Russian: Seminar of All Union Eng. Inst., Moscow, 4 August 1967.
219. David PEAT, In Search of Nikola Tesla, Ashgrove Press, Bath (1983).
220. Kenneth R. PELLETIER, Mind as Healer, Mind as Slayer, Delta, NY (1977).
221. Wilder PENFIELD, The Cerebral Cortex of Man, MacMillan, London (1957).
222. J. A. PERRY, Kirlian Photography, unpublished thesis, St Bartholomew's Hospital.
223. M. A. PERSINGER, ELF and VLF Electromagnetic Field Effects, Plenum Press, New York (1974).
224. Max PERUTZ, F.R.S., The Birth of Protein Engineering, New Scientist, 13 June 1985, pp. 12-15.
225. Dr William PETERSON, The Patient and the Weather, University of Illinois.
226. Prof. G. PICCARDI, Phénomènes Astrophysiques et évenements terrestres, Conference at Palais de la Couverture, Jan. 1959.
227. Dr John C. PIERRAKOS, The Energy Field in Man and Nature, Inst. of Bioenergetic Analysis, NY.
228. PIRUZYAN et al., How a Static Magnetic Field influenced the Tumour Sarcoma 37e. IVZ. Akad. Nauk.USSR. Seria Biol. 6. 893-898 (1969).
229. Colin PITTENDRIGH and V. G. BRUCE, Daily Rhythms as Coupled Oscillator Systems. Photoperiodism and Related Phenomena in Plants and Animals. AAAS Washington DC (1959).
230. PLATO of Athens, Timaeus (Trans. Desmond Lee), Penguin Books, Middx (6th edn, 1979).
231. Guy Lyon PLAYFAIR, The Unknown Power, Panther Books, St Albans (1977): also (with Scott Hill); The Cycles of Heaven, Souvenir Press, London (1978).
232. Jean du PLESSIS, The Electronic Reactions of Abrams. Blanch and Jeanne R. Abrams Memorial Foundation, Chicago (1922).

233. Herbert POHL, The Euglena Gracilis Expts., Zeitschr. fur Naturf. 36: 367 (1948). Cancer Research Lab., Stillwater, Okl.
234. F. M. POTTENGER, Pottenger's Cats, Price-Pottenger Nutrition Foundation, La Mesa, Calif. (1983).
235. Alexandr S. PRESMAN, Electromagnetic Fields and Life, Plenum Press, NY and London (1970).
236. Shirley PRICE, Aromatherapy, Thorsons, Wellingborough (1985).
237. Weston A. PRICE, Nutrition and Physical Degeneration, Price-Pottenger Nutritional Foundation, La Mesa, Calif. (1970).
238. Andrija PUHARICH, The Sacred Mushroom, Key to the Door of Eternity, Doubleday Books, Garden City, NY (1959).
239. Andrija PUHARICH, Beyond Telepathy, Darton Longman & Todd (1962).
240. Andrija PUHARICH, Uri: A Journal of the Mystery of Uri Geller, Doubleday Books, New York (1974).
241. PYTHAGORAS of Samos, ed. H. Diels. I.p. 27. Fragmente der Vorsokratiker, Berlin (1922).
242. Otto RAHN, Invisible Radiations of Organisms. Gebrüder Borntraeger, Berlin (1936).
243. P. E. RAPP, An Atlas of Cellular Oscillations. Jnl. Exptl. Biol. 81, pp. 281-306 (1979).
244. Wilhelm REICH, The Cancer Biopathy, Noonday Books, New York (1973).
245. Baron Karl L. F. Von REICHENBACH, Researches into the Forces of Magnetism, Electricity, Heat and Light, in Relation to the Force of Life. (trans. William GREGORY) J. S. Redfield, New York (2nd edn, 1851).
246. Dr Glen REIN, Scientific Investigations of the Human Energy Field, unpublished paper, undated.
247. Drs REJDAK and KURZ, Czech Report on Nelya Mikhailova, on telekinesis, Czech Pravda, 14 and 21 June 1968 (trans. in Paraphysics Intl., Jnl. Vol. 2, No. 3).
248. Dr White ROBERTSON, Electro Pathology (1918).
249. A.H. ROSE, Chemical Microbiology. Butterworths, London (3rd edn, 1976).
250. Dr Charles RUSS, An instrument which is set in motion by vision or by proximity of the human body, The Lancet, 30 July 1921, p. 222.
251. Walter RUSSELL, The Russell Radio Generative Concept. L. Middleditch, New York (1930).
252. D. RUSSELL DAVIS An Introduction to Psychopathology. Oxford University Press, Oxford (1957).
253. Shiro SAITO, Man and Magnetism - Biomagnetic Effects of Magnetic Fields. Jikei University Medical School, Tokyo (1975).
254. E. M. SAMUDZHAN, Effect of functionally weakened cerebral cortex on growth of innoculated tumors in mice. Med.Zhurn., A.N. Ukrainian USSR (1954) 24 (3), 10-14.
255. William SARGENT, Battle for the Mind. Pan Books, London (2nd edn, 1960).
256. Omar SATTAUR, How HTLV causes Leukaemia, New Scientist, 2 Aug. 1984, p.35.
257. Omar SATTAUR, Sharper Tests for AIDS, New Scientist, 2 May 1985, p. 23.

258. Bill SCHUL and Ed PETTIT, The Secret Power of Pyramids, Coronet Books/ Hodder Fawcett, London (1976).
259. Rupert SHELDRAKE, A New Science of Life, Granada (1983); Blond & Briggs (1981).
260. André SIMONETON, Radiations des Aliments, ondes Humaines, et Santé. Le Courrier du Livre, Paris (1971).
261. Carl and Stephanie SIMONTON, Getting Well Again, Bantam Books, NY (1978).
262. Brian SNELGROVE, The Unseen Self: Hidden Potential, privately published (1979).
263. Edward SOLLY, The Influence of Electricity on Vegetation (1845).
264. Fred SOYKA with Alan EDMONDS, The Ion Effect, Bantam Books (E.P. Dutton & Co.), Illinois, USA (1977).
265. Dr Aleksej D. SPERANSKY, Grundlagen der Theorie in der Medizin (Basis of Medical Theory), Verlag, Berlin (1950).
266. Dr Aaron H. STEINBERG, Upgrading Cellular Activity with Electromagnetism, Jnl. of Borderland Research.
267. S. STEWART and T. S. L. BESWICK, Bacteriology, Virology and Immunity, Bailliere Tindall, London (10th edn, 1977); Cassell & Collier MacMillan, Cassell.
268. Henry STILL, Of Time, Tides and Inner Clocks, Harrisburg Pa., Stackpole Books (1972).
269. C. H. STUART-HARRIS and G. C. SCHILD, Influenza, Edward Arnold, London (1975) p. 122.
270. Halliday SUTHERLAND, Control of Life. Burns Oates (1951).
271. G. SWANBECK, To UVB or to UVB? Editorial, Photodermatology, 1984, 1:2.
272. Albert SZENT-GYORGYI, Introduction to Submolecular Biology (1960).
273. Moki TANAKA, Flocculation of blood affected by sun and sunspots. Arch. Met.Geophysics. Bioklimat. 486 (1951).
274. David TANSLEY, Radionics, Element Books, Shaftesbury (1985).
275. R. THOM, Structural Stability and Morphogenesis, Benjamin, Reading, Mass. (1975).
276. David THOMPSON, Human Force Fields and Sergeyev's Transmitters, Macleans Magazine, September, 1968.
277. Sylvanus THOMPSON, Magnetism in Growth (8th Robert Boyle Lecture), Henry Frowde, London (1902).
278. THUCYDIDES, History of the Peloponnesian War, Book Two, 46-9, Dent & Dutton, NY and London (1910) (ed. 1957).
279. William A.TILLER, Kirlian Photography - Its Scientific Foundations and Future Potential Dept. of Materials Science, Stanford University, unpublished (1975).
280. William A. TILLER, Radionics, Radioesthesia, and Physics. Unpublished Mss. presented at Symposium on the Varieties of Healing. (Amer. Acad. Paraps. and Med.).
281. Peter TOMPKINS and Christopher BIRD, The Secret Life of Plants. Allen Lane (Harper & Row, USA). London. (2nd edn, 1974).
282. TOULMIN and GOODFIELD, The Architecture of Matter. Penguin Books.
283. L. TURENNE, Waves from Forms France (unknown date).
284. A. E. VINES and N. REES, Plant and Animal Biology, Pitman Books, Lon-

BIBLIOGRAPHY

don (4th edn, 1982).
285. George VITHOULKAS, Homoeopathy, Medicine of the New Man, Thorsons, Wellingborough (1985).
286. Dr Norman W. WALKER, Natural Weight Control. O'Sullivan Woodside & Co., Phoenix, Ariz. (1981).
287. Ritchie R. WARD, The Living Clocks, New York, Alfred A. Knopf (1971).
288. W. Grey WALTER, The Living Brain, Duckworth (1953).
289. G. D. WASSERMANN, An Outline of Field Theory, CIBA Foundation on ESP, Churchill, London (1956).
290. Professor Bernard WATSON, Medical Electronics and Physics at Bart's, 1964-1986 (February 1987).
291. James D. WATSON, The Double Helix, Weidenfeld & Nicolson, London (1968).
292. Lyall WATSON, Supernature, Coronet Books (Hodder & Stoughton) London (1973).
293. Lyall WATSON, Gifts of Unknown Things, Coronet Books (Hodder & Stoughton), London (1976).
294. Lyall WATSON, Lifetide, Hodder & Stoughton, London (1979).
295. Lyall WATSON, Heavens Breath, Coronet Books (Hodder & Stoughton), London (1984).
296. Lyall WATSON, Beyond Supernature, Hodder & Stoughton, London (1986).
297. Janet WATTS Article in Observer Colour Supplement, 12 April 1987.
298. Tony WEBB and Dr Tim LANG, Food Irradiation, The Facts, Thorsons, Wellingborough (1987).
299. Louis WEINSTEIN, Article: The Influenza Epidemic of 1918, New England Jnl. of Medicine, May, 1976.
300. P. M. WEST et al., An observed correlation between psychological factors and growth rate of cancer in man, Cancer Research 12. 306-7 (1952).
301. Olive WHICHER and George ADAMS, The Living Plant and Science of Physical and Ethereal Spaces: also Plant, Sun and Earth, Verlag Freires Geisteleben, Stuttgart (1949).
302. R. H. WHITEHOUSE and A. J. GROVE, The Dissection of the Earthworm, University Tutorial Press, London (1943).
303. Ann WIGMORE, Recipes for Longer Life, Rising Sun Publications, Mass. (1978).
304. Roger J. WILLIAMS and D. K. KALITA, A Physician's Handbook on Orthomolecular Medicine, Keats Publishing Co., New Canaan, Conn. (1977).
305. Thomas WILLIS, De Cerebri Anatome, London (1664).
306. Frank A. WILSON, Crystal and Cosmos, Coventure, London (1977).
307. Sir John WOODROFFE The Serpent Power, Luzac and Co., 1919.
308. WORLD HEALTH ORGANISATION Extremely Low Frequency (ELF) Fields, Env. Health Criteria No. 35. HMSO, London.
309. Dean Matthew WREN, Annotations to Thos. Browne's Pseudodoxia Epidemica, Bodl. 0.2, 26 Art Seld., p. 178.
310. Michael YUDKIN and Robin OFFORD, A Guidebook to Biochemistry, Cambridge University Press (4th edn, 1980).
311. Gary ZUKAV, The Dancing Wu Li Masters, Rider/Hutchinson (1979).
312. ZWEIG et al. Proc Natl. Acad. Sci. (1966) 56. 515-520.

Index

Page numbers in italic type refer to illustrations

Abbas, Ali 159
Abrams, Dr Albert 47-9, 52, 66, 100, 106
Acquired Immune Deficiency Syndrome
   see AIDS
acupuncture 108, 124, 129-30
adenine 119, *120*
adinovirus *31*, 32
AIDS
   brain tissue destroyed by 30, 216, 217-18
   causation 218-19
   diagnosis 70
   electrocrystal therapy for 82
   fighting back mentally delays end 196
   government campaigns 216
   Haiti, prevalent in 180
   Kirlian print of sufferer *217*
   opportunistic viruses associated with, size of 180-1
   seriousness of 172, 216, 217-18
   size of virus enabling penetration of myelin sheath 28
   stress, and 196
   symptoms 196
   T- and B-lymphocytes lost in 122
   T4 helper cells in 30
   treatments 218
Allen, C. M. 42
Allende, Carlos 72-3, 74
allergies 192
alpha rhythms 197
alternative medicines 58, 124-7, 153
Aly, Carl Otto 208
amethysts 149
amino acids 30, 117-22, 180, 186
amoebae 38
amputation 108
anaemia 167
ångström unit 55n
animal magnetism 45
applied kinesiology 190-1
Aristotle 21
Ark of the Covenant 49
aromatherapy 124, 167
Arrhenius, Svante 181
arthritis 207-9
ascorbic acid 12

astrology 9, 21, 44
Athens, plague of 28-9
Atlantis 50-1, 148-9
Attilj, Dr 203
aura, human 92-4
Aurora Borealis 46
auto-suggestion 16

Bach, Edward 44, 56-8
bacteriology 57, 195-6
Balitsky, K. P. 99
Balkwill, Dr Frances 184, 186
Beck, Robert 17
Becker, Robert 17, 158, 168, 208
Bentham-Oldfield scanner 135
Berger, Hans 197
Berlitz, Charles 60
Bertholon, Abbé 44
bio-electronic regulatory control techniques (BER) 191-2
bioflavonoids 167
bioplasma 107-8
Bircher-Benner, Max 162, 163, 167
Bitter, Dr Francis 71
blood
   diagnosis by 48
   disease of 98, 122, 183-4
   orgone energy carried by 49-50
bones, crystalline nature of 158
Bonewitz, Ra 58, 155, 157
Bose, Sir Jagadis C. 154-5
Bovis, André 55
brain signals
   cell replacement, and 103
   nature of 187
   reception of 11-12, 180, 221-2
   stress affecting 26, 27
   wavelength 29-30
   weakened 26, 196-7
brain-waves 197
breast-feeding 172
Brekhman, Prof. Israel 168
Bright's disease 164
Brown, John 87-8
Brownian Motion 15, 124
Butler, W. E. 93-4

258

INDEX

C, Vitamin 12
Callender, Sheila 183-4
cancer
   breast 83
   case studies 203, 206-7
   causes, proposed 184, 200, 202-3
   cells mucus-encased 166
   diagnosis 49, 79, 97, 98, 99, 198-200, 202
   fresh fruit good for 32
   gastric 97
   geraniums, in 66
   kidney 33-4
   Kirlian photographs of 32, 79, *198-9*, 199-200, 201
   lung 33-4
   mastitis presaging 83
   Pierce-Brown 99
   radiotherapy for 83-4
   raw foods, and 163, 166
   skin 27, 98-9, 116
   soil radiation as cause 184
   stress-related 32, 34, 57, 200, 202
   treatments 185, 201-2
   visualisation, and 33
   wart a kind of 30
   will-power, and 33
cannibalism 179-80
Catchpole, John 90, 91
Cayce, Edgar 51
cells
   cancerous 166
   communication between 117
   division 113, 186-7
   malnutrition of 161
   replacement 26-7, 95, 98-9, 103
cerebral Mass Action 101, 223
cerebral spasms 159
chemotherapy 106, 165, 185, 202, 224-5
Cheney, Margaret 70
Chladni figures 97, 103
chromosome 32
Clement, Mark 69-70, 209
cold virus 12
colitis 166
colonic cleansing 196
colour therapy 124-5
cooking methods, relative effect on corona discharge 174
covalent bonding 104, 116, 117, 155
Cox, Dr Len 47
'cluster' diseases 14-15
Creighton, James 33, 34
Crick, Francis 22, 72, 122
crowd control 17
crystals (*see also* electrocrystal therapy)
   amethysts 149
   characteristics 146
   corona discharge, beneficial effect on 145
   forms 156

growth 112, 158-9
healing 145, 146, 148
holograms of 154
Kirlian photography of 143-4
morphogenetic fields of 158-9
nature of 155-6, 158
quartz 138, 143-5, 149, 150, 155
sensitivity *149*, 157
sound generated from 153-4
stability 150-1
cutin 40
cytosine 119

DNA
   amino acids not manufactured by 30
   cloning 37
   composition of 25-6, 117, 119, 178-9, 186, 221
   electrical nature of 68, *102*, *109*, 178-9
   identification by 24, 28, 48, 104
   magnetism's effect on 98, 99, 100
   miscoding 27
   replication *68*
   ultraviolet radiation's effect on 30, 181-3, 184
   uracil not found in 118-19
Dana, James White 156
Darwin, Charles 23
Davis, Russell 189
Day, Langston 53
Delbruck, Max 74
Deltoid muscle test 190-1
dematerialisation 72, 74
dental decay 163-4
deoxyribonucleic acid *see* DNA
depression 191, 223
Descartes, René 197
diathermy 66
dimerisation *182*
disease, causology 58, 187-9
   environmental 188
   hereditary 188, 188-9
   psychosomatic 188
   socio-economic 188
   structural 188
Douglass, Dr John 166
dowsing 125-7
Driech, H. 101
Drown, Ruth 42
drug industry 165, 185, 223-4
Duane-Behrendt experiments 16
Dumitrescu, Ion 96, 97-8, 100-1, 102
dysbiosis 195-6

EMI whole body scanner 191-2
earthworms 23, 24, 36-7
Edison, Thomas 46
Egyptians, ancient 43, 50, 126
Ehret, Arnold 164

Einstein, Albert
  Manhattan Project, and 42
  part-time scientist 10
  relativity, theory of 100
  Tesla, and 60, 65
  US Navy work 60, 70-1, 72
electricity
  food alive with 167
  living organisms depend on 109-10
  power lines, effect of on human emotion 17, 158, 223
electrochemical transmission 26-7, 187
electrocrystal therapy
  diagnosis 128-45, 219-20
  electroscanning method (ESM) 135-45
  equipment 134-5
  human proximity in 111
  Oldfield's early work with 79-89
  rationale 146
  safety precautions 134
  side effects 148
  treatment 145-59, 215
electrography 96
electromagnetism *see also* magnetism
  brain affected by 11
  controllability 125
  effect on atoms 35
  homoeopathy explained in terms of 123-4
  image transmission 15
  orgone energy 50
  traffic of 17, 19, 158
  weapons using 17, 59, 71, 158
electronography 96, 98
eloptic energy 61
encephalitis 218
entelechy 101
enzymes, pancreatic 167
epidemics 12-13, 14
epidermis
  function of 40-1
  impervious to ultraviolet radiation 40
  plants' 40
Eppinger, Hans 166
Essen, Lars Erik 208
Essenes 163
explosives 71
eye-contact 16

fertilisers 44-5, 46, 113, 169, 224
fibro-adenosis 83
Finger Loop test 190
Florey, Ernst 110
fluoroacetates, poisoning by 54
food
  additives reduce nutritive value 170
  cooking, effect on nutritive value 173-4
  denatured 170, 172-3
  freshness 170, 176
  frozen 176

  irradiation 171-2, 173, 175
  politics, and 171, 172
  preservation 176-7
  raw 160-8, 201, 207-8, 214
football matches, influence of spectators on players' performance 16
Fractal Geometric Figures 89-90
Francé, Le Vicomte Henry de 126-7
Francé, Raol H. 46
Franklin, Rosalind 22, 179, 189
Froelich, Herb 107

Galvani, Luigi 45, 110
Gamow, George 70-1
genetics 22-3
Gerson, Max 162-3
ginseng 175-6
Glasser, Dr Ronald 33-4
Goethe, Johann Wolfgang von 66
Golla, Prof. F. 199
Goodfield, June 74
gout 26, 159
Gregory, William 45
Gribbin, John 104
guanine 119
Guilbault, George 145
Gurwitsch, Alexander 162

Hahnemann, Samuel 57, 122
Haiti 180
Hardy, Sir Alister 101
harmonics 114-15, 116, 157
headache 27 *see also* migraine
Headington School's flu epidemic 14
Health Education Council 172
heart disease 164
Hell, Maximilian 45
herpes 14, 119
Hieronymus, T. Galen 61
high-tension cables 17, 158, 223
Hippocrates 12
histidine 119
Hoffman, Sam 48
holograms 154
homoeopathy 122-4, 192, 193, 202
homoeotron 54-5, 58-9
Hoyle, Fred 12, 13, 14
hydra 39
hydrogen atom, light, and 35
hydrogen bonds 117-19
hypnosis 108, 202

INDUMED magnetic field therapy 193
influenza 12-14, 123
infra-red 184
infrasound 63-4
intention tremor 215
interference 35, 48, 75
interferon 184-6

INDEX

intestinal flora 195-6
invisibility 60, 70, 71-4
Inyushin, Vladimir M. 107
ionic bonds 155
ions 51-2
irradiation (of food) 19, 171-2, 173, 175
isoleucine 119

Jenny, Hans 15, 103
Jericho, Battle of 43, 49
Jessup, Dr M. K. 42
Jordan, Pascual 97
Joshua 42-3, 49

Kajinski, Bernard 16
Kamensky, Yuri 16
Kaposi's sarcoma 82, 180
Karstrom, Dr Henning 167
Kenton, L. and S. 168, 195, 207
Kenyon, Dr Julian 99, 191, 195-6, 197, 201
Kepler, Johann 9, 21
kidney disease 164
kinesiology, applied 190-1
Kircher, Athanasius 44
Kirlian, Semyon 64
Kirlian photography
  acupuncture, and 108
  cancer diagnosis 97
  discounted 95-6
  explained 92, 94, 95, 96-7, 107, 116, 122
  hypnosis, and 108
  method
    angle of incidence in fingertip studies 238-9
    barometric pressure control 234
    basic principles 227-30
    equipment 240-1
    exposure time 237-8
    film characteristics 234-7
    frequency and pulse repetition rates 239
    humidity control 233
    object/specimen topological features and mass 232-3
    plate pressure of specimen 238
    stability of equipment 231-2
    temperature control 233
    human subjects – procedure 244
    inanimate objects – procedure 241-4
  parapsychological use 108
  pattern-forms 106
  radioactive tracers' effect on 78-9
  safety 134, 226, 245
  three-dimensional 80, 130-3
  uses 95
Kollath, Werner 160
Konikiewicz, Leonard 198
Konneci, Dr 17
Kuhne 93

Kundalini 89
Kuratsune, Dr Masanore 165
kuru 179, 180

Lakhovsky, George, 66-9, 107, 161, 184, 208
Lang, Dr T. 171, 172
laser light 151-3
Lashley, K. R. 101
learning, morphogenetic fields, and 112
Lemström, Selim 46
leucine 119
leukaemia 98, 183-4
light
  blue around pyramids 50
  laser 151-3
  life dependent on 168
  nature of 34-5
  organically produced 66
  polar 46
  therapeutic use of 124-5
Linden, Diederich Wessel 126
lizards 38, 39
Lodge, Sir Oliver 46
Lomonosov, Mikhail 16
love, romantic 16, 112
Lowenstein 98
Lund, Prof. E. J. 69, 168
lupus lesions 163
lysine 119, 122

MORA therapy 192-4
McCarrison, Sir Robert 166
McCausland, Colonel 78
magic 16
magnetism *see also* electromagnetism
  DNA and RNA affected by 98-9, 99, 100
  earth 36
  effect on physical size of materials 142
  health related to 44, 159
  soundwaves produced by 142-3
  therapeutic use of 99-100
Maimbray 44, 102
Majajakrom 98
malaria 48, 106
man as machine 197
Manhattan Project 42
Margrassi, Prof. F. 12-13
Mars equations 9
mastitis 83
Matthews, Brian 210
Maxwell, James Clerk 36, 46
medical terms 32
meditation 197
mental illness 189
Mesmer, Dr Franz Anton 42, 45
methionine 119
microwaves 17, 19
migraine 162-3
Miller, Stanley 122, 219

mitochondria 26
mitosis 113, 119, 186-7
Moore, William 42, 60
molecular chemistry 187
morphogenetic fields
    artificial 25
    crystal growth, and 112, 158-9
    defined 20
    electromagnetics, and 24
    learning, and 112
    measuring 112
    mystery of 20-1
    nature of 24, 101-2, 112
    origins 110-11
    resonance in 53, 97
    study of 23
    ultraviolet light, and 24
Morphogenetic Radiation Field Hypothesis 223
multiple sclerosis
    case study 85-7
    causation 210, 212, 213-14
    distribution 211
    effects 26, 27, 211-12
    scaly cells 40
    treatment 213, 214-15
multiwave oscillator 67, 204, 207, 209
Munro, Dr Jean 19
Murr, Dr Larry 102
music 125, 154
myelin 26, 28

Neiper, Hans 167
nervous system 37, 40, 57, 187
New Guinea 179
Newman, John 46
Newton, Sir Isaac 9, 21
Nolfi, Dr Kristine 164
Nollet, Jean Antoine 44
non-phenomena 35
nuclear magnetic resonance (NMR) 191-2
nutrition 160-77

Odyle energy 45
Oldfield, Harry 139
    early career 76-9
    electrocrystal therapy 79-89
    family life 82
    homoeopathy 80
    research 89-91
oranges 170-1
orgone energy 49-50
Ostrander, Sheila 61-3
ovulation 168

pain
    cancer, in 84
    cause of 27
papovaviruses 30-2, 186

Paracelsus 44, 122
Pauling, Linus 104, 186
Penfield, Wilder 101
pest-control 46, 48, 54-5, 100, 160, 224
Pettit, Ed 50
phantom leaf effect 62-3
    discounted by Dumitrescu 95-6
    explained 116, 122, 222
    morphogenetic fields, and 25, 64
    pulsed high frequency, and 113
    replicable 97
phenylalanine 119
phenylketonuria 27, 119
Philadelphia Experiment 59-60, 70-4, 111
photography, aerial 54-5
photons 34-5, 107
photosynthesis 113, 167
planaria 39
planetary motion, theory of 9
plants *see also* pest-control; phantom leaf effect
    Alpine 113
    amino acids created by 118, 169
    barometric pressure, and 113
    circadian cyclical radiation pattern 175
    communication between 47
    electrically influenced 44, 45, 46, 49, 88, 102
    epidermal cells of 40
    fertilisation 113, 169
    growth of 69, 88, 102-3, 113, 168
    immunity to disease 169
    medicinal 44, 57-8
    pollution, and 113
Plato 50-1, 111, 148
Pneumocystis Carinii Pneumonia 180, 216
Pohl, Herbert 107
pollution 113, 203
poltergeists 15
polyunsaturates 174-5
Pottenger, Francis M. 164-5
prayer 16
Presman, Alexandr S. 98
Price, Shirley 167
Price, Weston 162, 163-4
Priestley, Joseph 21
psoriasis 27, 29, 115-16, 180, 215-16
psychic attack 16
pulsed high frequency 113-15, 146
pyramids 50-1
pyrimidine dimerisation 182, 183
Pythagoras of Samos 43, 163

quartz 138, 144-5, 146, 150, 155

RNA 26, 68, 104, 106, 119
radiation
    bio-electrical 44-5, 66-9, 116-17, 169-70
    diagnostic use 220
    diseased tissue, of 47-8, 117

INDEX

ionising 27, 202
  sunbathing 98-9, 116
  treatment for cancer 202
radio fields, coexistence with electrical fields 107
radionics 52-5, 94-5
Rahn, Otto 61
Ramsdale, Mallory 85-7
reflexology 125
regeneration, physical 23-4, 29, 38-40
Reich, Dr Wilhelm 42, 49-50, 52
Reichenbach, Baron Karl von 45
Rein, Glen 78-9
replication of experiments 9, 54
resonance 43, 53, 59-61, 63-4, 97, 104, 111
ribonucleic acid *see* RNA
Richards, Dr Guyon 52-3
Riviere 99
Rollright stones 138
Rose, Prof. A. H. 181-3
Ross, William 45
Russell effect 106-7
Russell, Bertrand 72

sarcoma 27, 29, 82, 98, 203, 206
Schild, G. C. 14
Schroder, Lynn 61-3
Schrodinger equation 34
Schul, Bill 50
Schurin, S. P. 103, 162
science
  history of 21
  scepticism, and 35, 69
  specialisation in 22
scrapie 179, 180
segmental electrogram (SEG) 191, 192
semen 218-19
Serov, Dr 16
Shapiro 98
Sharaf, Myron 50
Sheldrake, Rupert 101, 110-11, 112, 113, 158
Simonton, Carl and Stephanie 33, 34
skin disease 27
Skin Hydration Test 198
Smith, Dr Cyril 19
smoking 202
Solly, Edward 45
spiritualism 15
sponges 39-40, 195
Stern, Otto 42
Stiner, O. 166, 207-8
stomach 47
stone circles, megalithic 138
stress
  brain signals affected by 26, 27, 32, 34
  disease-related 86, 116, 189, 196, 202
  gastro-intestinal membrane affected by 196
strophalomancy 126

Stuart-Harris, C. H. 14
Studitsky, Dr Alexander 108
sun 107, 167
sunbathing 202
sunspots 36, 46
superoxide dismutase 208
surgery 201
surveillance theory 34
Szent-Georgyi, Albert 208

Taylor, Eve 167
telepathy 15-16, 126
teleradiaesthesia 126
televisition, harmful effects possible 157-8
Tesla, Nikola 47, 59, 60, 64, 65, 70-1, 134
  high-frequency machine 205
Tesla coil 132, 229
Thomas, Robert 14
Thompson, Sylvanus 46
Thouvenel, De 126
threonine 119
Thucydides 29
thunderstorms 102
thymine 120
Tiller, Dr. W. A. 94-5
tinnitus 87-8
toning 125
Troskin, Dr 16
tryptophan 119
tuberculosis 163
turtles 39
twins, identical 16

UKA Co. 54-5, 58-9
ultraviolet radiation
  aura, human, may be composed of 92-3
  bacteria affected by 183
  DNA affected by 30, 104, 181-3
  earthworm sensitive to 24, 29
  energy 184
  psoriasis treated by 29, 115-16
  skin cancer caused by 27, 116
  wavelengths 184
Upton, Armstrong and Knuth 42, 54-5, 58-9
uracil 30, 118-19
urology 124

valine 119
Vegatest 191, 192
viral communication 103, 178
viruses 12, 103, 178, 180-1, 219
vision 93, 184
vitamins 12, 166
Vithoulkas, George 123-4
Voll, Dr 192

Walker, Dr Norman W. 164
Warr, de la, George 42, 53-4

warts 30-2, 186
Waters, June 115-16, 215-16
Watson, Prof. Bernard 74, 108
Watson, James 22
Watson, Lyall 39-40, 63, 66, 194, 195
waveforms
    glandular 94-5
    insect 48
    pulsed high frequency 113-15
    sea 43
    therapeutic 125, 222
    types *18*, *239*
Webb, T. 171, 172
Wessel Linden, Diederich 126
Whitwell, Anne 82-5
Wickramasinghe, Chandra 12, 13, 14
Wienstein, Louis 13
Wigmore, Ann 164

Wilkins, Maurice 22
will-power in fighting disease 196, 201-2
Williams, Roger 161
witchcraft 43
Woodpecker, Operation 158
Woolley-Hart, Dr Anne 84
Wren, Christopher 21, 22
Wren, Dean 221

X-rays 47, 97, 98, 156, 178

Yang, D. Kim S. 99
Yannon, Sam 17-19
yin and yang 89
yoga 89, 124
Young, Thomas 34

zapping 19